New Schools for a New Century

edited by

Diane Ravitch and

Joseph P. Viteritti

NEW
SCHOOLS
FOR A NEW
CENTURY

The Redesign of Urban Education

Yale University

Press • New Haven

and London

Printed in the United States of America.

Library of Congress Cataloging-in-Publication Data

New schools for a new century : the redesign of urban education / edited by Diane Ravitch and Joseph P. Viteritti.
p.   cm.   Includes bibliographical references and index.
ISBN 0-300-07046-2 (cloth : alk. paper)
1. Education, Urban—United States—Case studies.   2. School management and organization—United States—Case studies. 3. Educational change—United States—Case studies.   I. Ravitch, Diane.   II. Viteritti, Joseph P., 1946–
LC5131.N29   1997
370'.973'091732—dc21   96-39929

A catalogue record for this book is available from the British Library.

The paper in this book meets the guidelines for permanence and durability of the Committee on Production Guidelines for Book Longevity of the Council on Library Resources.

10   9   8   7   6   5   4   3   2   1

Contents

Preface

This book is the product of a seminar that the editors conducted at New York University between 1994 and 1996. The purpose of the seminar was to learn about the many efforts under way across the nation to change the management and organization of public education. We created a Working Group on School Organization and Educational Quality as a vehicle for meeting with school reformers and to hear about what they were doing to redefine public education.

What began as a research seminar eventually grew into large public meetings. These gatherings were attended by educators, government officials, journalists, business leaders, foundation executives, and other interested citizens. Members of the New York City Board of Education participated in some sessions, as well as state legislators and members of the New York Board of Regents. Among our speakers were Howard Fuller, the former superintendent of schools in Milwaukee, who supported the implementation of school choice for low-income children in that city; Deborah McGriff, a former superintendent of schools in Detroit, who had become vice president of the Edison Project; Ted Kolderie, one of the national leaders of the charter school movement; and Yvonne Chan, the principal of the Vaughn Learning Center, an exemplary charter school in Los Angeles, who has demonstrated in practice the potential of the charter school concept.

Our purpose was to listen and learn and to introduce an influential audience of New Yorkers to exciting ideas. In this effort, we were assisted by
the Manhattan Institute and the Democratic Leadership Council in New
York, which cosponsored several of the meetings.

As interest in the seminar grew, we realized that what we were learning
about the new face of school reform deserved a far larger audience than
could be reached through meetings and seminars. In assembling this collec-
tion, we have drawn together the work of a distinguished group of scholars
who are deeply involved with different kinds of organizational innovations.
Not all would be in full agreement on what form the redesign of schooling
should take. As we survey the contributions to this volume, however, certain common elements seem to define current thinking about the relation
between school organization and educational quality: that the factory-style
model of schooling characterized by bureaucratic organizational structures
and large, anonymous schools no longer meets the needs of our nation's
children; that educators at the school must have sufficient autonomy to
make decisions about their school's budget and staffing, as befits professionals; that parents, especially low-income parents, should have a wider
range of choices in selecting schools for their children; and, finally, that the
ultimate goal of school reform is both to strengthen public education and to
improve student performance.

The seminars and the conferences of the Working Group on School Organization and Educational Quality and the preparation of this book were
generously supported by the John M. Olin Foundation. We especially want
to thank Jim Piereson and Janice Riddell of the Olin Foundation for their
belief in this project. The book was produced with additional support from
the Lynde and Harry Bradley Foundation, the Alice M. and Thomas J. Tisch
Foundation, and the Smith Richardson Foundation. We also want to ex-
press our personal thanks to Peter Flanigan, who has been a tireless supporter of improved educational opportunities for poor children and an inspiration to both of us as well.

We thank John Covell of Yale University Press for his enthusiasm and
professionalism, and our editor Dan Heaton for his care and wit in bringing
the project to fruition. And finally, we thank our research assistants at New
York University—Brian Maxey, Gerald Russello, Malavika Valla, and Gisella
Westwater—for their hard work.

We hope that this book will help to inform the ongoing national discus-   ix
sion of school reform. From what we have learned, we are convinced that
public education is being redefined and reinvented to meet the increasingly
complex and challenging needs of American society and to prepare children
to be full participants. There are, of course, institutional and political obstacles to be overcome, which is hardly surprising. Still, Americans understand
that formal education—and the knowledge and skills that it creates—is intri-
cately connected to individual opportunity, economic growth, civic participation, and social progress. Given the central importance of education to
individuals and to our society, improving educational opportunity for all is
certain to have a high priority on our nation's agenda until it becomes a
reality for all American children.

New Schools for a New Century

Introduction

Diane Ravitch and Joseph P. Viteritti

This is an exciting period in American education. For the first time in a century, reformers are beginning to think "outside the box" of the industrial-era factory model of schooling. There is growing recognition that one-size-fits-all education does not fit everyone, and that schooling must be adaptive to the changing needs of children and society. In the past, that very rhetoric—"the changing needs of children and society"— was enlisted in the creation of our current inflexible bureaucratic system. That hierarchical system served the nation fairly well for many years, but over time it became more rigid, more inefficient, and less able to provide equal educational opportunity. It is not up to the challenges of the new century, nor is it capable of achieving the high standard of universal literacy that a modern economy and advanced society demand.

As a new century begins, reformers understand that no single plan can replace the existing system. Each chapter of this book describes one or more innovations that are intended to enhance the educational op-portunities of those children who have been least well served by the status quo. We believe that this kind of restructuring will invigorate public education and renew its promise. What is heartening about the current national scene is the diversity of innovative approaches that are being tried across the nation. Incorporation into broad-range public

2   policy of the ideas behind charter schools, contracting arrangements, and choice would redefine public education. Such a redefinition demands the reordering of political agendas and of an administrative apparatus that has operated urban public schools for most of this century. These changes could also liberate imaginative educators from overregulation, promote accountability at the school level, and give all parents opportunities to choose from a wider variety of schools.

Restructuring urban education will not be easy. The constraints are apparent in most of the following chapters. As Chester Finn suggests in Chapter 9, the political and institutional obstacles to meaningful change are huge. When we envision city schools as they might be from the perspective of how they are, it is clear that reform will proceed incrementally, against large odds. Yet we do not doubt that reform will happen, because our nation cannot afford to sustain an educational system in which significant numbers of children are poorly educated.

A Decrepit Factory

The factory model of schooling, which has come into such disfavor among innovators, is the product of the well-intentioned reforms of another era. Education reform was one aspect of the progressive agenda that was enacted at the turn of the century to rid cities of rampant political corruption and to socialize a generation of immigrants into the American way of life. At the time, municipal government was controlled by political machines, whose decentralized structures allowed party bosses at the precinct level to control patronage, contracts, and decision making.[1] As an antidote to corruption, good-government advocates sought to centralize decision making in the hands of professional administrators. They became infatuated with the creed, then current in private industry, of scientific management, which promised to improve organizational performance and promote new levels of efficiency.[2]

Translating the factory model of reform from business to education came rather easily to turn-of-the-century school administrators. The idea of removing education from the reach of city politics was particularly welcome in the midst of such widespread corruption. Even the school board, which was to provide education with some semblance of democratic control, was conceived by progressives more as a sacred trust designed to protect the public interest than as a representative body.[3] And the rules of scientific management appealed to school administrators who wanted to remove challenges to their own authority and to establish professional rather than lay control of education.

The entire scheme was very attractive to the leaders of the new pedagogical profession. Forged at elite schools and tempered in the ideology of their emergent discipline, their newfound professionalism was enhanced by the hierarchic administrative structure of the age. Educationalists, after all, were the immediate beneficiaries of the tenets of scientific management; they were the experts who knew best when it came to education.[4] And nobody was about to challenge the expertise or wisdom of these "school men"—neither the army of young women who taught in the classrooms nor the hordes of barely literate immigrants whose children occupied them.

Through the middle of the twentieth century, the factory model worked remarkably well. It provided unparalleled educational opportunities to generations of immigrants who became literate and productive members of society. The large minority of children who did not enroll in school or left without graduating could count on finding a job that did not require much education, sometimes at good wages. Now, in a new century, the schools that were "good enough" several decades ago are inadequate. Built to process large numbers of students, they are incapable of connecting with and helping those youngsters whose lives have been disrupted by family breakdown or the stress of social conditions. The educational requirements of the economy continue to increase; few jobs are available for unskilled labor, and virtually none at good wages. Furthermore, the highhandedness and uniformity of the hierarchical bureaucratic system frustrate parents and teachers who want to be treated with respect. The system regularly affronts parents who seek a different program for their children and professionals who seek an opportunity to exercise initiative. As demands upon the system grow, its leaders assert their traditional claims of expertise, but few credit such claims as anything other than a shield against accountability and responsiveness. As we explain in Chapter 1, no city school system more epitomizes the old model than New York's: like a huge old factory it is hopelessly outdated, yet it has managed to withstand serious attempts at reform.

The pyramidal structure of authority, concentrated in the central headquarters of city school systems, is the major obstacle to innovation. The population sending its children to city schools today has become better

4   informed and more diverse. Not all parents have the same expectations and values, not every child has the same needs. Teachers want to be treated as professionals rather than interchangeable factory workers whose judgments and expertise are not taken seriously by officious bureaucrats. The premises of the old system must be redesigned so as to create an organization whose mission is education rather than self-perpetuation.

Autonomy

The most interesting structural innovations in American education are of recent vintage; few predate the 1990s. Some (like choice programs) have been resisted so fiercely that their very existence is always at risk; others (like charter schools) are so new that evaluations are scarce. The track record for these approaches, therefore, is thin, and it is undoubtedly too soon to assess their effect on educational quality or opportunity. But if the certainty of success were a prerequisite for innovation, we would still be waiting for the first aircraft to leave the ground, laser surgery would be performed only in science fiction novels, and the pages of this book would have been set by hand.

Although we cannot yet identify any particular strategy that will reliably improve education in big cities, what does *not* work seems by now to be well known. What undermines the effectiveness of principals and teachers? A school system that seeks to restrict initiative by imposing an elaborate command-and-control mechanism, that attempts to manage all of its employees through uniform and burdensome mandates and regulations, that stamps out efforts to find a different (perhaps better) way of educating children, and that lacks meaningful standards for what children should learn but has elaborate standards for the delivery of mediocre services. The school reformers of today prefer small autonomous schools, diverse approaches to school organization and pedagogy, and a willingness to be judged by student performance.

State governments have led the way in attempting to provide regulatory relief.[5] In 1995, Governor George W. Bush persuaded the Texas legislature to rewrite the state education law, cutting the list of rules imposed on local districts from 490 to 230.[6] As a result, school districts may choose their own textbooks and grant teaching permits to noncertified teachers. With the support of Governor John Engler, Michigan legislators revised their state education code, eliminating 205 of its 620 sections and modifying 65 others.[7] Governors in other states, such as Florida and California, have called for similar measures. Illinois is one of ten states that have established procedures through which school boards can request waivers from state imposed requirements.[8]

Deregulation at the state level, however, represents only part of the battle for school autonomy, and not necessarily the most daunting one. Often local boards and the bureaucracies they preside over have a greater stake in maintaining their hold on personnel in the schools than do politicians and administrators in the state capitol. In an effort to loosen the reins of local control, many school systems have experimented with site-based management, with different degrees of enthusiasm and sincerity. Site-based management is an attempt to shift decision making from the central administrative office to the school. Such initiatives have been varied in approach—principal centered, teacher centered, parent centered, or consultative.[9] The most ambitious of these plans delegate instructional, financial, and personnel decisions to the school. Local school boards institute versions of site-based management to quiet restive reformers. In Illinois the state legislature imposed a far-reaching plan in 1986, creating a Local School Council for each school in Chicago.[10] Chapter 7, by Anthony Bryk and his colleagues, assesses the progress of this reform.

Chicago's approach to decentralization is considered parent centered. Rochester, New York, and Dade County, Florida, in contrast, have launched programs that require a strong teacher role in governance, and Albuquerque, New Mexico, takes a principal-focused approach. In 1989 Boston established school-site councils composed of parents, teachers, and students, with power over instructional programs, budgeting, staffing, and purchasing. Under the Los Angeles Educational Alliance for Restructuring Now (LEARN), thirty-four schools in the district were officially granted decision-making and budgetary autonomy in 1993, and sixty more schools were added a year later.[11]

Thus far the research on site-based management suggests that school districts are unwilling to cede real authority to schools. Often decentralization is token and marginal. In such important areas of discretion as budgeting and personnel, local school boards and central administrators have a difficult time relinquishing power.[12] In part because site-based management has proved insufficient as a reform strategy and district administrators

6   have been reluctant to turn over control, innovators at the school level have begun to petition state legislatures to authorize creation of charter schools. But local efforts to promote site-based management continue, as does research. In their study of forty-four schools in eleven districts in the United States, Australia, and Canada, Priscilla Wohlstetter and her colleagues analyze those factors that contribute to the successful delegation of power to schools (Chapter 8).

Charters and Contracts

Charter schools are public schools. Some are newly created institutions, others are reconstituted public schools. Some are managed by private entrepreneurs, others by teachers, parents, or nonprofit organizations that have demonstrated a capacity to operate an educational institution. The first charter school law was passed in Minnesota in 1991, the second in California a year later. By September 1996, charter school legislation had been enacted in twenty-five states; many other states were debating such legislation, and nationally the number of charter schools had reached 421, with as many as eighty others on the drawing board.[13]

What distinguishes charter schools from other public schools is the nature of the charter itself. Depending on the statute, charters may be granted by a state department of education, a state university, a special governing board created just for that purpose, or sometimes a local school board. The last form of chartering arrangement is usually the least effective because one of the major objectives behind the charter school movement is to provide educators at the school level with autonomy from the local school board. As Louann Bierlein explains in Chapter 2, charter laws grant schools varying levels of autonomy. In exchange for autonomy, a school is held to a degree of accountability that is generally unheard of in public education. If the school fails to live up to the performance objectives defined in its original agreement with the chartering agency, the charter can be revoked and the school closed.

Contracting arrangements differ from charter schools in two respects. They usually originate with a local school district rather than at the state level, and the service provider is usually (though not always) a private entrepreneur. Private contractors have been involved in education for many years, providing transportation, delivering meals, performing custodial services, and even assuming responsibility for administrative functions. What is novel about the current discussion of contracting is that it involves not a supplementary service but the provision of instruction and management of schools.

Contracting caught the nation's attention when organizations like John Golle's Educational Alternatives, Inc. (EAI) and Chris Whittle's Edison Project began to seek contracts to run schools and even districts.[14] In 1993 EAI took over general management of the entire Hartford, Connecticut, school district and six schools in Baltimore, only to have both agreements revoked by the school boards amid controversy about the performance of each partner.[15] Edison developed a different and more cautious approach from that of EAI. John Chubb, Edison's senior vice president, describes in Chapter 4 how the enterprise scaled back its original ambitions and moved methodically, designing curricula, training its personnel, strategically investing its resources in capital and technology, and launching one school at a time. Another part of the educational market has attracted smaller firms that run specific instructional programs for public schools but leave the overall administration of the school to the district. Sylvan Learning Systems, for example, has contracted to provide remedial programs in three Newark, New Jersey, high schools, and it has similar projects in other cities, including Baltimore, Chicago, and St. Paul.[16]

Many critics have confused contracting with privatization. But like charter schools, contracted schools are public institutions, authorized by a public authority, financed by public funds, and accountable to a public board. The proof that contract schools are not privatized is that a public board can cancel the contract and resume control. Like charters, contract schools are an extraordinary vehicle through which to exchange autonomy for accountability—an unusual transaction in public education. Paul Hill, who has been studying the reinvention of public education for several years, explains in Chapter 3 how contracting may be broadly used as a reform strategy at either the local or state level.

Choice

Choice is one of the most controversial and misunderstood ideas in American education. It has been seen as a way of extending the reach of public

8   education and as a weapon to destroy it. It has been portrayed by some as an elitist scheme to benefit the most advantaged students and represented by others as a plan to expand the opportunities of the most disadvantaged. In fact, choice has many faces, depending upon how it is implemented by public authorities. The concept has evolved from a set of abstract principles that alarmed many defenders of public education to a set of programmatic initiatives that deserves the serious attention of anyone concerned about expanding the educational opportunities available to poor children. Choice has come to mean one of three approaches: the market model, the public school model, and the equal opportunity model.

THE MARKET MODEL

As early as 1955, the Nobel Prize–winning economist Milton Friedman sent shock waves through the education community when he proposed a free-market model of schooling that left little room for public institutions.[17] Friedman was disturbed by the government monopoly over public schools, which in his eyes promoted neither competition among institutions nor choices for parents. The system he envisioned would provide each parent with a voucher that could be used at a private institution.[18] The government would set standards for teaching and learning but would not run its own schools. Employing his own theory of market forces, Friedman predicted that his proposal would drive failing institutions out of business and offer incentives for those that remained to strive for the highest levels of performance.

    The market approach gained new prominence in 1990, when John Chubb and Terry Moe published their provocative indictment of public schooling in America, advocating its replacement with a system of private choice.[19] Chubb and Moe's book focused particular attention on the bureaucratic and political institutions that shape public education, shielding it from accountability, and drew on an extensive body of data to demonstrate that private and parochial institutions outperform public schools and produce higher student achievement. Their critique of the democratic process that surrounds public education—and its capture by such organized political interests as teachers unions—drew sharp criticism from fellow political scientists and educators alike.[20] But it also attracted attention to choice as a viable political and programmatic option in government circles.

The experience of public school districts with choice has been mixed. The early history of the approach can be traced to the desegregation battles that erupted around the *Brown* decision: segregationists used freedom of choice plans to preserve racial exclusivity until the practice was struck down by the Supreme Court.[21] Controlled choice and magnet school programs were implemented later on a widespread basis as an instrument for desegregation that was both less conflictual and more effective than forced busing plans.[22] By 1981 there were more than one thousand magnet schools in districts around the country.[23]

As the discussion of educational equality changed its focus from racial integration to school improvement, public choice programs also altered their orientation. Choice came to be viewed as a tool to expand the options available to minority children who had been isolated in failing inner-city schools. Some of the early programs instituted on a local level—such as those in Cambridge, Massachusetts, and White Plains, New York—linked the goals of racial integration with educational equality.[24] As state programs came into existence, the emphasis on educational opportunity allowed minority students to enroll in schools and districts that were outside the usual geographic range of options.

Minnesota enacted the first statewide interdistrict choice program in 1985. By 1995, twenty states had similar statutes.[25] Assessments of these initiatives have produced ambiguous findings. An initial evaluation of the Minnesota program conducted in 1990 showed it to be highly successful in attracting disadvantaged students and improving their performance.[26] A widely circulated report subsequently prepared by the Carnegie Foundation in 1992 indicated that most parents prefer sending their children to local schools and are not inclined to put them on a bus in order to attend an institution in a neighboring district—a point made by opponents of forced busing a generation earlier.[27] Some scholars have suggested that many parents—especially poor parents—are ill-equipped to make wise choices for their children, and that choice will lead to social and economic stratification.[28]

In reality, the outcome of choice programs—that is, who registers and who benefits—depends primarily upon the program's design.[29] One of the basic shortcomings of public school choice is the assumption that enough

10   spots are available in high-quality institutions to accommodate children
who might wish to leave poor schools. Unfortunately, that is often not the
case. Most interdistrict plans are voluntary, and school districts have limits
on the number of choice students they will (and can) accept from other
districts, especially when the choice students begin their bus ride in the
inner city and are perceived to have problems that many suburban parents
and educators want to avoid. In Massachusetts, for example, only 25 percent of the local districts participate in the statewide program, and none in
the twenty-nine-district suburban rim of Boston.[30]

Without a larger supply of high-quality schools accessible in or near the
central city, public school choice is an empty promise, available to a very
small number of children. It is more likely to promote competition among
parents and among disadvantaged students than among schools. Although
the charter school movement may serve to expand the number of desirable options for urban populations, the process, which has produced fewer
than five hundred small institutions nationwide, will be slow. We need to
explore other options for those children who are not successful in the current system.

THE EQUAL OPPORTUNITY MODEL

One way to expand the supply of viable educational alternatives is to provide the resources to attend private and parochial institutions for children
who cannot otherwise afford it. Many such institutions are found in the
inner city. As Valerie Lee explains in Chapter 6, parochial institutions have
an impressive track record in educating students who have traditionally
been underserved by public schools. Lee's chapter (based upon a book she
wrote with Anthony Bryk and Peter Holland), builds on the work of the late
James Coleman and his colleagues at the University of Chicago.[31] Lee takes
the analysis a step further by identifying those institutional variables associated with effective teaching and learning.

The equal opportunity model of school choice consists of governmental
programs that provide public scholarships for poor children to attend private and parochial schools.[32] These programs cannot damage or impair
public schools because they target only a small segment of the public school
population, most of whom are already at risk of failure in public schools.
Nor do such programs endanger public education because public officials
control the number of students who are eligible to participate. Such pro-

grams do not encourage "skimming" the best students because they supply scholarships only to the most disadvantaged children, who are statistically likely to be found at the low end of the achievement distribution.

Some economically disadvantaged parents, no doubt, are more or less aggressive in taking advantage of such programs than others, just as some are more successful at getting their children into good public schools under ordinary circumstances.[33] The point is to create as many new opportunities for the poor as possible by developing alternatives to failing institutions and closing them so that even children with the least aggressive parents have a realistic chance of ending up in a good school. Choice programs that give poor children access to high-quality private and parochial institutions and create competition for public schools aim to do that.

In Chapter 5, Paul Peterson and Chad Noyes describe and assess the first such program in the United States, which was instituted in Wisconsin in 1990 at the urging of Governor Tommy Thompson. Eligibility is limited to students from families whose income is 175 percent of the federal poverty level or less. In its original form the program included only nonsectarian private schools. In 1995 the statute was amended to allow religious schools to participate. A similar program has been enacted by the Ohio legislature for disadvantaged children in Cleveland. Both programs have been challenged in the courts.[34]

Scholarship programs designed to enhance the educational opportunities of the poor have been supported by the governors of several states, including Connecticut, Pennsylvania, Texas, Minnesota, and California. Income-based proposals have been considered by state legislatures in Arizona, Illinois, Maryland, and New Mexico. A similar plan was proposed in Congress for public school students in the District of Columbia, while another bill in Congress would have authorized a demonstration project on a limited national scale.[35]

Programs such as these are worthy of careful consideration because they move us beyond abstract notions of choice and define it in an actual policy context. These programs are not designed to destroy or supplant public education, or to deprive it of its best students or to help the children of the privileged. To the contrary, they aim to provide appropriate alternatives for the children who are least likely to succeed under current conditions. If such programs succeeded, public schools would continue to enroll the vast majority of children and to function as the nation's primary providers of

12 elementary and secondary education. The only difference would be that those disadvantaged children who are now failing or at risk in current institutions would have an opportunity to be educated in a different setting. Diane Ravitch returns to the subject of school choice in Chapter 10, discussing it in the context of charter schools and the broader reform agenda.

A New Century

The transformation of urban education from a monolithic system that imposes uniform rules on school administrators, teachers, and children to one that is dynamic and diverse will not occur overnight. Nevertheless, the signs of change are apparent, and they point to a fundamental restructuring of public education. This revolution has begun with signs of discontent among those who are most directly affected: teachers and principals. The most active within their ranks are resisting an established order that saps their energy and ignores their ability and initiative. This revolution is likely to grow because it has been joined by consumers, who are dissatisfied with the results and unwilling to have their concerns disregarded.

The acute vulnerability of the old regime is underscored by the multilateral assault upon it. First, many of its most talented and productive members want out. Current appeals for deregulation and site-based management indicate that creative educators no longer want to be shackled by requirements set by individuals who have only a remote idea of what principals, teachers, and children need. The conversion of existing schools into charter schools is welcomed by those teachers and principals who have longed for control over their resources and are willing to be held accountable for the consequences of their actions in exchange for greater autonomy.

Similar issues arose in Great Britain in the 1980s.[36] In 1988 the government launched a program that allows the parents of a school to vote to make it a "grant-maintained" school. If their application is approved, the school effectively opts out of the jurisdiction of the Local Education Authority (LEA). It receives its own per-capita budget and an allotment for administrative services, which is under the control of school-level personnel. In exchange for this autonomy, the school is expected to meet clearly defined performance standards based on a national curriculum and a national test. It is a liberating concept, one that has much in common with our own charter schools.

The British route encourages public schools to "opt out." The advantage of our own charter school movement is that it provides a vehicle to achieve autonomy, both for existing public schools and for new institutions. These are schools designed for the future rather than the past. So far, the limited experience with charter institutions shows that they tend to have much smaller enrollments than the old schools.[37] Research suggests that smaller institutions are more personalized than larger schools, have a more defined sense of purpose, and are more likely to promote high levels of student achievement.[38] As we earlier noted, the academic performance of charter schools has not yet been determined; given the diversity of charters, we expect that some will do very well, and others will not. The challenge for educators will be to heed lessons from those that do improve student learning, especially for students who were previously at risk of failure.

What would education be like in a city populated by such schools? It is not hard to visualize, for many cities already have sponsored numbers of experimental small schools without cutting them loose from the bureaucracy. One can imagine a universe of distinctive schools—small, autonomous, and unburdened by a large administrative structure, not unlike the parochial schools that currently dot the urban landscape. Catholic schools have demonstrated that high expectations can be translated into high performance, even in the inner city. In fact, the most effective schools—whether public, private, or parochial—share the same characteristics: they are relatively small, devote relatively few resources to administrative overhead, have high expectations for all students, have a common curriculum in which all students participate, and have a strong sense of mission and a well-defined culture. The goal is not to let a thousand flowers bloom but to encourage the development of schools committed to erasing the learning gap between advantaged and disadvantaged children.

This returns us to the issue of choice. The growth of charter schools will certainly have an impact on the viability of public school choice programs as mechanisms to improve the educational opportunities for all children. But the realization of this promise will come slowly, especially if charter schools remain small in size (as they should) and if their overall number is "capped" (as their opponents so often insist). The demand for private school choice programs for the poor is most compelling because disadvantaged children who are not likely to succeed in their current school placement cannot afford to wait for a better day to arrive. They need better alternatives now.

14   One point worth emphasizing, as we review recent school reform initiatives, is the critical role played by the states in the restructuring and "reinvention" of urban education. Part of that influence arises from the legal structure that governs schooling, which places important decision making in the hands of governors and state legislatures. But the real explanation is institutional. The pivotal issue is control. In a relative sense, states do not seem to have as strong an institutional stake in the bureaucratization of education as do local school boards, and the interest groups that are strongest in the city are sometimes not of equal strength in the state legislature. When faced with demands to alter a century of institutional history, such considerations are salient.

As school reform advances, school decentralization in the form of site-based management should be pursued vigorously. So should charter schools, established by the state, removed from the authority of local school boards, as laboratories in which to test the capacity of educators to meet high standards when freed of unnecessary rules, regulations, and bureaucratic administrivia. Contracting arrangements, which introduce new energy and talent to city school systems, offer a promising alternative, especially when local school boards recognize that contracting permits higher levels of accountability for results. States appear to be the likeliest initiators of charter schools, and local school boards seem to be the likeliest initiators of contracts for instructional services. In either case, the bottom line must be a readiness by both public officials and school leaders to ensure that children are meeting high and clear educational standards.

The introduction of charter schools and contract-managed schools into public education may be exactly the impetus that is needed to promote meaningful performance standards for students and schools; the very existence of such schools will cause educators within the existing system to demand clear standards by which to measure school performance, as well as their own. Until now, most public education systems have been content with minimum standards or standards that are so vague as to be meaningless.

Public education in America is undergoing a slow, steady transformation, and the changes on the horizon promise a new level of vitality and effectiveness. This promise requires that reinvention strategies—like charters, contracting, and choice—occur within a context of standards, assessments, and accountability. When public schools consistently perform poorly, when they are unable to help children learn, then they must be replaced by more effective organizations. Sometimes poor public schools have been reorganized and transformed, but sometimes it may be necessary to replace ineffective schools with new institutions altogether, such as charter schools and contract schools, and to provide scholarships for the neediest children.

Public education does not have to be defined solely as schools operated by the government and staffed by civil servants. Surely many traditional public schools (especially in the suburbs and rural areas) will continue to thrive; it may well be that most parents will prefer them to the new alternatives. That should be a matter of parental choice. But those parents who want a different education for their children should also have choices. To the extent that public officials and innovative educators can expand the definition of public education to encompass a diversity of institutions, public education will be strengthened even as it is redefined. Government will continue to have a decisive role in setting educational standards, assessing student performance, monitoring the fiscal probity of school administrations, reorganizing failing schools, and authorizing new schools. For government, this is a tall order. But government need not make all the decisions. The actual management of schools and decisions about organization and pedagogy should be left to educators in the schools, who are likeliest to know what they must do to educate their pupils.

As Paul Hill suggests, one of the most valuable instruments to appear in the current wave of reform is the performance contract, which grants autonomy in exchange for accountability. Whether called a contract or a charter, such performance agreements should help to define the relation between public authorities and educational providers, whether they manage charter schools, contract schools, or government-run schools. Private and parochial schools that accept tuition vouchers for poor children should expect to be held to the same performance standards.

Setting standards does not mean intrusion on the design of instructional programs or imposition of a cookie-cutter approach to staffing, schedules, or organization. New schools are likely to be created by universities, groups of teachers, nonprofit organizations, and for-profit organizations, as they have been in those states that have authorized charter schools. They will differ in their pedagogy. They are likely to include many different approaches; some will be progressive schools, outward-bound schools, family-style schools,

16   single-sex schools, theme schools, back to basic schools, and classical academies. The range of options will be as vast as the imagination of creative educators.

For more than a century, we have held the means of education constant —a regulated, uniform, one-size-fits-all approach—and allowed the ends to vary in terms of student achievement. Our focus on means and our disregard of ends has fostered extremes of inequality. We must reverse the order, varying the means to accommodate a more diverse student population while holding constant the ends in order to promote improved outcomes for all children. We do not maintain a large and expensive public education system merely to provide custodial care for young people, nor should we be satisfied to educate a significant minority extremely well. Our goal must be the education of every young American, and our means must encompass and encourage every reasonable and effective approach that brings us closer to that goal.

New York: The Obsolete Factory

Diane Ravitch and

Joseph P. Viteritti

It is difficult to imagine an organizational structure as hapless or incorrigible as the New York City public school system. By any reasonable measure of educational effectiveness, the system is not working well. Sprawling, rigid, machinelike, uncompromising, it is the premiere example of factory model schooling. Its centennial in 1996 passed uncelebrated and unremarked, possibly because its multitude of embarrassments made celebration unseemly. The school system has become a symbol of unresponsive bureaucracy that somehow rebuffs all efforts to change it. It is the creature of another era, designed as a machine in which orders flowed from the top and were quickly implemented below with no regard for the ideas or opinions of either its workers or customers.[1]

The system worked well enough in an earlier age. In its first half century, the percentage of graduates increased in each decade, and steady progress seemed the order of the day. The economy also had good jobs for students who left school without graduating. But today, progress has stalled: little more than 50 percent of the youngsters who start high school reach graduation, and the economy has few places for high school

18   dropouts. What is needed today are schools that educate almost all who enter; what is needed is a school system that is equally intolerant of social promotion and of school failure. What is required today is something that the current system has never supplied: the ability to provide a high level of universal education.

Today the system retains its original structure, with additions that were grafted on in 1969 (creating decentralized local school boards) and 1996 (removing the hiring powers of the local boards). Now the system is both centralized (with a central board) and decentralized (with thirty-two elected school boards). Its structure defies reason, with authority so broadly dispersed that no one is ultimately accountable for the quality of education.[2] Mired in bureaucracy and entrenched in local politics, this cumbersome system stands as an obstacle to meaningful change at a time when other cities are reforming their school systems. The organizational structure consumes resources needlessly, wears down energetic educators, and marginalizes even the best-conceived efforts at innovation.

The situation is not entirely hopeless. New Yorkers point with pride to the extraordinary number of students who become Westinghouse scholars, and to the system's educational jewels, like Stuyvesant High School in Manhattan, the Bronx High School of Science, and La Guardia High School of the Performing Arts, which sits across from Lincoln Center. Also noteworthy are the success stories found in educational experiments like the public choice program in East Harlem or the Wildcat Academy in lower Manhattan, which serves some of the city's most troubled youth.[3] But these are exceptions rather than the rule. Far too many students in New York City are assigned to schools that are too large, too decrepit, too overcrowded, or too dispirited to provide good education. Wave after wave of reform has washed over the system, promising changes that never materialized.

New York City has always exhibited an extraordinary capacity to produce and attract talented people. However, even the most gifted educators and boldest leaders are no match for a system that has outlived its usefulness and lacks the capacity to change. In 1996 the Board of Education swore in its eighth chancellor in twelve years. Each time the position becomes vacant, the city indulges itself in the hope that some man or woman with magical powers will arrive on the scene to successfully navigate the political and managerial minefields on behalf of one million school children. But each administration ends with more casualties. Chancellors are the most obvious casualties of a system that has proven to be ungovernable. More damaging to the city, however, is the demoralization suffered by the many dedicated professionals who toil in more than one thousand schools and are confronted with a culture of bureaucratic regulation that makes it impossible for them to perform their jobs well.[4] Most tragic of all are the many thousands of youngsters whose lives are blighted because they are not well educated.

The Bureaucracy

Although never the subject of song or story, the bureaucracy at 110 Livingston Street is justly fabled.[5] With nearly 120,000 employees and a budget of approximately $8 billion, it is the largest government agency in the United States outside of Washington, D.C.[6] Atop this massive structure sits a seven-member Board of Education, appointed by six political authorities: two members are appointed by the mayor, the others by the five borough presidents. Even at the highest level, it is impossible to discern who is ultimately responsible for what happens in the school system. The most important function of the board is to appoint a chancellor, who acts as the system's chief executive officer. Usually when the board is called upon to select a new chancellor, the process degenerates into an embarrassing spectacle that reveals the political divisions among its six appointing authorities.

There is no simple way to describe the bureaucracy at 110 Livingston Street. Even metaphors fail, for no one living species in the animal, plant, or marine kingdom suffices to capture its essence. Like a huge dinosaur, it is not particularly smart, has an insatiable appetite, moves awkwardly, yet exudes great power. Like wisteria, it is impossible to control; clip it back and it grows more vigorously than before. Like a giant octopus, its many tentacles reach fearlessly into every aspect of the school system. Livingston Street oversees personnel, budgetary, and building functions; determines who gets what supplies; oversees maintenance of the system's enormous inventory of buildings; supervises student transportation and the delivery of school breakfasts and lunches; and operates numerous educational and "support" functions, including special education, bilingual education, and school safety. It also runs the high schools.

The numbers of children served in the school system clearly require a large budget, but the system's administrators never seem to be able to

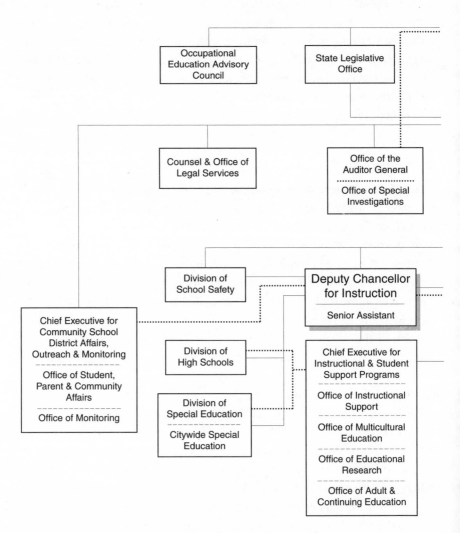

FIG. I.I New York City Board of Education organization chart

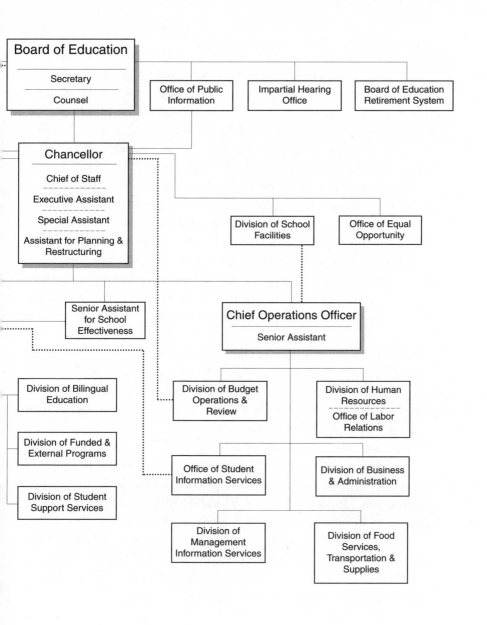

Board of Education

Secretary

Counsel

Office of Public Information

Impartial Hearing Office

Board of Education Retirement System

Chancellor

Chief of Staff

Executive Assistant

Special Assistant

Assistant for Planning & Restructuring

Division of School Facilities

Office of Equal Opportunity

Senior Assistant for School Effectiveness

Chief Operations Officer

Senior Assistant

Division of Bilingual Education

Division of Funded & External Programs

Division of Student Support Services

Division of Budget Operations & Review

Division of Human Resources

Office of Labor Relations

Office of Student Information Services

Division of Business & Administration

Division of Management Information Services

Division of Food Services, Transportation & Supplies

22   manage the budget so that schools are well maintained, teachers are well paid, and materials are in good supply. In early 1996, newly appointed Chancellor Rudolph Crew released a fifty-five-page reorganization plan designed to "create the opportunity for cost savings" and "minimize, if not completely eliminate, organizational redundancies and inefficiencies." The proposal resulted in a net savings of $271,503 from a budget of $8 billion.[7] One of the great misfortunes associated with the large expenditure of resources by the city school system is that the average classroom benefits relatively little. According to the board's own systemwide figures, only 42.2 percent of the school budget was spent on instruction in 1995–1996.[8]

This diversion of funds from the classroom to administrative and support functions in the bureaucracy is typical of large American cities, but it stands in bold contrast to better-functioning systems in Europe and Asia, where the majority of professionals are in the classroom.[9] Certain nonclassroom costs are unavoidable, like the expense of heating and repairing buildings, and the salaries of bus drivers, librarians, custodians, security guards, and cafeteria workers. Yet it is also clear that most of the necessary functions are overadministered and undersupervised. Some of these functions (school meals, for example) could be managed with greater efficiency by individual schools, and others could be delivered by municipal agencies (financial auditing by the Comptroller's Office, for example, and the screening and training of security guards by the Police Department).

There is a substantial body of research in the field of organizational studies that correlates organizational size with performance. It shows that economies of scale accompany growth to a certain point; then the pattern reverses, and "diseconomies" are associated with exceptionally large institutions.[10] By most measures, Livingston Street has passed the threshold of inefficiency. It has a long history of mismanagement, waste, and corruption. An overview of the major divisions of the board suggests the complexity of the overall organization, which tends to be managed by inertia rather than by plan.

DIVISION OF SCHOOL SAFETY

The Division of School Safety is one of the largest urban police forces in the country. With a $70 million budget, it deploys a 3,000-person security force throughout city schools. Although unarmed, members of its uniformed force have been granted special officer status by the New York City Police Department, which empowers them to make arrests. The executive director of the division decides what kind of security is provided to each school. The principal has no control over the school's security detail, whose members are appointed by central authorities and report to them. The division has been the subject of numerous studies and investigations.[11] In 1992, the Special Commissioner of Investigation for the New York City School District issued a report documenting financial improprieties and nepotism in the upper ranks of the division.[12] School safety officers themselves have been arrested for drug abuse, the sale of narcotics, and sexual misconduct with students. Mayor Rudolph Giuliani has sought to transfer school security to the Police Department, while the Board of Education insists that the function must remain within its control.

BUREAU OF SUPPLIES

The Bureau of Supplies administers a $160 million budget under which everything from pencils, books, and chalk to computers, desks, and filing cabinets are purchased and allocated. In 1994, the U.S. Attorney, in cooperation with the Special Commissioner of Investigation, uncovered a system of fraud in which more than $125,000 was diverted for private use. Instead of using the funds to purchase school supplies, twenty-five employees conspired to apply the money toward personal expenses, financing, for example, vacations to Puerto Rico, mortgage and credit card payments, and jewelry purchases. A report prepared by the Special Commissioner described these findings as the "tip of the iceberg" and documented a procurement and purchasing system that invited corruption.[13] In another incident a local news reporter for CBS made a video recording that showed employees from the bureau loading their private vehicles with items taken from the storehouse. People familiar with the workings of the school system often joke about the dead bodies buried in the bureaucracy. In early 1995 the figure of speech turned to reality when the remains of two skeletons were found in the furnace room of a warehouse. Investigators have tied the discovery to corruption within the bureau, but the case remains open. Many school principals believe that they could purchase supplies for their schools at lower cost than does the Bureau of Supplies and could be sure of having them available when needed instead of at the bureau's convenience.

The Bureau of Supplies is administered by the same school official as the Office of Food and Nutrition Services. Despite the widely publicized incidents of corruption that were uncovered in the division, the chancellor and the Board of Education permitted the executive director to retain his position. In June 1995 the Special Commissioner of Investigation uncovered gross mismanagement practices in Food Services. Outdated and rancid food was being served to schoolchildren while funds were stolen by employees. Two-year-old turkeys, sixteen-month-old ground beef, and twenty-month-old beans, cheese, and corn were among the items being served in school cafeterias.[14] The investigation was inspired by incidents of food poisoning among students. Mismanagement aside, there is reason to wonder why a single agency sets the menu for more than one million children every day and why this agency delivers precooked meals to schools that have their own kitchens and staff. Intelligent experimentation in a limited number of schools would quickly determine whether schools could do a better job of preparing nutritious meals than does the Office of Food and Nutrition Services, but the will to try something different has been lacking.

SCHOOL CONSTRUCTION AUTHORITY AND DIVISION OF SCHOOL FACILITIES

A number of units within the school system are responsible for the quality and condition of its thousand-plus school buildings. Among these are the School Construction Authority (SCA) and the Division of School Facilities. The SCA, which commands a $4 billion capital budget, oversees the construction and renovation of school buildings. It was created in 1988 as a separate authority with its own board because of dissatisfaction with the Board of Education's Division of School Buildings. That division, which had responsibility for construction and renovation as well as maintenance, had been plagued by allegations of incompetence and impropriety. The Division of School Facilities, which supervises maintenance and custodial services, is the remnant of that former unit. In 1994 school custodians signed a new contract with the city, which promised to give principals increased authority over custodians and to demand more accountability. These organizational and contractual changes, as bold as they seemed at their inception, have proven to be largely ineffectual. The overwhelming majority of schools continue to have custodians who report to "central," not to the principal;

and the handful of schools that have "privatized" custodians have no role in selecting the company that provides these services: the central bureaucracy is in charge of that, too.

Most teachers and principals would agree that custodians have more control over the quality of their everyday lives than any other building personnel. Custodians have long enjoyed an unusually exalted position in the schools. They belong to one of the most powerful labor unions in the system and enjoy civil service protections, yet they operate as private entrepreneurs with the authority to hire their own employees. Functioning as a "quasi-independent contractor," each building custodian is given a budget ranging from $80,000 to $1,200,000—depending upon the size of the school —from which he hires helpers, buys equipment, and draws a salary.[15]

For many years, few restrictions were placed on the employment practices of custodians, and it was customary for them to hire relatives. Some custodians have worked their way around more recent nepotism rules by hiring each other's relatives. Although the 1994 contract was supposed to give principals more supervisory authority over their building custodians, these personnel still report to the Division of School Facilities, which determines their assignment, retention, and terms of employment. Principals do evaluate their custodians, but the report is of little consequence. As recently as March 1996 an audit of the division's $188 million payroll by the city comptroller detailed widespread waste, mismanagement, and fraud in the overtime paid to custodial helpers.[16] Previous inquiries had documented instances when custodians did not show up for work and maintained other jobs while under contract with the school system.

In June 1995 a blue-ribbon panel composed of executives from the real estate, financial, and corporate sectors prepared a thirty-eight-page report for Chancellor Ramon Cortines, documenting the deplorable conditions in school construction. Buildings were literally collapsing, the panel reported; crumbling walls, leaking roofs, and falling plaster were common. The study warned, "Unless immediate steps are taken to fix the buildings, we believe that school children, teachers and staff will be hurt or even killed."[17] In spite of the alarming warning, no immediate action was taken.

In April 1996 reports emerged in the press concerning the mismanagement of the Board of Education's $170 million leasing program for private space to accommodate increasing enrollments. The Manhattan District Attorney launched an investigation of a $12 million lease agreement that

26   had been negotiated by an employee who had resigned from the board to work for the landlord who won the contract.[18] In some instances, the board leased space from tenants who made a huge profit by subletting, or from individuals who did not even own the building until after completing a lucrative contract with the board. Almost simultaneously, an inquiry by the state senate disclosed "serious problems"—delays, cost overruns, and dangerous conditions—in thirty of fifty-four building or renovation projects under the direction of the SCA.[19] When leasing is necessary, it makes more sense for the board to engage commercial agents who are paid only for their performance, rather than using their own inexperienced employees.

DIVISION OF BILINGUAL EDUCATION

The Division of Bilingual Education administers programs to children with limited English proficiency. These programs are supposed to help approximately 150,000 immigrant students learn English. Under state law, students are not permitted to spend more than three years in bilingual programs unless the board applies for individual waivers from the state Department of Education. In 1994 the Board of Education released a report showing that tens of thousands of students had been permitted to languish in the programs for up to six years. The study indicated three-year exit rates of 37.9 percent for students entering in second grade, 15.0 percent for those entering in sixth grade, and 11.4 percent for those entering in ninth grade.[20] The study highlighted great disparities in exit rates between bilingual programs, where classes are taught primarily in the students' native language, and English as a second language programs, where classes are conducted primarily in English. The board's report showed that students in ESL programs entered the English-speaking mainstream much faster than students in bilingual programs. A 1974 consent decree made it very easy for students to be assigned to bilingual classes.[21] Any student who has a Hispanic surname or comes from a home in which no one speaks English is given an English language test. Students who score in the bottom 40 percent are assigned to bilingual education, even those who know more English than Spanish and hear English spoken at home. Once placed in bilingual education, the student finds it difficult to withdraw. The negative findings about the effects of bilingual education, as compared with English as a second language instruction, led to no substantive changes.

Shortly after the release of the board's 1994 report, the Bushwick Parents

Association filed a suit seeking to end a practice whereby the state education commissioner routinely issues blanket waivers of the three-year limit at the request of local bilingual coordinators. The group, representing 150 Brooklyn families, complained that many of the teachers in the program do not speak English and contended that local administrators strive to keep enrollments high in order to protect their jobs. Although their claims have merit, the Bushwick parents face an uphill battle in court. Because the state commissioner was "following procedure," the practice was upheld by the trial court.[22] The bilingual program continues to operate in response to the requirements of its administrators, rather than the students or their families. In a more rational setting, the program would be judged by its results, and its supposed beneficiaries would be allowed to choose whether to participate or enroll elsewhere.

Community Boards

The Decentralization Law enacted by the state legislature in 1969 was actually a political compromise that perpetuated the centralized bureaucratic system and parceled out control of the elementary and middle schools to elected local boards in thirty-two school districts. An outgrowth of the community power movement of the 1960s, the law was explicitly designed to create an institutional mechanism for giving parents access to and participation in educational decision making.[23] By the middle of the decade, black and Hispanic children were a majority of the enrollment in the school system. Many parents within minority communities believed that the centralized bureaucracy was indifferent to the needs of their children. Political activists, especially antipoverty workers in minority communities, wanted to create power centers with control over budgets and hiring rather than continue to trust the closed system that had prevailed for more than a half century.

As the ancient Chinese curse augurs, the reformers of the day had their wish granted. Politics they wanted, and it was politics they got. The transfer of power was grudging and only partial. Demands for community control set the stage for one of the most divisive political struggles in the history of the city, with a variety of community activists on one side, bolstered by Mayor John Lindsay and the Ford Foundation, arrayed against the teachers union on the other.[24] Because most of the community activists were black

28   and the educators were predominantly white and Jewish, the contest had
an ugly racial and religious undertone that tainted local politics for years.

The decentralization law requires that school board elections be held
every three years to elect nine-member boards in each of the thirty-two
districts. School board elections have seldom drawn a turnout of more than
10 percent of eligible voters. The 5.2 percent turnout in 1996 was the lowest
yet. Some would argue that the low turnout is a function of the electoral
system itself—a confusing proportional voting scheme, using paper ballots
that are cast in early May rather than on election day in November. It is also
true that the communities are artificially drawn and that few eligible voters
know or care who is running for the local school board. Or the participation
rate may be a true barometer of the confidence that people have in the
voting process and the boards that are elected. Whatever the reason, school
board elections can hardly be viewed as models of democratic politics. The
low turnout makes the elections fair game for organized interest groups,
such as unions, political parties, and small bands of opportunists who see
school politics as a well of patronage.

In 1993, the Special Commissioner of Investigation completed an inquiry
into the school board election process that revealed "widespread fraud and
corruption as well as administrative mismanagement."[25] In one Manhattan
district an undercover investigator was allowed to vote fifteen times under
fifteen fictitious names; another did the same ten times in a neighboring
district. This corruption spills over to the actual governance of the districts,
where school boards control more than $100 million in funds, as well as the
power to appoint district superintendents, administrators, principals, and
thousands of paraprofessionals. It is not uncommon for teachers and paraprofessionals to be forced into political servitude by local board members—
collecting petitions, fund raising, electioneering—as a price for professional
advancement.

The story of wrongdoing within the districts has been told many times.[26]
One can pick up a New York newspaper almost weekly and read about jobs
that were sold, nepotism in the hiring of principals, teachers who were
pressured to attend political events for board members, money that was
misappropriated for private use, or sex scandals or drug abuse involving
school board members. Every year the chancellor goes through the almost
ritualistic practice of suspending school boards for some kind of misconduct

or just plain incompetence. The event usually attracts a great deal of media attention and head shaking by local politicians. But more often than not the same board members who were removed by the chancellor for malfeasance subsequently manage to get reelected in a political process that defies any form of accountability. The persistence of scandals involving local school boards finally prompted the state legislature to pass legislation in December 1996 that removed from the local boards the power to hire their district superintendent and shifted that decision to the chancellor. Decentralization has now been transformed to recentralization; the local elected school boards have been allowed to continue existing, albeit with greatly curtailed authority.

School decentralization in New York City is a conspicuous example of distorted public priorities. It allowed the elementary and middle schools of the city to develop into arenas for adult ambition and greed rather than as institutions dedicated to the well-being of children. A survey conducted by the *Daily News* in 1995, to which 236 out of 288 school board members responded, indicated that only 38 percent had children in the school system.[27] Nearly 80 percent of the respondents did not know the size of their district budget or such basic information as enrollment data or test scores.[28] Nearly half could not identify the landmark *Brown v. Board of Education* Supreme Court decision. New York may be unique in the way it permitted local politics to take the place of meaningful parent participation.

In its twenty-seven-year history, decentralization has produced change, but not necessarily change for the better. One of the first casualties of decentralization was the Board of Examiners, which administered examinations to teachers and administrators. Whatever the shortcomings of the examination system, there was at least consideration of merit in decisions about hiring and promotion. With the elimination of the examinations, such decisions are now routinely based on race and ethnicity at both the central board and the new local school districts. Meanwhile, the old factory still thrives at Livingston Street: issuing orders, writing regulations, imposing requirements; controlling all purchasing, maintenance, hiring, and assignment of personnel. For teachers and principals, the shift from decentralization to recentralization will scarcely be noticeable because most of the major functions of the schools never left Livingston Street. The old factory was always in control.

Student Achievement

In January 1997 the commissioner of education released a new "state report card," measuring the performance of every public school in New York State.[29] The devastating report revealed a dramatic performance gap between New York City schools and those in the rest of the state, a gap that persisted even when the socioeconomic characteristics of students were considered. Only 59 percent of third-graders and 64 percent of sixth-graders were found to be reading above the minimum competency level, compared with 90 percent of the third-graders and 91 percent of the sixth-graders in the rest of the state. This meant that 89 percent of all elementary schools in the city failed to meet the state's minimum expectation for performance (requiring 90 percent of a school's students to be reading at standard).

The math results were more positive—88 percent of the third-graders and 84 percent of the sixth-graders in the city meeting the standard—but they still showed city children to be lagging behind the rest of the state, where 99 percent of third-graders and 98 percent of sixth-graders met minimum standards. These disparities were also evident at the high school level, where only 32 percent passed the English Regents exam, compared with 52 percent in the rest of the state, and 45 percent of the ninth-graders passed the math Regents exam. The data are particularly disturbing when viewed in light of the large number of youngsters who never finish high school.[30] Only 44.3 percent of high school students graduate within four years, less than 60 percent in five years.[31]

The State Board of Regents regularly publishes a list of poorly performing schools throughout the state. As of 1996, a statewide list of ninety-eight such schools included ninety in New York City. The total could easily be doubled with the addition of city schools that have consistently demonstrated poor academic performance. When the state commissioner first published a list of the poorest performing schools in 1985, the criteria were more rigorous and there were 393 identified in New York City. These ninety institutions, now called Schools Under Registration Review (SURR Schools), epitomize the high tolerance for persistent failure exhibited by policy makers in the city and state. At the end of 1995, a newly appointed state education commissioner ordered the city Board of Education to take corrective action in sixteen of the schools or run the risk that those schools would be closed or reorganized.[32] He set a deadline of two years for fourteen of the schools, and gave the other two an extra year to show improvement. Many of these schools had been on the failure list since 1989. No mention was made of the other seventy-four schools on the list. In July 1996 the regents announced that standards would be upgraded for determining when schools might be placed on the list and ultimately be eligible for closing.

Imagine being the parent of a child in a SURR school. If she had entered first grade in 1989, she might have spent all of her elementary school years in a failing institution. If she had entered school more recently and was in one of the sixteen institutions slated for corrective action, then she minimally might expect to spend about half her elementary school experience in a school recognized by state officials as totally inadequate. When we look at the performance goals set for these schools by the state, the prognosis for the child is even more discouraging. For PS 154 in Harlem, the 1995 target was to get 34.6 percent of the children in the third grade at or above the third-grade reading level; for PS 157 in the Bronx, the hope was to have 26.9 percent of the third-graders reading at or above grade level; and PS 304 in Brooklyn aspired to boost 12.3 percent of its third-graders to that standard. Most communities would find these low aspirations insulting.

Certain patterns are obvious in the list of SURR schools in New York City. The schools tend to be located in the poorest areas of town that are populated mostly by black and Hispanic families. A disproportionate number of these families are headed by a single mother and derive at least a part of their income from public assistance. For years, some educators have insisted that the entire story of school failure can be explained by demographics. There is, however, ample evidence that certain schools have been successfully educating students with a similar profile. Some are public schools in New York City and other big cities (such as the Wesley School in Houston), and others are parochial schools that flourish in the same communities as the SURR schools.

In 1992 the state commissioner of education convened a blue-ribbon panel, chaired by former governor Hugh Carey, to examine Catholic education in the state. The study demonstrates how these institutions, much like other parochial schools around the country, have managed to excel within inner-city communities while nearby public schools fail. There was a significant difference, for example, found in the percentage of elementary school students performing at the third-grade level in reading (60 percent in public schools vs. 77 percent in Catholic) and mathematics (81 percent vs. 90 per-

32 cent) and a dramatic difference in the passing rate on Regents Competency Examinations for high school students in mathematics (57 percent public vs. 78 percent Catholic), science (63 percent vs. 89 percent), writing (62 percent vs. 81 percent), and reading (62 percent vs. 91 percent).[33] Contrary to the common perception about selectivity in Catholic schools, Catholic school students in the city were as likely as their public school counterparts to exhibit multiple risk factors that are associated with poor performance (for example, family income below $15,000, single-parent household, parents who did not complete high school).

The study also found a notable difference between the two sectors in per pupil spending ($8,374 for public, $1,364 Catholic elementary, $2,925 Catholic high school).[34] We focus on these differences not to disparage public schools but to highlight two specific points that are relevant to the public policy issues woven throughout this volume. First, the data demonstrate that the structure of schools has an impact on their performance levels. The organizational variables that enhance parochial school performance and distinguish them from public schools will be discussed extensively by Valerie Lee in Chapter 6. Second, the data underscore the inutility and wastefulness of compelling children to remain in institutions like SURR schools, waiting for them to get better somehow, when more desirable options could be made available to poor children through the implementation of choice programs.

The argument for choice is bolstered by a private initiative begun in New York City in 1986 called the Student Sponsor Partnership. The program matches children from disadvantaged families with private donors, who subsidize their tuition in Catholic high schools. When the program was launched, it involved 46 students and 46 sponsors. As of 1996, there were 929 students and 757 sponsors. Of the 319 students entering in the 1995–1996 school year, 77 percent were from single-parent households and 64 percent were from families receiving public assistance.[35] The program is a remarkable success story, with a 75 percent graduation rate since its inception. Approximately 89 percent of the graduates go on to college, and 80 percent of those graduate from college within four or five years. The Partnership would be an appropriate model for a public school choice experiment, but the prospects for such a program in New York are discouraging.

Prospects and Politics

New Yorkers have an extraordinary self-image. No matter what the issue, they like to think of themselves as more knowledgeable than the rest of the nation. Sometimes it is even true. But when it comes to school reform, big dreams get deflated by political realities. In 1989, New York flirted with the idea of school choice when the state commissioner of education included it in a larger proposal he had prepared for the Board of Regents. A minor provision within a broader educational initiative called the New Compact for Learning, the commissioner's proposal would have provided educational vouchers to poor children who had been attending failing public schools. It would have given students trapped in dysfunctional educational settings an opportunity to attend private or parochial schools at public expense. The proposal died. As Commissioner Thomas Sobol explained it, "The teachers' unions and the school board associations and the PTA's were up in arms. They basically told us they would kill everything if we persisted with the voucher proposal."[36]

Two years later the regents attempted to enact their own pilot program when they considered vouchers for five thousand poor children from the state's worst public schools. It was one of the few occasions when Governor Mario Cuomo personally met with the board to argue a position on an education issue. He appeared to explain how providing vouchers for poor children to attend better schools would harm public education. The proposal was struck down by a vote of eight to six. A similar proposal was defeated in 1996.[37]

The teachers union is one of the most powerful political forces in the state capitol. It is virtually impossible for an education bill to emerge from the legislature without the union's support. Year after year, when the state publishes data on funds spent by various interest groups for lobbying activities in Albany, the teachers union appears near the top. In 1995, for example, New York State United Teachers spent $1,165,447, second only to the Greater New York Hospital Association ($1,181,706).[38] The teachers' expenditure exceeds the hospitals' if we factor in spending by the United Federation of Teachers ($400,519), the New York City affiliate of the state teachers association.

The power of the union is unparalleled: no major decision is made by the

34 Central Board of Education without conferring with the UFT. The union president exercises virtual veto power in the selection of a chancellor. With all the talk of community power, the union still fields one of the most viable slates in local school board elections. Within every school building, it is the rules and procedures negotiated by the union in contracts, regulations, and statutes that set the tone of activity.

Union leaders like to think that the union is in the vanguard of reform. When confronted with proposals that threaten to reduce their power, positions, or long-held prerogatives, however, they bring their full influence to bear on public officials. In the spring of 1996, the City Council of New York held a public hearing to consider alternative ways for providing public educational services.[39] High on the agenda were charter schools and contracting arrangements. The union sent five representatives to the meeting to oppose the proposals, some from the Washington office of the American Federation of Teachers, and others from the local UFT. They scolded the elected officials on the podium for raising such a provocative set of questions.

Unfortunately, the union's power in Albany and at Board of Education headquarters has not translated into real gains for the city's teachers compared with others in the region. New York City teachers have lower salaries and worse working conditions, and there is a constant talent drain to higher-paying suburban districts.

The Board of Education had approved a citywide choice program in 1991, which theoretically gave every child the right to attend the public school of his or her choice, so long as space was available. Unfortunately, most desirable schools are filled, and there are many applicants for each new place. Only six of thirty-two districts in the city even pretend to practice choice.[40] At the high school level, the immensely popular educational option schools like Edward R. Murrow reject far more students than they accept. (Some highly desirable schools receive eight applications for every opening.) For most children, public school choice is an empty promise.

Former chancellor Joseph Fernandez was a strong proponent of school-based management. He had instituted it in Miami before being recruited to New York; he had begun to develop a national reputation around the concept. In 1990 he announced that school-based management was being implemented in New York. What emerged had a definite New York flavor to it, resulting in no real autonomy at the school level and compromising precious little of the authority wielded by Livingston Street. School-site councils dominated by representatives of the teachers union were convened to discuss marginal instructional issues, but the big decisions about personnel and budget remained downtown.[41] The greatest disappointment of the 1996 school governance bill passed in Albany is that it did not result in any transfer of decision-making authority to the school level.

In the spring of 1995, the Annenberg Foundation announced the award of a $50 million gift to New York for the development and replication of innovative schools.[42] After much negotiation between the Board of Education, the chancellor, the teachers union, and a host of education groups, it was decided that the grant would be administered through four private organizations, under the umbrella of another not-for-profit institution called New Visions for Public Schools, which has its own governing board. While not so labeled, the experiment is the closest thing the school system has ever had to a private contracting arrangement for instructional services, although it does not have any of the accountability mechanisms that are built into contracting arrangements in other cities.

Educational reformers look to the Annenberg project with great hope. All of the groups behind it have articulated a commitment to small, autonomous schools. Some have called these relatively new institutions "charterlike schools." However, these institutions do not have control over their budget, they have limited control of personnel, they are fettered by the bureaucracy's red tape, they file the same reports as large schools, and central administrators determine which children from which boroughs may choose to attend them. Unlike charter schools, no clear performance standards have been agreed upon by which they will be evaluated. Many defenders of the status quo, including members of the central board, use these "charterlike schools" to fend off demands for real charter schools. Ironically, charter legislation may be the likeliest way to preserve the experimental nature of the Annenberg schools and to prevent their eventual assimilation into the larger system. Charter legislation would also define the student performance standards that these schools must meet.

One can appreciate the durability of the old factory by contemplating the timidity of those efforts that have offered the most promise to dismantle it. Rather than apply a wrecking ball to its walls, reformers in New York toss the biggest snowballs they can find and, after a few forceful heaves, often come to the conclusion that it is much warmer inside the building. We must keep a close watch on the Annenberg schools, for they are the best hope for

36 change in New York. We hope that they will resist the relentless pressure to be absorbed by the system; we hope that they will eventually realize that their prized authority will disappear unless they demand that schools be allowed to control their budget and staff. Otherwise, the time will come when the valiant pioneers will retire and the new schools will quietly merge into the bureaucratic system. Even if the Annenberg project succeeds in attaining its goal—one hundred small schools enrolling a total of fifty thousand students—it will reach less than 5 percent of the public school enrollment. Even if it provides good schools for those children, it is not an answer to the more systemic problem.

As we approach a new century, the old factory still stands. A few bricks have been loosened, but the tired old machinery continues to clank and grind. No one believes anymore that it is run by the wisest and best educators in the land. The giant factory no longer commands the respect and admiration that it once did. Its assembly line is ragged, and its products frequently fail. But it endures. The people who control the operation are unwilling to change it in any fundamental way.

The factory system must be replaced, just as other obsolete top-down hierarchical structures in other sectors of society have been replaced. It cannot meet the needs of the vast majority of children in New York City for a high-quality education. We imagine a public school system that values performance, flexibility, innovation, and responsiveness. We imagine a public school system in which public authorities set clear academic standards and assess student performance; approve the opening of new schools and close failing schools; act as ombudsmen for the children; engage in long-range planning; and audit schools for educational and fiscal performance. We imagine a public school system in which each school has a large measure of autonomy to manage its resources and staff; in which parents select the school that is best for their child; in which there is a diversity of schools to meet a diversity of student needs; and in which the goal for all children is an education that will prepare them for further learning, skilled employment, and active citizenship.

Perhaps one day parents, the business community, and civic leaders will agree that the city can no longer afford a school system that does not work for so many children. If that day ever comes, the educational factory of New York City will be dismantled and replaced by educating structures that are able to meet the demands of a different age.

2 The Charter School Movement

Louann A. Bierlein

This charter school law is my license to dream, to do what I have always known needed to be done for kids, but was not doable because of the system, too many excuses, and a lack of accountability.

Charter school founder, California

I believe that charter schools give us a way to be innovative within the public school rubric. They give us a way to move forward on a new notion of a system of public schools. I think that it is an innovation worth trying.

Public school district superintendent, Wisconsin

Charter schools are experiments at best and will do little more than take money away from the traditional public school system. There really is no need for such schools since things are generally fine as they are.

Teachers union leader, Los Angeles

38   A distractor from real educational reform, that's all charter schools
really are.
University professor, New York state

These are among the many comments I hear as I visit charter schools across
the country, work with policy makers implementing such laws, and speak
with those opposed to the concept. Talk to those involved with creating
charter schools or laws, and they are very committed to the concept. Talk
with those who oppose the creation of such entities and they are equally
committed. No other recent education reform initiative has sparked such
interest and controversy, and none has grown so rapidly. What are charter
schools and what is their appeal? Where did the idea come from? What has
happened to date across the country? What does the research show? And,
finally, what is the long-term chance for survival of this concept?

Charter Schools: The Concept and Its Appeal

A charter school is a public institution that is conceptualized, organized, and
eventually operated by any public or private person or organization.[1] The
school operates under a charter contract that has been negotiated between
the school's organizers (teachers or parents, for example) and a sponsor
(such as a local school board, a state board of education, or a university),
which oversees the provisions of the charter. The charter describes the
school's instructional plan, specific educational outcomes and measures,
and its management and financial plan. Charter schools may be formed
using an existing school's personnel and facilities, a portion of such a school
(called a school-within-a-school), or a completely new entity with its own
facilities and staff. Some states allow the conversion of private nonsectarian
schools to public charter schools.

    Charter schools are independent legal entities with the ability to hire and
fire, sue and be sued, award contracts for outside services, and control their
finances. Such schools are public schools: they receive state funding, are
nonsectarian, and are prohibited from selective student admission or charg-
ing tuition. They are also schools of choice for teachers, students, and parents; if a charter school fails to attract these individuals or violates any terms
of its charter, it goes out of business. Charter schools are freed from most state
laws and local board policies (except for health, safety, civil rights, and fiscal

and pupil accountability) and are granted full authority over the public funding, which follows students. In exchange for freedom from regulations, charter schools agree to be accountable for improved student outcomes.

Charter schools are an appealing reform concept for many. They focus on results, not inputs; create more educational choices for teachers, parents, and students; allow school-site personnel and parents to make administrative and instructional decisions and hold them legally liable for them; and create a more consumer-driven educational system.[2] Charter schools also encourage questions about conventional public school management, instructional, and accountability practices: Why should only local school boards have the right to govern schools? Why can't school personnel and parents have full control over all funds associated with their student count, including salaries? Hasn't the time come when educators, as part of a collective school entity, must demonstrate progress or risk their employment?

The ultimate appeal of charter schools is that they are public entities, incorporating perhaps the best of both the current public school world (for example, protection for students and public funds) and the private school world (for example, competition, full site control). Two types of accountability are involved—schools must both attract students and demonstrate specific results—or go out of business.

A number of individuals and groups, however, remain critical of the charter school concept. They contend that policy makers are using this issue to distract from other broad-based education reforms. Some believe that charter schools represent a first step that will lead inevitably to private school vouchers. Critics fear resegregation and elitist schools. They warn that hard-fought salary and benefit levels may be undermined by "non-professionals" employed by charter schools. Many are concerned simply because the creation of such schools challenges long-held "truths" regarding governance and accountability within public education.

The Charter School Explosion

The charter school concept can be traced to a California alternative education association, which in 1985 began advocating that teachers be granted the power to establish public schools.[3] A bill to this effect was proposed during 1987 but didn't go far in the California legislature. A 1989 article by Ray Budde caught the attention of a few individuals across the country,

40   notably Albert Shanker, head of the American Federation of Teachers (AFT), who began to promote the idea.[4] Minnesota's Democratic Senator Ember Reichgott Junge heard Shanker speak in 1989 and decided to work for charter school legislation.

After a tough political battle, Minnesota enacted the nation's first charter school law in 1991, with California following the next year. Six more states —Colorado, Massachusetts, Michigan, Wisconsin, New Mexico, and Georgia—passed similar legislation in 1993.[5] Within less than five years, twenty-five states and the District of Columbia had enacted charter school–type legislation.[6] Active legislative discussions have occurred in at least fifteen other states. In Washington a citizen group bypassed legislators and spearheaded a voter initiative to place a charter school–type proposal on the fall 1996 ballot.[7]

The bipartisan appeal of the charter school concept has fed the movement's steady growth. Both the Clinton administration and the Republican-controlled Congress support this idea (one of the few education-related issues they agree on). At the state level, nearly all Republican legislators favor the concept because of its free-market and choice components. Democrats are split; many like the empowerment aspect of charter schools (and strongly dislike vouchers), but others are opposed because of union objections and potential student equity issues. Because of these latter concerns, charter schools are often perceived as a "Republican" issue with some Democratic support.

But strong Democratic support is apparent at the state level. Of the first nineteen states that enacted charter school legislation, twelve had Democratically controlled senate chambers, and eleven had Democratically controlled house chambers (a twelfth house chamber was evenly split).[8] Even in the seven states with the strongest charter school laws, Democrats controlled five senate chambers and four house chambers (again, one house chamber was split). Charter school supporters may follow party lines within a particular state, but viewed in the aggregate, charter school reform efforts have been bipartisan.

Critical Charter School Law Components

Political battles over charter schools remain intense. State policy makers face many constraints when translating the pure charter school concept into law, including state constitutional provisions, school financing systems, tradition, and, perhaps most critical of all, the political clout of various education groups. As a result, only a few states allow an unlimited number of charter schools as strictly defined. In these states with strong charter school laws, such schools can be sponsored by entities other than local boards, are granted a great deal of financial and legal autonomy, and are automatically free from most state and local rules.

In states with weaker laws, charter schools are essentially no more than enhanced site-based decision-making experiments: schools must remain part of the school district, have limited control over budget and personnel matters, and must seek waivers from regulations on a case-by-case basis. Given the variation among charter school laws, it would be an error to view all laws (and the resulting charter schools) as equal.

Table 2.1 summarizes the seven essential components to creating charter schools capable of challenging status quo elements of the system and ultimately producing positive reform results.[9]

1. A charter school must be allowed to seek sponsorship from a public entity other than a local school board and/or be allowed to appeal a school board decision.

School boards have historically been the sole providers of, and primary decision makers for, public education in their communities. They hold a monopoly over the public education industry and do not give up power willingly or easily. History also suggests that local boards are not known for innovation and are unlikely to push for sweeping changes. Political pressures often ensure a level of "sameness" within a district in the areas of curriculum, management, salaries, and benefits. Charter school applicants must therefore have the ability to appeal an unfavorable local board decision to some higher authority or to bypass their local boards completely, going directly to an alternate sponsor (such as a state board or university).

An appeals process puts pressures on local boards to carefully consider charter proposals based on the soundness of the plan (not politics), while the availability of alternate sponsors forces local boards to compete for their students. For example, many local boards in Arizona began actively to solicit charter proposals in the hope that groups would stay with them rather than go to one of two state boards authorized to grant charter approvals. In

TABLE 2.1 Initial Twenty Charter School Laws: Analysis of "Stronger" Components

	Stronger														Weaker					
	AZ ('94)	DE ('95)	NH ('95)	MA ('93)	MI ('94)	TX ('95)	CA ('92)	NJ ('96)	MN ('91)	CO ('93)	LA ('95)	WI ('93)	HI ('94)	WY ('95)	NM ('93)	RI ('95)	GA ('93)	KS ('94)	AR ('95)	AK ('95)
1) Nonlocal board sponsor available OR Appeal process exists	✓	✓		✓	✓	✓	✓	✓	✓	✓					✓					
2) Any individual or group can attempt to organize a charter proposal	✓		✓	✓	✓	✓ [a]	✓	✓ [b]	✓	✓	✓	✓	✓	✓		✓		✓		✓
3) Automatic exemptions from state laws/rules & local policies	✓	✓	✓	✓	✓	✓	✓		✓		✓	✓ [c]	✓							
4) Fiscal autonomy—school has control over funds generated by its student count (including salaries)	✓	✓	✓	✓	✓	✓	✓ [d]		✓	✓ [e]	✓		✓							
5) Legal autonomy (e.g., teachers are school, not district, employees) OR the charter (not the law) determines level of legal autonomy	✓	✓	✓	✓	✓	✓	✓		✓	✓ [c]	✓									
6) No (or very high) limits on number of charter schools that can be formed (compared with total population)	✓	✓	✓	✓	✓	✓	✓	✓	✓	✓	✓	✓	✓	✓			✓		✓	

TABLE 2.1 *Continued*

| | Stronger | | | | | | | | | | | | | Weaker | | | | | | |
	AZ	DE	NH	MA	MI	TX	CA	NJ	MN	CO	LA	WI	HI	WY	NM	RI	GA	KS	AR	AK
7) Some % noncertified individuals can teach at charter school (without having to seek a waiver or alternate certification)	✓	f	✓	✓	g	✓	✓				✓									
Total "stronger" components	7	7	7	6	6	6	6	5	5	5	5	3	3	2	1	1	1	1	1	1

Note: "Stronger" charter school law components are those which are most true to the charter school concept, challenge the status quo aspects of the system, and theoretically may lead to broader student impacts and ripple effects. Component #1 (availability of nonlocal board sponsorship or appeal) is considered a vital component in order to get an adequate number of charter schools started.

[a] Based upon "open enrollment" charter school portion of Texas's charter school bill. Eligible organizers are limited to public or private higher education institutions or a nonprofit or governmental entity.

[b] In New Jersey, any teachers or parents within a district may themselves, or in conjunction with any in-state higher education institution or private entity, establish a charter school; such schools are eligible for at least 90% of the local levy budget per pupil; and district collective bargaining provisions automatically apply to converted public schools, while salaries within new charter schools must fall within the range established by the district in which the school is located.

[c] In Wisconsin, charter schools are automatically exempt from most state laws and rules, not local board policies. Also, recently enacted provisions strengthen the law for potential charter schools within the Milwaukee district only in that such schools can become legally and financially autonomous and have access to a state appeals process.

[d] California's charter schools are allowed by law to be legally and fiscally autonomous, but this depends upon the provisions of a given school's charter.

[e] Legally, Colorado's charter schools are to remain a part of the local school district and to receive at least 80% of their funds; in practice, however, many are operating quite autonomously.

[f] In Delaware, up to 35% noncertified teachers may be utilized if no qualified alternative certification program exists (and currently there is no such program in the state).

[g] In Michigan, the issue of automatic law exemptions is still unclear, and certification is required except in university-sponsored schools where higher education faculty can teach.

44 response to the charter law in Massachusetts (where proposals go directly to the commissioner of education), the Boston public schools and the teachers union initiated their own charter school process.

2. Any individual or group should be allowed to develop and submit a charter school proposal.

Creative energies from outside the traditional public education system are necessary to support serious reform efforts. Limiting the creation of charter schools to those currently in the system (certified teachers and existing public schools) ensures that a large percentage of the population continues to be excluded. Policies should allow and encourage "outsiders" to become an active part of the solution, especially given limited educational resources and growing needs.

The idea of allowing outsiders to form charter schools has been challenged by many in education circles. Some are concerned that religious groups will gain access to public funds, while others fear that profiteering will corrupt education. Although some caution is warranted, many creative partnerships and charter schools have resulted from this openness. For example, Skills for Tomorrow Charter School, a vocational/technical school in Minnesota, is being run with support from the Teamsters Union, and Woodward Academy, a Detroit-based residential charter school, is operated by the U.S. Drug Enforcement Administration. Such external groups have the potential to offer new insights into the educational process. And if they fail to deliver the outcomes promised, their charter contracts will be revoked.

3. Charter schools must automatically be exempt from most state laws, regulations, and local policies (except health, safety, civil rights, and fiscal and pupil accountability).

Some states, rather than offering automatic blanket exemptions, require charter schools to seek individual waivers from specific regulations. This limitation weakens the concept in a number of ways. First, all existing laws and policies remain in place, and efforts to remove barriers must be expended. Innovation is constrained because it is more difficult to remove an obstruction than to proceed with no obstruction at the outset. Second, research has found that although a number of states have waiver provisions on the books, only modest impacts have resulted. (This is true for public

schools in general, not just charter schools.)[10] A lack of knowledge regarding what can be done under a given law may be more of a barrier than the
law itself. Volumes of state and local regulations scare away many from
restructuring efforts; for others they provide an excuse for not trying at all.
Automatic exemptions are important in that they immediately set the stage
for "no excuses" planning for charter schools.

4. and 5. Charter schools must have fiscal and legal autonomy.

It is difficult, and perhaps unfair, to hold individuals or entities responsible for progress when they do not have full control over all resources. When
charter laws require schools to negotiate over the amount of funding they
will receive, the balance of power continues to reside with the local board.
Providing full funding to successful charter school applicants minimizes
disputes that can arise in the negotiation process. Charter schools, in turn,
can still subcontract with their district for some services.

Legal autonomy for charter schools is also essential. First, local boards
should not be legally liable for the actions of the charter school. If charter
schools gain full control over funding and decision making, then those
within the school should be fully responsible for their actions (the charter
school gets sued, for example, not the local school board). Second, education is personnel-intensive, and charter schools must therefore have control
over salaries, evaluations, and employment terms.

6. There should be no limits on the number of charter schools that can be
established within a given state.

Lack of political commitment is communicated when just a few charter
schools are allowed relative to the state's overall student population. Potential charter organizers are discouraged when the legal limit is small and may
conclude, "Why bother?" Given that a critical mass of such schools is necessary to evaluate the merits of the concept, those with sound ideas should
not be rejected simply because a certain arbitrary limit has been reached.

7. Charter schools must be permitted to employ noncertified teachers.

This component challenges one of the education system's most strongly
held beliefs—state teacher certification requirements. Completion of a set

46 number of pedagogy courses and a student teaching practicum has long been the minimum standard required for entry into the teaching profession. Teachers often must also take graduate-level courses to maintain certification. Universities benefit from the steady stream of students (especially at the graduate level), while the teaching profession benefits by becoming a "closed shop."

Allowing noncertified individuals to teach in a charter school does not mean that anyone off the street should be placed in a classroom. Instead, it tests whether a focus on results (student learning), rather than inputs (certified teachers) will improve student performance. When a school is placed on a contract, will it still choose to include only certified teachers or might it include some part-time specialists, such as retired engineers or college professors? Stronger charter school laws allow this type of question to be tested.

Current Status of Charter School Laws

Table 2.1 also depicts how the seven components of a strong charter school law are distributed across the twenty initial charter school states. Only three states—Arizona, Delaware, and New Hampshire—have charter school laws that contain each of the essential provisions. In seven other states—Massachusetts, Michigan, Texas, California, New Jersey, Minnesota, and Colorado—although one or more of the seven key components are absent, an alternate sponsor or appeals process is present, and the resulting charter schools tend to be fiscally and legally autonomous entities. Laws in the other ten states (with the exception of Louisiana, which is missing only the nonlocal board sponsor component) do little to challenge the status quo or to create internal and external pressures for change. The charter school concept has been watered down in a number of states.

Why have so many weak laws been enacted? In many states, groups opposed to charter schools promote weak charter legislation rather than trying to kill the bill completely.[11] Weak charter school laws have the benefits (for opponents) of holding voucher proponents at bay while limiting any chartering activity. Unfortunately, a weak charter school law is perhaps worse than no law at all because it fools people into believing that reform is under way. For example, both Kansas and Arizona passed charter laws in 1994. Within two years, Arizona's stronger law resulted in the opening of forty-six charter schools, but not even one had opened in Kansas, with its weak law.

What Do We Know About the Initial Charter Schools?

What is actually happening within the initial set of charter school states? This ostensibly simple question raises several issues relevant to any data-related inquiry regarding charter schools. No national charter school clearinghouse existed as of summer 1996 to track charter school activity, nor did every state department of education uniformly monitor such entities (primarily because of lack of funding). One national survey of all existing charter schools has been conducted, and a few university and/or federal laboratory-based researchers have published reports. Some site-specific data is also emerging, but aggregate impact data are essentially nonexistent. Many charter school critics are using this "data void" to their advantage.

To help rectify this problem, two nationally based studies are currently under way. The first is a two-year study funded by the Pew Charitable Trusts Foundation, in which Hudson Institute–affiliated researchers are conducting case studies of thirty-five charter schools across seven states. Researchers for this project (including this author) are conducting hundreds of site-based interviews, gathering qualitative information on initial implementation issues. This study was initiated mid-1995; this chapter presents preliminary observations.

The second significant study is funded by the federal government. Awarded to RPP International, a research firm based in Berkeley, California, this four-year study began during late 1995 and will be gathering a variety of qualitative and quantitative data. These researchers are collecting achievement data as part of a comparison between charter school students and non–charter school students. Preliminary data from this study should be available during 1997.

HOW MANY CHARTER SCHOOLS ARE THERE?

Table 2.2 lists those states with charter school laws on the books long enough to have allowed charter schools to be in operation (at least since 1995). These figures were gathered from state department of education personnel or others closely affiliated with the charter school program within each state.

These data clearly show that the character of a given law significantly determines the number of charter schools that open their doors. In the six initial states with strong laws, 365 charter schools are known to be operating, compared with 25 in the five initial states with weaker laws. As we

48 **TABLE 2.2** Operating Charter Schools (June 1996)

	State	Year Passed	Number
"Stronger"	Minnesota	1991	19
Charter Law	California	1992	108
States	Colorado	1993	32
	Massachusetts	1993	22
	Michigan	1994	77
	Arizona	1994	107
	Total		365
"Weaker"	Georgia	1993	10
Charter Law	New Mexico	1993	5
States	Wisconsin	1993	9
	Hawaii	1994	1
	Kansas	1994	0
	Total		25

have seen, if the majority of the seven critical elements are not present in a charter law, few charter schools open.

WHAT DO THESE CHARTER SCHOOLS LOOK LIKE, AND WHO IS BEING SERVED?

No two charter schools are exactly alike. They come in every size, shape, and flavor. Unlike the "one-size-fits-all" scenario typically found within school districts, many charter schools offer the best of what alternative education has to offer (smaller schools, experiential learning, teachers who want to work with students in nontraditional settings), with the added features of true site control, limited rules and regulations, and a contract that requires results. Some have a special emphasis, such as science or the arts; others serve a special population, such as dropouts. Many are housed in nontraditional educational facilities, like community recreational facilities or old church buildings. Others are housed in regular school buildings, having converted from an existing school rather than starting from scratch. Numbers of students range from a low of ten to more than twelve hundred in a school.

A few examples illustrate this variety. The Boys and Girls Academy is a middle school for 100 students run by a Boys' and Girls' Club in Mesa, Arizona, using an arts-based curriculum; Northlane Math and Science Academy is a hands-on, focused school housed in a home/garage in Free-

TABLE 2.3 Operating Charter School Enrollments (January 1996)

Enrollment	AZ	CA	CO	MA	MN	MI	Total
0–100	19	23	8	5	14	18	87
	(41%)	(35%)	(33%)	(34%)	(82%)	(45%)	(42%)
101–250	18	11	10	7	3	19	68
	(39%)	(17%)	(42%)	(47%)	(18%)	(48%)	(33%)
251–500	7	8	6	2		3	26
	(15%)	(12%)	(25%)	(13%)		(8%)	(13%)
501–1000	2	19		1			22
	(4%)	(29%)		(7%)			(11%)
1001+		5					5
		(8%)					(2%)
Total	46	66	24	15	17	40	208

Note: Data extracted from individual state summaries provided by state departments or individuals working closely with charter schools in the state. Complete data were not available for California.

land, Michigan, serving 40 students ages six to twelve; Boston Renaissance Charter School, a K–5 inner-city school for 630 students that is open 210 days per year, twelve hours per day, employs the Edison Project design; the Community of Learners, a middle school in Durango, Colorado, focuses on student-centered and self-directed learning for about 60 students; and the Choice 2000 Online High School offers 200 students an educational program through "cyberspace," using file servers based in Perris, California.

Many charter schools have been developed to serve K–5 elementary populations (about one third of those in operation during 1995–96 in the six states with the most charter schools), although a growing number of schools are being targeted toward students at the middle and high school levels or some combination of these grades.[12] Several schools are trying to create "one room schoolhouses" by serving a broad range of students within a given school: one tenth serve grades K–12, and one fifth serve grades K–8. Many others plan to expand into such groupings. This is in sharp contrast to most traditional public schools, which have moved away from such groupings (especially K–12), unless forced by geographic isolation to maintain them.

Existing charter schools are on average very small. Table 2.3 indicates that within the six states with the most charter schools, 42 percent have enrollments of one hundred students or fewer. Nearly half of these schools have fewer than fifty students. With the exception of California, where

50   a large percentage of their charter schools are converted public schools, nearly every charter school is designed to serve fewer than five hundred pupils. Considering that many charter schools serve students in the middle and/or high school levels, these schools are significantly smaller than traditional public schools.

Why are charter schools so small? First and perhaps foremost, many charter schools are established on the premise that smaller class sizes and overall school populations enhance student learning. Although budgetary constraints are often cited by regular public schools as the reason for not creating smaller schools, charter schools accomplish this goal, often with significantly less funding. Private contracting for certain services, as well as a focus on a specific mission, appear to be key ingredients. For example, charter schools do not offer a large array of electives or athletic programs, which pull funds from core academic classes. Second, except in Massachusetts, charter schools do not have access to local bond funds generated for the construction and/or purchase of school facilities. Charter schools must therefore expend a portion of their operating funds to obtain facilities. The resulting facilities are often former warehouses or other commercial spaces that are small in comparison to most traditional school facilities and campuses.

WHO ARE THE STUDENTS BEING SERVED?

Critics often assert that charter schools will "skim off" the best and brightest students and that minority and/or special needs students will not be served. Preliminary data, however, reveal that charter schools do indeed serve minority students. Table 2.4 illustrates the percentage of African-American, Hispanic, and Native American students being served within charter schools as a whole compared to those in the total public school population within five states. Charter schools are generally attracting a disproportionately high number of such students. This is especially true for African-American students. Many charter schools have been established within inner-city environments, often by minority leaders in those communities.

Others argue that income levels will be a determining factor both in where charter schools will be established and who will ultimately attend. Definitive nationwide data on the enrollment of low-income students do not exist, although either side of the argument can be supported with existing state-based data. Preliminary findings from UCLA researchers suggest that less affluent communities (and often therefore largely minority

TABLE 2.4 Charter School Racial/Ethnic Enrollments (percentages)

	African-American		Hispanic		Native American	
	Charter School	Public School	Charter School	Public School	Charter School	Public School
Arizona (Sept. 1995)	12	4	22	29	8	7
Colorado (Sept. 1994)	3	5	13	17	4	1
Massachusetts (June 1995)	21	8	17	9	1	<1
Michigan (Oct. 1995)	39	16	5	3	6	<1
Minnesota (Oct. 1994)	15	4	2	2	7	2
Composite	18	7	12	12	5	2

Note: In some states, these types of data were just in the process of being collected and do not always represent complete charter school profiles [Arizona = 38 schools (of 46 operating); Colorado = 14 of 14 operating that year; Massachusetts = 15 of 15 operating; Michigan = 23 of 40 operating; Minnesota = 13 of 13 operating that year]. All data were provided by department of education personnel within each state.

communities) in southern California frequently lack the wherewithal to establish charter schools.[13] Another recent study by the Southwest Regional Laboratory (SWRL) confirms that California's current charter schools enroll fewer low-income students than the comparison schools in their study.[14] An earlier study, however, found that California's metropolitan charter schools served high concentrations of low achievers, minority students, and students with limited English proficiency (LEP).[15] A survey of Michigan's initial charter schools revealed that five of six schools had higher percentages of low-income students than the neighboring districts.[16]

The data also remain somewhat mixed in reference to students with special needs. Many charter schools are focused on dropout retrieval, troubled youth, or students with learning disabilities. For example, the Macomb Academy in Michigan targets educable mentally impaired students, while the Metro Deaf Charter School in Minnesota provides a day program for deaf students; City Academy in Minnesota and YouthBuild Charter School in Boston were designed to attract dropouts; and the Success School is run in conjunction with Arizona's correctional department. A nationwide

52   survey of charter schools conducted during spring 1995 finds that one half
of those responding were designed to serve at-risk students.[17] A recent
SWRL report holds that California's charter schools are serving three times
as many students who had previously been retained in grade than surrounding public schools, and twice as many former dropouts. On the other
hand, it also notes that California's charter schools report fewer special
education students than are found in comparison schools.

Overall, definitive student profile data do not currently exist. Early information, however, does not support the claim that charter schools are "white
enclaves," or that they skim the best and brightest students. Indeed, many
charter school operators contend they are attracting more than their share
of students who were not succeeding in the traditional public school system.

What Effects Are Charter Schools Having?

STUDENT OUTCOMES

> People in this school really care about what I learn. At my other school,
> it was easy to hang back and do nothing; no one really pushed you to
> try harder.
> *Charter school student, Minnesota*

The quotation above depicts the attitude of many students enrolled in charter schools.[18] Students are pleased by the individualized attention they are
receiving, and many report they are being academically challenged for the
first time.

In reference to actual student achievement, however, self-reports represent the only source of data currently available. Although our ability to
generalize is hampered by the fact that such reports are not yet uniformly
collected, several charter schools claim tangible student improvements. Examples include:

City Academy, St. Paul, Minnesota, reports that of its forty-two graduates
    through June 1995 (all former dropouts), 100 percent were accepted
    into postsecondary programs.
Horizon Instructional Systems, a charter school near Sacramento, California,
    that uses an individualized education plan for each student, notes that its

test scores increased an average of 10 percent compared with the rest of the district.

Vaughn Next Century Learning Center in Los Angeles, an existing public school of more than twelve hundred students that converted to charter status, reports that its language arts scores improved from the ninth percentile to the thirty-ninth, while its math scores increased from the fourteenth percentile to the fifty-seventh.[19]

In view of the smaller school and class sizes of most charter schools, many critics respond to such data by noting that charter schools "should" be getting such results. But the question must be, if charter schools can accomplish these results with many at-risk students and limited resources, why can't regular public schools? On the other hand, we don't have adequate data at this point to know whether these examples represent the norm for charter schools.

PARENTAL INVOLVEMENT AND SATISFACTION

Our children came from traditional public schools, where everyone basically learns at the same pace in the same manner. In this charter school, children are treated as individuals, each with their own unique talents, strengths, and style of learning. Incredible things are happening. *Charter school parent, Michigan*

Parents appear to be quite satisfied with the charter schools their children attend. A survey of Minnesota charter school parents reveals satisfaction with the schools' curricula, teachers, and staff, as well as such school features as small classes, longer classes, and a wider range of school resources.[20] The curricular focus was the primary reason parents chose a given charter school, followed by school features (for example, small classes, location, and environment), and unhappiness with a prior school. Only a small percentage of parents were dissatisfied with such issues as lack of resources, transportation, space, and first-year "growing pains" in the charter schools.

Parents of charter school students also appear to be very involved in education-related activities. A recent study focused on such activities within California's charter schools, especially relative to the use of parent contracts.[21] Researchers found that parents at charter schools were substantially more involved in the daily life of the school than were parents at

54 nearby district-managed public schools. There was more effort on behalf of charter school teachers to involve parents than in comparison schools. On the other hand, the researchers raised a concern that charter schools may be using contracts as a means of excluding those parents who are not supportive and educationally involved.

Observations I made as part of the Hudson Institute study provide additional case data depicting increased parental involvement and satisfaction. I gained these insights during site visits to four new "start-up" charter schools during fall 1995: City Academy, a dropout retrieval program serving about 60 students in St. Paul, Minnesota; Emily Charter School, a K–8 rural Minnesota school of 75 students using a multiage, thematic focus; West Michigan Academy of Environmental Science, a K–8 school of nearly 350 students located in Grand Rapids, Michigan; and Concord Academy, a K–12 school of about 220 students, using an integrated fine and performing arts focus, in Petoskey, Michigan. Despite the small sample size, there was striking consistency in comments across the sites. None of the schools had formal parent contracts, yet each noted extremely high levels of parental involvement. Across the four schools, eighteen parents were interviewed (nearly half of whom considered themselves low-income), and all were extremely pleased with their school. When asked to describe how the charter school differed from their children's previous educational settings, the parents offered the following general comments:

More open to parents. The charter school is more receptive to parents, and the ideas and suggestions of the parents are welcomed and acted upon.

Higher student expectations. There are much higher standards for all students, who are expected to take responsibility for their own learning and to meet certain outcomes.

Improved curriculum. The curriculum is thematic and well connected so that students understand what and why they are learning something. There are many hands-on experiences and few worksheets, there is much more flexibility and individualization, and enrichment activities are an integral part of the curriculum, not part of a pull-out program.

Dedicated teachers. The teachers work a lot harder to meet the needs of every student. There are no more passive teacher lectures and bored students, and the teachers are allowed to teach—to be professionals.

Family feeling. There are smaller, multiage, integrated classrooms, and the "one-room schoolhouse" concept allows students to move academically and socially at their own pace.

When asked why they believed these things are occurring within the charter schools but not at the public schools that their children previously attended, parents offered the following types of responses:

Less bureaucracy. Regular public schools are too big, regulated, and complacent, but at this school there is no bureaucracy or teachers union dictat-
ing how things are to be done.
More accountability. Regular public schools currently have a monopoly and
feel no real pressure to improve what they are doing, while teachers in
charter schools know that they must be accountable or they will be
gone—there is no tenure or union to protect them.

Reports of long waiting lists for charter school openings represent further evidence of parental satisfaction. For example, Massachusetts reported 1,934 students on waiting lists in June 1995, compared with 2,667 students being served.[22] The recent Hudson Institute report also notes that the ma-jority of charter schools in its seven-state sample had long waiting lists.[23] This is true even though most of these schools are located in nontraditional educational facilities and struggle with poor conditions, including limited space and inadequate resources. (One, for example, is housed in an old coliseum and recently had to completely pack up and move out for a four-day dog show.) A casual observer might think twice about placing his or her children in such environments, yet most parents are pleased to have their children in these schools. Many note that the school may not "look like much," but the staff's commitment and the family feeling far outweighs its appearance.

TEACHER ATTRACTION, SATISFACTION, AND PROFESSIONALISM

For an educator, it's like you died and went to heaven. We are creating
as we go. This is what charter schools are about, you build from scratch.
Charter school teacher, Massachusetts

The recent Hudson Institute report found that excellent teachers are flock-ing to charter schools.[24] They crave the chance to work with colleagues and parents who share their philosophy, and they are often willing to make

56 trade-offs for this opportunity, including longer hours, risk of failure, uncertainty, minimal facilities, and modest pay for the work involved. In spite of lower pay (in some cases), charter schools have no difficulty in finding qualified teachers, most of whom are state certified.

Who are these teachers and why do they choose to work in a charter school? Many are individuals who had previously taught in public schools, but had left for a number of reasons—to raise children, to work in the business world, to relocate, to avoid school violence. A few are first-time teachers, a few others are coming directly from other public school districts, and some come from private schools or home schooling arrangements. When asked why they have chosen to work in a charter school, teachers offered the following general comments:

Freedom and flexibility. There is less red tape and useless paperwork, and teachers are allowed to write their own curricula based upon the needs of the students.

Positive climate for teaching and learning. Teachers and students learn together and exhibit respect for one another and the school. Classes are much smaller and offer opportunities for real team-teaching, as well as a greater focus on discipline. Many things tolerated in regular schools—name-calling, talking back to the teachers—are not allowed here.

Increased decision making. Every decision in the school is focused on the students, not on tradition, regulations, or what is easier for the teachers. Teachers have more control over decision making and budgets, and they receive ample parent and administrative support.

Dedicated staff. The staff is more stable, committed, and caring, and although the workload is greater, they are willing to take it on.

Enhanced accountability. Teachers cannot blame anyone else in this school. A much stronger feeling of accountability exists, and expectations for both the teachers and the students are much higher than in other schools.

When asked about disadvantages to working in a charter school, respondents referred to a lack of resources, inadequate facilities, some stress because of the demands of working with more at-risk students, and issues associated with wearing many hats (both as teachers and decision makers). The lower salaries were never mentioned; when asked about this factor, nearly all respondents noted that they "didn't go into teaching for the money." In spite of these negatives, nearly all of the teachers commented

that they felt like real professionals for the first time in their teaching careers. At this point one can only speculate regarding whether these findings
will occur in all charter schools and whether this level of commitment can
continue indefinitely.

OTHER VISIBLE IMPACTS

> Having a charter school in our community has resulted in a sense that
> there is some competition out there, and that there is a need for the
> schools to reach out to parents and teachers and treat them more like
> customers.
> *Local school board member, Michigan*

Data on other charter school impacts are also beginning to surface. These
include both salutary "ripple" effects across the system and more effective
resource allocation.[25]

Charter schools are intended not only to serve their own students but to
help initiate changes within the broader system as well. Several examples of
ripple effects illustrate that this is beginning to occur. A Montessori-type
program is now offered by one Minnesota district after parents sought to
establish such a program under the charter law. Several Colorado local
school districts approved alternative or special-focus schools shortly after
the enactment of their state's charter school legislation.[26] Parents and
teacher supporters of these programs had long been advocating district action without success and believe the pressure of a potential charter school
forced their local districts to act. Other districts are now telling their staffs to
"treat our parents and students more like customers." As noted by one
researcher: "Even the skeptical must acknowledge that, in a relatively short
time, the ripples are spreading—and the effects they bring are precisely
those sought by reformers elsewhere in a variety of ways and with varying
success."[27]

Some schools are also securing the allocation of larger portions of the
budget for instructional activities. A good example is Vaughn Next Century
Learning Center, a charter school in Los Angeles. Under the leadership of a
dynamic principal, the school ended its first year as a charter school with a
surplus of more than $1 million out of a $4.6 million budget, even after
reducing class sizes and restoring a districtwide teacher pay cut. These funds
were used in part to purchase and raze two adjacent crack houses and to

58   build additional classrooms. Sound fiscal management, in conjunction with
private contracting for some services, helped accomplish reallocation of
resources. As another example, the Johnson Urban League Charter School
in San Diego, found that it could procure food services much cheaper than
the local district, freeing up additional funds for classroom instruction.[28]

Barriers and Strong Opposing Forces

There are a number of inherent barriers and forces working against the
long-term success of charter schools.[29] Some result from the overlay of
charter schools onto an existing education and school financing structure.
Others are attributable to the vast resources and lobbying efforts of special
interest groups that are trying to weaken or derail such reform efforts. Still
others stem from many educators' lack of business experience and from
skepticism toward entrepreneurial efforts in education.

A number of charter school developers have difficulties with the business
aspects of operating a school. State education financing and reporting procedures are complex, and charter school founders often underestimate the
time and management skills required to run a school. Although only two
charter schools to date—Los Angeles–based Edutrain and Citizen 2000 in
Phoenix—have had their charters revoked for financial mismanagement,
many struggle until they gain the necessary expertise.[30]

Nearly every charter school, except for those that convert from existing
schools, has difficulties securing an appropriate facility and funds to reno-
vate and/or otherwise equip that facility. Charter schools do not have the
ability to generate capital revenues—they have no taxing authority—and
thus begin their struggle for survival with significantly less funding per
student than regular public schools. Yet they must still find adequate facilities, often leasing retail space, old church buildings, community recreational
centers, and the like. Some have been offered school buildings by supportive
districts, others have been fortunate to find local universities or businesses
that are willing to lend them good facilities at no (or low) cost. Still others
must spend a large portion of their operating funds in order to bring their
facilities up to health and safety codes. A few states provide minimal start-up
funds, and a new federal grant program will provide some relief to select
schools. Many charter school developers, however, have been forced to rely
on their personal funds—remortgaged homes and "maxed-out" credit cards

—to cover start-up expenses. Some approved charter contracts have been unable to open because an adequate facility could not be financed.

Opposition from teachers unions and school board associations presents perhaps the greatest threat to strong charter school laws (and to the schools themselves once laws are enacted). Such organizations generally support charter schools only as a means to ward off private school vouchers, and they work hard to ensure that only weak laws are enacted.[31] For example, the director of City Academy charter school in Minnesota was recently informed that the National Education Association, of which she is a member, had spent more than $12 million to defeat charter school legislation.[32] Her membership dues were being used to undermine the success of her own charter school!

Once charter school laws are enacted, the battle continues. A recent report from a California policy organization cites numerous activities undertaken by the California Teachers' Association (an NEA affiliate) to prevent charter schools from being established.[33] According to this report, for example, the San Diego Teachers' Association circulated rumors, leaked documents, and rigged elections in their efforts to undermine a charter school proposed by the Urban League of San Diego for inner-city youth. I have heard similar reports from teachers at several Michigan charter schools. One twenty-five-year veteran public school teacher and former union member spoke bitterly of the Michigan Education Association's key role in getting Michigan's first charter school law declared unconstitutional, effectively stopping funding at midyear to her charter school. She maintained that her former union has lost sight of what public education is all about.

Many school district administrators and boards are also active opponents of charter schools. When local boards are the sole sponsors allowed, many strings are often placed on the charter school proposals, and sometimes only schools serving populations of students at very high risk are being approved.[34] If the district no longer has control over charter school approvals because of alternative sponsorship options, then pressure is applied at the state level and elsewhere. For example, a Michigan school superintendent recently sent a letter to Central Michigan University stating that the district would no longer accept student teachers from that university or recommend that its graduates attend CMU.[35] What had CMU done to provoke such a threat? It had chartered more than thirty schools in the state and was actively working with others.

60 What Does the Future Hold for Charter Schools?

> For those who seem to be intimidated or afraid of educational reform,
> we would like to offer a challenge: put politics, money, and special
> interests aside momentarily and spend a day at [the charter school my
> children attend], observing and interacting with the kids, then join our
> family for dinner afterwards. Ask questions and listen to the kids'
> answers, then make your decisions.
> *Charter school parent, Michigan*

The crystal ball is still cloudy on the future of charter schools. On one hand, strong charter school legislation continues to be at the top of many legislators' educational reform agendas, and the number of charter schools—and of their success stories—continues to grow. On the other hand, the opposing forces are powerful, and many charter school operators are wearying of their efforts to overcome the barriers inherent in operating a highly accountable school while battling the opposition.

Even if charter schools win the political battle, other questions remain. Can they continue to overcome the economic disadvantages of being small while operating within financing systems designed to fund districts, not schools? Are the teachers attracted to charter schools adequately prepared to teach the many at-risk students served? Are too many charter schools approved and implemented without adequate long-term planning? Can a small number of charter schools really change the broader system of more than eighty-five thousand public schools?

In spite of these lingering questions, preliminary data reveal that charter schools hold great promise for America's public education system. They are already successfully educating a number of students and forcing reforms to occur within some districts. They are serving as powerful tools for many policy makers, educators, parents, and community leaders who believe that long-held traditions and structures surrounding public education need serious reexamination. And, although charter schools are not a panacea, many believe that they are an important component of long-term education reform efforts.

3 Contracting in Public Education

Paul T. Hill

"Contracting out" has recently joined vouchers and outcomes-based programs among the true hot-button issues in public education. In the past few years, Minneapolis; Chelsea, Massachusetts; and Hartford, Connecticut, have hired contractors to act as de facto school superintendents. Miami; Baltimore; Wichita, Kansas; Sherman, Texas; and Wilkinsburg, Pennsylvania, have hired for-profit firms to operate whole schools, and twenty-five states have authorized charter schools, which are public schools operated by independent organizations under contract with public authorities. Dozens of other localities, including Nashville, Chicago, and Dallas have considered or are now debating contracting-out proposals.

Contracting in public education is not a new idea. Public school systems have used contractors for decades, primarily for such noninstructional services as construction, repairs, transportation, accounting, and legal representation. Some districts, moreover, have contracted out for limited instructional services—foreign language, arts, and music—and many have hired independent contractors for teaching required by fed-

62 eral programs, particularly compensatory education and education for the handicapped. Sylvan Learning Systems provides remedial reading instruction in Washington, D.C., and several other major public school systems, and organizations like Dialogos offer foreign language instruction in public schools as well as through businesses and adult education institutions. Some districts have also entered into contracts with special private schools for severely handicapped students and for "alternative" high schools that serve students on the verge of dropping out. As school board members and the public lose confidence in the public schools—especially in the big cities—such efforts to diversify the systems' offerings through contracting out for discrete services are likely to grow.

Two elements are new about recent contracting proposals: First, many would allow private parties to operate whole districts or whole schools, not just discrete programs. Second, the districts and schools thus operated would be designed to serve mainstream students, not merely those with special needs. Unlike former contracting arrangements, under which school districts purchased services they did not want to provide themselves, current proposals invite private parties to enter the core business of public school systems—taking full responsibility for education of regular students. In January 1996, *U.S. News and World Report* claimed that private firms were managing twenty schools in seven states, serving 14,900 students.[1] Four private companies—Whittle Communications' Edison Project, Sabis International, Education Alternatives Incorporated (EAI), and Alternative Public Schools (APS)—are running public schools under contract.

Controversy has made educational contracting a household word. When the Dade County Public Schools hired EAI to manage one public school in Miami Beach, the event was reported in the education trade press, but it was not in the newspapers outside Miami. However, when Baltimore's mayor and school board hired the same Minnesota-based firm to run a number of failing inner-city schools, the ensuing controversy was covered in newspapers and TV newscasts across the nation. The difference between the Miami and Baltimore events was the position of the teachers union: the United Teachers of Dade was a full partner in the decision to hire EAI and did not expect the results to threaten its members' jobs. The Baltimore teachers union, on the other hand, felt excluded from the decision and declared all-out opposition when EAI replaced unionized classroom aides with lower-paid recent college graduates. Teachers union opposition has since solidified: unions threatened legal action and strikes in Washington, D.C., Hartford, and Wilkinsburg; unions have also opposed enactment of state charter schools laws and have sued to block implementation of enacted charter laws in Massachusetts and Michigan.

Teachers union concern about contracting is easy to understand: private contractors might hire teachers who are not part of union bargaining units and might establish wage and working condition precedents that threaten existing collective bargaining agreements. Contracting also gives school boards an alternative to bargaining with unionized teachers: by arranging to have schools operated by independent parties that will each hire their own teaching staffs, school boards can bypass the need to reach agreement with the teachers union.

Unions are not, however, the only sources of opposition to whole-school contracting proposals. Many lay people, accustomed to thinking of public schools as run by a politically accountable central bureaucracy and staffed by lifelong civil servants, are uncomfortable with any proposed change. Many of the strongest supporters of public schools—especially education school professors and civil-rights lawyers—fear that without detailed political controls publicly funded schools will become segregated and that schools with good reputations will become elitist.

Although the idea of contracting for whole schools and districts has scarcely been tried, the early results have not resolved fears or opposition. EAI, the first firm to seek contracts aggressively, lost its agreement in Baltimore in late 1995 amid controversy over its performance. The Dade County Schools did not renew EAI's one-school contract, saying that it could now run the school as well as the contractor. Also in late 1995, EAI's contract to run the Hartford school system teetered on the brink of collapse for months, as the local school board anguished about how much control over individual schools it wanted to cede to the contractor. The contract was finally canceled in January 1996, at the end of a period of wrangling over whether the Hartford board had arbitrarily changed the definition of the cost savings that determined the contractor's pay. Hartford refused to reimburse more than $10 million that EAI claimed to have spent.

EAI's trials and missteps have not, however, stopped the movement toward public school contracting. Although it is not clear whether any more districts will try to contract out their central office operations, the number of contracts for operation of whole schools is growing rapidly. As Dean Millot

64 noted in 1995, a majority of the more than 250 charter schools then existing operated under some form of contract between a school board (or another state agency) and a private organization.[2] Most of these private contractors are ad hoc organizations created only to run one charter school. A significant minority of contractors, however, are established organizations that manage a variety of social services or, like Edison and Sabis International, are in business to operate schools in any state and locality that has the authority to hire them.

Three recent charter agreements in Massachusetts might set the pattern for growth in contracting for whole schools. In each a local group sought a charter from the state, thus gaining the authority to create schools and receive state funds for each enrolled student. The charter holders then entered contracts with firms from outside the state, Edison and Sabis, to operate the schools. Edison and Sabis therefore work as subcontractors to community groups that hold state charters, and they are subject to firing or replacement if they do not perform. These arrangements provide a promising mixture of clear contractual accountability, professional school management, and community control. Large national providers, like Edison and Sabis, are not necessary for such an arrangement to work; local professional organizations, even teachers unions, might establish similar relationships with charter holders.

The vast majority of contract public schools have been established since 1993, and it is much too soon to say whether the existing schools will succeed in providing coherent instructional programs or producing positive student outcomes. The great promise of contracting is that it can clarify the relations between individual schools and public authorities. As a result, schools can pursue their instructional missions free from the continual changes in policy and mandates that political school boards inevitably create. At the same time, public authorities can establish exact performance standards to which schools will be held accountable, as well as define the circumstances under which schools might lose standing to receive public funds.

Issues to Be Resolved

It is already clear, however, that contracting cannot reach its potential unless it leads to real agreements between two legally competent and independent parties. School boards must fully intend to rely on a contractor to provide a particular service, and boards must be prepared to sustain or cancel the contract according to clearly defined expectations for results. Contractors must be unambiguously in charge of providing services and fully accountable for performance. Three sets of issues about contracting in public education must be resolved:

Scope. What decisions can contractors control and what decisions must still be cleared with or controlled by school boards?

Accountability. How, in detail, can contractors be held accountable and rewarded for the performance of the schools or services they manage?

Legal status. Do state laws governing public education allow contracting for whole schools, and if not, what changes are necessary?

SCOPE OF CONTRACTS

Contract management of entire local school systems is attractive because it appears to promise an end to political gridlock that makes it impossible for school boards to act decisively toward school improvement. Putting discretion in private hands can, in theory, allow definitive action in trimming waste, restaffing schools, retraining teachers, and upgrading curricula. It assumes, however, that local school boards will truly delegate all their powers to independent organizations.

It appears unlikely that school boards will ever fully delegate their basic powers. The Chelsea School Board and Boston University have contended for years about their respective responsibility for fund raising and instructional improvement. In the first year of EAI's contract in Hartford, the contractor and school board were unable to establish a clear division of responsibilities, and the contract nearly fell apart several times over questions of fiscal control and the contractor's claims for payment. Relations between the Minneapolis board and the Public Strategies Group, led by contractor-superintendent Peter Hutchinson, have been more harmonious. However, Public Strategies has limited the scope of its activities. In the first two years of the contract, Hutchinson's group concentrated on improvements in fiscal management and teacher training but did not change the basic structure of teacher-administration-union relations within the schools. In the 1995–1996 school year, for the first time, Hutchinson began to discuss the possibility of entering contracts for operation of individual schools, to be managed either by local site councils under the state's charter schools law or by private organizations like Edison.

In practice, systemwide contract management has fallen far short of expectations. Both contractors and school boards have been so eager to enter arrangements that promised school improvement that they have been careless in establishing goals, responsibilities, and expectations. Provisions in Chelsea's and EAI's contracts for whole-district management were so vague that neither the contractor nor the school board could confidently expect to enforce its rights in court. The Hartford experience illustrates the pitfalls of ambiguous contracts and Hollywood-style payment clauses that do not define such key factors as gross and net costs and how savings can be calculated.

Existing "contracts" for management of whole districts are much more like engagements than marriages: both parties expect to discover their own needs and interests as they go along, and neither party's expectations of the other can be strictly enforced. Minneapolis's contract, which strictly limits the superintendent-firm's powers but leaves room for incremental expansion by mutual agreement, provides a sounder precedent.

EAI's recent experience in contracting both for whole districts and individual schools has revealed serious uncertainty about the meaning of the word *contract* in education. In its relation with the Hartford school board, EAI expected to gain control over basic district financing and to be able to reorganize and restaff failing schools (including contracting for their operation by additional independent organizations). In fact, EAI's contract was ambiguous about the residual powers of the school board, and the board effectively seized back most of them before the contract fell completely apart.

Although districtwide contract management looks like a route to rapid change, the forces opposing real delegation of central office management to contractors are enormous. Every interested party—even reform groups that want deregulation and innovation—can see the risk in allowing districtwide decisions to be made by private parties. Boards are, therefore, likely to come under constant pressure to undelegate and repoliticize decisions that the contractor is nominally supposed to make. Thus, future districtwide management contracts, if any, are likely to preserve board powers in ways that strictly limit contractors' freedom of action. As *U.S. News and World Report* concluded in a recent review of business opportunities in public education, prudent entrepreneurs should steer clear of districtwide contracting.[3]

In all likelihood, the straightest route toward an all-contract school system is through a gradual increase in the number of individual schools run under contract rather than through contract management of entire districts.

Meanwhile, the use of narrow-scope contracts, for specialized instruction in language, arts, and advanced technology, is likely to grow. As public school systems come to terms with stable or shrinking per-pupil revenues, many are searching for ways of providing "the extras" at lower cost. Districts also need to develop financial flexibility so that they can expand and contract specialized services as their budgets rise and fall. Contracting out allows districts to provide specialized services when they can afford them without assuming permanent obligations to employ civil service–protected teachers.

ACCOUNTABILITY AND PAYMENT

In Hartford, EAI expected to derive its profits from savings obtained by contracting out financial management, custodial, and building maintenance services, as well as streamlining schools' administrative structures and teacher's aide arrangements. Although the board prevented the expected changes in schools, EAI was able to introduce efficiencies in ancillary services. However, because the board had to pay unexpected costs in areas not covered by EAI's contracting-out program, it claimed that it had no basis on which to pay the company's claim.

EAI's Baltimore experience was problematic for different reasons. Its original contract with Baltimore called for evaluation on the basis of student test scores, attendance rates, and parental satisfaction, among other criteria. But the contract did not specify the exact measures, performance standards, or schedules by which its schools would be evaluated. EAI and the Baltimore schools did not seriously address the issue of evaluation until after the Baltimore Federation of Teachers, an avowed opponent of the contracting plan, issued a scathing review of EAI's first-year performance. Although EAI's own measures of student progress were positive, these were significantly different from the tests by which all Baltimore schools were evaluated.[4] EAI was never able to work as a full partner in defining the terms by which its schools were evaluated. An independent evaluation done by a University of Maryland branch campus, also using the Baltimore city tests, provided the final negative assessment that sped the cancellation of EAI's contract.

68   EAI's Baltimore experience shows that contracts made on handshake agreements can be disrupted by third parties that oppose the idea. It was EAI's misfortune to be party to the contracts that taught such lessons to other school boards and potential contractors. As we shall see, more carefully constructed contracting arrangements might resolve such issues.

LEGAL STATUS

Under most state legal frameworks, responsibility for public education is held by the state and delegated to local school boards. In some states, authority thus delegated cannot be delegated further. State courts have differed in their interpretation of contracting out by school boards. Some have held that it is a routine choice of means of service delivery, while others have construed contracting as an impermissible redelegation of governmental authority.

Some state teacher collective bargaining laws also make contracting difficult. Laws that require school boards to bargain with a single agent for all teachers usually preclude any proposal that would make individual schools the employers of teachers. Although districtwide collective bargaining is not wholly incompatible with contracting, it can impose strict limits on contractors' independence and control of their schools. Under most existing collective bargaining agreements, schools would be bound to employ only teachers who were members of the districtwide bargaining unit and might have to accept teachers on the basis of seniority rather than their fit with the contractor's approach to schooling.

Some state charter schools laws resolve these issues, but most do not. In general, the basic legal underpinnings that might make contracting a true alternative to bureaucratic management of public education have not yet been established.

A Systemic Solution

The foregoing issues can be resolved comprehensively through a whole-system design that would provide new options, for teachers and others who want the freedom to run effective public schools and for school board members and other public officials who want to find ways to support effective schools.

This proposal includes elements of contracting for entire school systems and for individual schools. It does so by relieving local school boards of the responsibility of running schools, yet it does not contract out such basic policy decisions as who will run individual schools, what mixture of school types a local system will provide, and how schools can be evaluated. These decisions will remain in the hands of a democratically elected local school board. School boards will then provide individual schools indirectly, through contracting with independent parties, rather than, as now, bureaucratically, by creating a pyramid of civil service units, with schools at the bottom.

The system design is based on a simple insight about effective schools. Schools whose students learn quickly and deeply are not uniform products of a bureaucratic culture. This is true for schools that educate the most advantaged children and those most at risk. Virtually all schools that make a dramatic difference in their students' knowledge and abilities have something that sets them apart: a warrant to be different. This warrant supersedes many of the rules that govern the public education system as a whole. Effective schools often select, train, and evaluate staff differently than do other schools and make rigorous academic and behavioral demands on students. The warrants for being different in these ways are sometimes explicit and sometimes based only on tacit agreement among the authorities responsible for the broader public education system, the school staff, and outside financial supporters. But in any case the agreements on which such schools are based are essentially contracts, specifying what mission the school will perform, whom it will serve and how, and on what grounds the school's special status will be continued or revoked. The governance system sketched out in this chapter would apply the principle of contracting to all public schools, not just a few.

Contracting for schools responds to the belief that public schools can be effective only if they are freed from micromanagement by political bodies and helped to develop specific approaches to education, so that staff members can feel responsible for what they produce and parents can hold them accountable. Schools with definite missions and approaches to education give teachers and principals a strong incentive to collaborate, press one another for good performance, weed out weak staff members, and work as hard as necessary to build their school's clientele. As an alternative approach to public education governance, contracting is intended to permit

70   all public schools to have these characteristics. It builds on the charter
schools movement in the United States, which permits groups to run publicly funded schools under explicit contracts with the local school board.[5]
Unlike the charter schools concept, which designates a few schools for contracts and leaves all others governed as before, this system design calls for
contracting for all the public schools in a local system. Contracting for public
education is also consistent with the British idea of social markets.[6]

Under a contracting system, schools would be independent enterprises,
operating under applicable national and state laws and the terms of explicit
contracts specifying what kinds of instruction are to be delivered, to and by
whom, and to what effect. As in the completely free market system proposed by John E. Chubb and Terry M. Moe in their 1990 book *Politics,
Markets, and America's Schools,* students and teachers would choose and be
chosen by schools: no one would have an automatic right to administer,
teach in, or attend a particular school. In contrast with Chubb and Moe's
fully privatized system, the independent organizations that run schools
would not necessarily have to build or equip them. If public school facilities
exist, contract schools could use them; where no school facilities now exist,
local school boards could build them and allow school contractors to use
them. School facilities would be government owned, contractor operated.
Contractors operating schools would not have to make major construction
or lease investments or risk major losses while they were building a reputation and clientele. Contractors would be guaranteed a minimum level of
income for the duration of the contract, ideally a period of five years. Contracts would, however, specify that schools failing to attract a minimum
level of enrollment or failing to produce the specified student outcomes
could be closed and their funding terminated.

State public school boards could create standards that would apply to all
contract schools. These standards could, like state licensing and student
graduation standards for private schools, limit the range of possible schooling approaches, but they must not be so specific that they force all schools to
be alike. Each contract would specify the school's mission, instructional
emphasis, admissions practices, and student outcome expectations. Contracts would run for specific periods and be automatically renewed only if
all aspects of performance were satisfactory. Contractors whose performance was mediocre could be forced to compete for renewals.

Under a contracting scheme, a public school would be one run under contract with a public education authority. The contractor could be any of a wide variety of private nonprofit and profit-making organizations, including ad hoc organizations created by the parents and staff of an existing public school. But local school boards would not run schools themselves or create public bureaucracies to do so.

Any organization able to obtain a business license would be eligible to enter into a contract to manage one or more schools. State and local school boards could set minimum qualifications for potential contractors, but these must be broad enough to allow organizations other than those currently involved in the management of schools to offer to develop and manage schools. Contractors could include local neighborhood groups, alliances of teachers and parents working together in existing public schools, social service agencies, colleges and universities, civic groups, businesses, church groups, teacher cooperatives, teachers unions, and other organizations put together expressly to serve a particular group or use a particular instructional method. Entrepreneurial organizations, such as EAI and the Edison Project, could also enter contracts to provide schools.

Contractors would use public school buildings at no cost, and the local public education authority would provide a negotiated amount for utilities, incidental repairs, and maintenance; capital expenditures not specific to the contractor's instructional methods would be made by the public education authority.

HOW WOULD PUBLIC FUNDS BE ALLOCATED TO CONTRACT SCHOOLS?

Public funds for schools would continue to be raised from a combination of national, state, and local grants. The local public authority would pay contractors by combining funds from all sources. Contracts would, in the vast majority of cases, be based on a standard local amount per pupil. A local school board would be free, however, to negotiate a slightly higher than average per-pupil rate for schools in the lowest income areas, where children often need extra supportive services, and small classes are often necessary.

Total funding would be based on estimated enrollment and would be

72   adjusted in light of experience. In order to stabilize school services, contractors would start each school year with a guaranteed minimum amount of funds, which would be increased immediately if enrollment exceeded expectations. In schools whose enrollment was equal to or higher than anticipated by the contract, total funding would equal the average per-pupil expenditure (less a small amount kept out to pay the school system's contract administration costs) times the number of students enrolled. After a year in which enrollment fell below expectations, a contract would provide for a reduction in the guaranteed minimum funding for a school. If a school's enrollment fell below a minimum specified level, either party (the contractor or the public education authority) would be free to terminate the contract.

Contracting could allow for, but not automatically require, differential funding for students from different demographic and income groups. In the United States, absolute equality in local per-pupil funding would be a major benefit for disadvantaged groups. Since 1964, federal and state governments have provided "categorical" grants to pay for extra services to low-income, handicapped, and language minority children. These grants can add as much as 20 percent to a school's funding. As several recent studies and lawsuits have shown, however, the schools that get most of the categorical grant money are frequently shortchanged in the distribution of other resources. Because the highest-paid senior teachers cluster in middle-class schools, schools in low-income areas of a school district often have younger, less experienced, and cheaper staff members, many of whom can teach only because they have been granted waivers of normal certification requirements. The result, as was demonstrated in the 1992 Los Angeles case *Rodriguez v. Anton,* is that local spending in low-income area schools is often only one half to one third of what is spent in higher-income areas. The categorical grant funds that cluster in the low-income schools are too small to equalize funding. Thus, in spite of a declared policy of providing extra resources to the neediest schools, most localities in fact give them much less.

By bringing all the schools within a district up to true equality of funding, contracting will dramatically increase the funding for schools in the most troubled inner-city neighborhoods. All schools in a city might still suffer from less-than-optimal funding levels—a problem that can be remedied only by statewide school finance reform. But the city district would no longer misallocate its funds in favor of schools in privileged areas. The first contracts negotiated for schools in low-income neighborhoods could, therefore, be based on the localitywide average per-pupil expenditure. If it became clear that competent providers could not operate in those areas without supplementary funding, higher per pupil rates could be negotiated in future contracts.

WHAT WOULD CONTRACT SCHOOLS TEACH, AND BY WHAT METHODS?

The core purpose of contracting is to create schools that have clear and simple missions and definite strategies for motivating students and delivering instruction. Contracts would therefore specify the goals and methods that will be used in a particular school. These goals and methods could be formulated by the potential contractors themselves. In Baltimore, for example, Education Alternatives Incorporated secured a school board contract to manage six schools based on extensive use of computer-paced instruction. Goals and methods can also be formulated by a public education authority seeking to provide a school that meets a defined need (for example, a school that emphasizes apprenticeship-style education) or to meet an organized demand (for example, a school with high academic standards that emphasizes arts or cultural and historical studies).

Regardless of the method by which a school's mission and approach are formulated, however, they would be written into the contract. The contract provisions and the basic licensing and student graduation requirements that apply to all private schools would become the sole method of public control over a school's curriculum and pedagogy.

State or local school boards could require that all contractors cover certain core subjects and that all students pass certain examinations, but they could not specify curricula so tightly that all contractors were forced to run identical schools.

Contracting would require school boards to make educational decisions on a school-by-school basis rather than by enacting policies that constrain all schools alike. In considering a particular contract, the board need not ask whether a school concept is right for all the students in the locality or whether some groups would dislike a particular school. All the board would need to ask is whether there is a demand for a particular school and whether the people proposing to run it have plausible credentials for doing so.

WHO WOULD TEACH IN CONTRACT SCHOOLS?

Schools, or the contractors that run them, would be the employers of teachers. A local school board that hired a large number of new contractors

74 would inevitably create a great deal of teacher mobility, as teachers from schools that were closed or put under new management sought placements. A board that sought to enter into contracts with the staff of some of its existing schools might experience less teacher turnover.

School contractors, whether cooperatives of staff members of existing schools or new organizations created to run schools, would hire teachers on the open market or from a registry of certified teachers. The school board could set minimum teacher pay scales. But decisions about hiring, promotion, and assignment of individuals would be made by the contractor, subject only to laws governing normal private employment. Contractors could also choose to pay extra for teachers with rare or indispensable skills and to give bonuses for exceptional performance. Teacher groups that became contractors could decide that all should be paid the same; alternatively, some teachers may act as owners or managers and pay themselves far more than other teachers, who would be employees.

Contractors could choose to hire teachers through the local teachers union, which might operate as a guild hiring hall, brokering teachers into schools that fit them and suggesting additional training for teachers who have not been picked up by any school. The union might receive some funding from the school board and from schools that use its teacher referral services. It could use these funds to pay teachers who were looking for school placements and for training. As Ted Kolderie has suggested, teacher cooperatives organized outside the union could also serve as subcontractors to many schools, offering instructional programs in particular areas of expertise, such as science or art.[7]

Schools would be independent enterprises. School boards might set minimum qualifications for teachers and principals, but they could not specify a single mix of teachers, administrators, uncertified academic specialists, or aides. A given school might decide to hire a relatively small number of highly paid teachers or a larger number of less expensive, less experienced teachers. But most institutions would, like private schools, be forced to live within their budgets by employing a mix of staff members, from a few highly experienced mainstays to the more numerous new college graduates who are current on subject matter but may lack experience in pedagogy. No school could afford to have a large staff entirely composed of highly paid senior teachers (as is often the case in U.S. urban secondary schools), and few schools could maintain the necessary reputation for quality if they relied entirely on low-cost, inexperienced teachers (as many public grade schools in low-income urban areas are now forced to do).

HOW WOULD STUDENTS BE ADMITTED TO CONTRACT SCHOOLS?

Each school's processes and standards for student admission would be set by its contract. In general, to avoid charges of discrimination, all school contracts would call for admission by random selection from the list of all who apply. No contractor would be allowed to handpick students or to set admissions standards not unambiguously derived from the school's mission. Thus, for example, a performing arts school might require auditions, and a school focused on higher mathematics could require prerequisite courses. But schools could not set admissions requirements based on measures of general academic ability.

Although virtually any student could gain admission to a particular school, the school would be free to impose student effort requirements, as long as those requirements were explicit and uniformly applied. Schools would also be obligated to publish their methods for helping students experiencing academic difficulty. Students who failed to do the required work could be suspended or expelled. The local school board could require, however, that a consistent pattern of failure among disadvantaged or minority students would lead to a review of the school's contract.

Even though students would be free to apply to any school, the local school board might want to be especially vigilant about the educational opportunities available to low-income and minority-group students. Parents in poverty areas might find it especially difficult to transport their children elsewhere, and local residents and merchants might want to keep a school to anchor the community. In such cases, local school boards might want to attract contractors who would be willing to operate in difficult environments, and require that they give neighborhood children first preference on admissions. School boards could offer special inducements in the form of higher than average per-pupil revenues for contractors operating in low-income areas or serving a primarily disadvantaged clientele. Organizations operating more than one school on contract might also be required to run a specified number of schools in low-income or otherwise troubled areas. This would guarantee that the most capable contractor organizations could not evade the toughest problems. It would create an incentive for all contractors to develop competency in educating multiproblem students. A

76   contractor that wanted to avoid being responsible for a school with a bad reputation would need to ensure that none of its schools was considered a "dumping ground" for troublesome students and staff.

School contracts would include specific agreements on the kinds and levels of student outcomes expected and the methods whereby those outcomes would be assessed. These outcomes could be linked to national or state standards or could be tailored to a particular kind of school. Career-oriented schools, for example, aspire to outcomes that regular academic schools do not. Contractors who failed to provide instruction as promised, or whose students' outcomes were unsatisfactory and not improving as anticipated, could be fired or faced with new contract terms.

Like private schools, schools run under contract would have responsibility for the in-service training of their own teachers and for quality control. These functions, which in bureaucratic school systems are centrally administered and therefore unresponsive to individual schools' needs, would be performed by the contractors themselves. Contracts must include reasonable funding for staff training, schools' self-assessment, and adoption of promising new teaching methods and technologies.

One important technique for ensuring the effectiveness of schools' quality control and self-improvement efforts is contracting with intermediary organizations that would run multiple schools. Universities, teachers unions, social service agencies, churches willing to provide nonsectarian instruction, and private firms like the Edison Project could operate several local schools under one contract. They might run all the schools in a given neighborhood or region of the city or run a network of elementary, middle, and high schools, all based on a common approach or philosophy.

Such organizations could act as intermediaries between the school board and the individual schools. The intermediary organizations would, in effect, be the school board's prime contractors. Intermediary organizations could take responsibility for school self-evaluation, staff development, and quality control; they would also have a decisive interest in making sure that their stronger schools help their weaker ones. Dealing with intermediary organizations would immeasurably simplify the work of school boards, which would then have to supervise and evaluate a far smaller number of contractors.

State and local school boards might encourage creation of such inter- mediary organizations as teacher cooperatives. A local board could also enter contracts with similar organizations established in other localities.

As such locally based intermediary organizations developed reputations for quality, they might become regional or national in scope, offering to run schools in many localities. Intermediary organizations could develop distinctive approaches to education and capitalize on the recognition and consumer confidence that a "brand name" can engender. Individual schools are likely to benefit from economies of scale in designing curriculum and staff development. As Mary Beth Celio has shown, the stronger schools in a network can assist the weaker ones, and staff can be transferred from one school to another, both to shore up weak programs and to increase exposure to high-performance organizations.[8]

Intermediary organizations would have costs, and these would be paid from contract funds received by the schools. A school might join an intermediary organization for a fee, or an intermediary organization running several schools could deduct its operating costs before sending money to the schools. Estimates of these costs vary. In the United States, Catholic diocesan school systems typically charge schools between $10 and $25 per student to pay for testing, consulting, and financial management services. Assuming a school size of five hundred, the upper range of these costs would be about $12,500 per school. A secular organization might pay its employees twice as much, therefore requiring $50 per student or $25,000 per school. If the average per-pupil expenditure were $5,000, the intermediary organization costs would be about 1 percent of the school's budget. Another cost estimate can be based on the Edison Project's rule of thumb that the corporate central office would have one staff member per two thousand students. If the average school size were five hundred students, one staff member would be required per four schools. If these staff members cost an average of $100,000 each, the cost per school would again be $25,000 or 1 percent of a school's budget.

HOW WOULD STUDENTS BE PROTECTED AGAINST CONTRACT SCHOOL FAILURE?

The local public school board would retain ultimate responsibility for the education and protection of children. It would fulfill that responsibility by maintaining a portfolio of contracts serving two objectives: first, to ensure that the local system as a whole offers a range of approaches and services

78 that matches the diversity of needs of local children; and second, to ensure that no child receives a low-quality education. The school board would identify the need for particular kinds of schools, identify contractors potentially able to provide such schools, solicit proposals, and negotiate contracts. It would also continuously evaluate contractors' performance, both to prepare for the time when a contract must either be renewed or reopened to competition and to identify contractors who were not delivering on their promises or, for any reason, failing to produce positive student results.

If a school were found to be failing its students, the school board could demand improvements or replace the contractor. Parents could also take their children out of poorly performing schools at any time and move them into better-performing ones. Local school boards would be responsible to inform parents whenever a school was failing to meet its commitment. They would also need to make sure, by constantly tending the portfolio of contracts, that children who left a failing school had someplace better to go.

There would still be some need for school superintendents and local district administrative offices. These offices would give school boards and parents fair, unbiased information about school performance. Boards would also need staff or contractor assistance in identifying needs for new types of schools, finding promising potential contractors, and monitoring contract performance. Many of these functions could be performed by contractors, though not the same ones that operate the schools. But the evaluation and contractor identification process could not be neglected or performed for free: these would be the main mechanisms by which the public was assured that its children were being well cared for and its money carefully used. Given public authorities' tendency to underfund research and evaluation, state law might require each local authority to set aside some percentage of their gross revenue, perhaps 2½ percent, for school assessment contracts.

WHAT INCENTIVES WOULD CONTRACT SCHOOLS HAVE
TO INNOVATE AND SOLVE PROBLEMS?

Because contracting makes schools independent and competitive enterprises, it can be far more effective than the bureaucratic system in encouraging school initiative. Under contracting a school must attract students in order to survive. A school must therefore offer something that sets it apart— a distinctive curriculum, social climate, or extracurricular program—that

attracts the interest of potential students and their parents. It must deliver
what it promises and avoid major disruptions in the program. In addition to
maintaining a distinctive and consistent program, a school must develop a
reputation for quality, such that parents expect their children's opportunities for jobs and higher education to be enhanced, not compromised. It must
deliver on its promises well enough to keep current students from transferring out, create "brand loyalty" among families with several children, and
attract enough new families to fill the entering class each year.

That is a demanding set of requirements, but it is not unusual. Private schools of all descriptions face the need to differentiate their products
and maintain consumer loyalty. Even religious schools, which benefit from
parents' attachment to the sponsoring institutions, live and die on their
reputations for consistency and quality. As Celio has documented, many
of the Catholic schools that closed in the 1970s did so because their traditional clients concluded that they offered little to set them apart from
public schools. Conversely, the Catholic schools that survived were the
ones with well-founded educational traditions and a capacity to maintain quality.[9]

The need for product differentiation encourages a number of behaviors
that "effective schools" advocates have tried to create in public school staffs.
Principals and other administrators of contract schools would have strong
incentives to articulate a mission and to ensure that all elements of the
school contribute to its attainment. The mission must also be easy to com-
municate and meaningful to parents: it must be focused on what children
will experience in school and what they will be able to do upon leaving it,
not on subtleties of educational technique that may matter only to professionals. Teachers would also have strong incentives to work in teams and to
be concerned about the overall effectiveness of the school. A school mission
stated in terms of the desired attributes of students leaving the school helps
teachers understand how their particular class or subject matter contributes
to their school's final product. As studies of exceptional public schools have
shown, this focus on mission makes teachers understand how they depend
on one another and encourages them to identify the school's deficiencies
and help remedy them.[10] The demands of sheer economic survival also
make teachers concerned about the performance of the school as a whole.
In a contracting system, when a school is forced to close because too few

80   students want to attend it, all teachers have to find new jobs, no matter how well they taught their own classes. Teachers therefore have strong incentives to help one another, identify weaknesses, and ensure that variations in teacher performance do not harm the school's ultimate product and reputation.

WHAT INCENTIVES WOULD CONTRACT SCHOOLS HAVE FOR
HIGH PERFORMANCE?

The need to attract students encourages high performance. It both rewards schools that gain reputations for quality and leads to declining enrollments and termination of contracts for schools with bad records. Local school boards would also play a role in quality assurance because they would be charged to replace low-performing contractors, either at the end of their contract terms or, if performance were bad enough, even earlier.

On the positive side, because the local board's administrative office would be reduced to a contracting agency, more money would go directly to the school level. Based on a number of studies of U.S. central office spending, cutting spending there by one third would increase school-level funding, now approximately 80 percent of total spending, to nearly 90 percent.[11] Each school would also be free to allocate its income as needed: if it chose to spend less on driver's training, substitute teachers, or elective courses and more to hire a highly qualified mathematics teacher or to send a literature teacher for retraining, it could do so. No particular staff development programs would be mandated from on high, but the schools would have the money and freedom to buy what they need.

Under contracting, school boards would retain ultimate responsibility for school quality. They could replace a contractor (or force an intermediary organization to make substantial quality improvements) as soon as performance fell below acceptable levels. A local school board could also continually "prune" its portfolio of contractors. If the average duration of a school contract were five years, a district would review one fifth of its schools every year. When contracts came up for renewal, contractors whose schools fell below some set level of performance (say, the tenth percentile of all local schools) could be eliminated from consideration. By this mechanism, the contracting system ensures unrelenting work on the lowest-performing schools and should, over time, substantially raise the average performance level of all district schools.

Contracting creates a more equitable allocation of resources among schools than the bureaucratic system, but it lacks a sure solution to the problems of unequal per-pupil funding among localities within a state and of resource instability caused by rising and falling government revenues.

Contracting allocates cash in the form of a fixed per capita reimbursement payment from the local education authority to the school. A school would be guaranteed a minimum annual income, which it would receive until its pupil count reached a set level. Beyond the minimum a school would receive a fixed per-pupil amount for any additional students.

All school costs would be forced out into the open. Schools would negotiate wage and benefit packages with each individual teacher or administrator. No entity other than the school itself could pick up such "hidden" costs as fringe benefits or retirement pay. Schools that affiliated with intermediary organizations might receive services ranging from staff training and recruitment to benefit and retirement packages. But these would all be funded solely from the cash payments made to the school by the public education authority, and these payments would be based solely on the per-pupil payment.

HOW COULD PUBLIC SCHOOL BOARDS RESPOND TO CONTRACT SCHOOL FAILURE?

Under contracting, parents could withdraw their children from a failing school instantly and enroll them somewhere else. But that is not the only way that children might be protected against school failure. The school board could threaten to cancel the contract of a failing school and award it to another provider. The contractor, whether at a single school or an intermediary organization managing many schools, would have to respond successfully or lose its contract.

An intermediary organization running a troubled school would have many choices. It could fire or retrain staff, swap key staff members with stronger schools run by the same organization, or have the school run temporarily by a SWAT team of experts from the intermediary organization's headquarters. The existence of intermediary organizations would also increase local school boards' options. A board could assign a failing school to an organization with a good track record. Some problem schools might even be shared among intermediary organizations as assigned risks.

82   The success of the contracting system in dealing with school failure depends on the existence of a good supply of alternatives. Contracting limits the risks of starting a school by guaranteeing contractors a fixed minimum income and full reimbursement for all costs for students enrolled above the minimum expected number. It can also lower entrepreneurs' front-end costs by allowing contract schools to use existing school facilities and equipment. These lower costs and risks do not guarantee that entrepreneurs and social service agencies will offer to run schools. Schools will remain hard to run and profits may be elusive. But contractors need not fear the outright losses that market system entrepreneurs would suffer if they decided to open a school but nobody came. Under contracting, organizations motivated by professional or social justice concerns (teachers unions, community groups, or interfaith coalitions of churches, for example) could afford to try running schools.

COULD CONTRACT SCHOOLS RELY ON THEIR AGREEMENTS WITH SCHOOL BOARDS?

Contracting tries to protect schools from the turbulence of educational politics. It does so in part by limiting the inherent powers of school boards: they can provide schools only by finding contractors to run them, and they can change valid contracts only through equitable negotiation with independent parties. Boards could not dictate unilateral changes in valid contracts. Disputes between school operators and school boards could ultimately be decided in civil court, and accumulating case law would further define both parties' contractual obligations.

Contracting does not eliminate the political pressures that now lead boards to micromanage schools, but it gives school boards a stable and plausible method for managing such political pressures. It does so by building a way around the need to create a broad social consensus on curriculum and pedagogy, by fostering diversity on precisely those issues on which people have the greatest difficulty agreeing.

Commitment to diversity in schooling may be the only way to free schools from the burdens of regulation.[12] State and local school boards now act as little legislatures, receiving demands from all parts of the community and finding ways to respond, in some minimally acceptable way, to all of them. Like all legislatures, school boards handle demands through the processes of compromise and logrolling. When boards reach compromises among competing demands, they encode the results in rules of general applicability that constrain how teachers use their time and specify how particular issues or groups of students are to be served. The result, in either case, is to sustain what historian David Tyack calls fragmented centralization—control of the schools by multiple uncoordinated mandates and reporting requirements, not by comprehensive plans or designs.[13]

Contracting implies a commitment to a system of individually strong schools. It replaces bureaucratic micromanagement with a totally different supply process, whereby individual schools are commissioned to provide particular approaches to education. Basic civil rights guarantees and employee protections would still apply to all schools, but a school would not be required to take actions incompatible with its basic mission or approach. For example, a school commissioned to provide bilingual instruction to immigrant children would not be required to offer the same courses to all native-born pupils. A school commissioned to provide a particular curriculum would not be required to change it just because one parent complained that it did not meet her child's needs. Most importantly, a group that desired a particular form of multicultural curriculum might be able to obtain it for a particular school without that curriculum's being mandated for all schools sponsored by the same local school board.

Such diversity permits schools to focus on a defined mission and to differentiate their products, as private schools do. If no one approach to schooling is universally required, there is no need to resolve differences through political means. Different tastes and preferences can find expression in different schools. Under contracting it would be possible for individual schools or small groups of schools to adopt and rigorously pursue definite theories of pedagogy. The success of networks of schools connected with Montessori, Waldorf, Paideia, and the Jesuits and other religious groups attests to the power of schools based on strong theories.

Diversity is not an end in itself but an inevitable by-product of a reform based on contracting, which would force schools to differentiate themselves on the basis of curriculum, climate, or some other feature that might attract parents. Given the wide range of social, cultural, and language groups served by public education, schools will inevitably come to set different goals and pursue different approaches.

School boards would still have to make some difficult decisions about whether to contract with ideological fringe groups or with people who lack traditional qualifications as educators. Some boards might resolve such

84   issues by contracting only with intermediary organizations that have established track records. But some may face the need to make official decisions about whether to contract for schools on the boundaries of traditional educational practice or content. Such decisions will inevitably involve balancing the interests of competing groups—they will, that is, be political. But these decisions will define the fringes and boundaries of what can be delivered as public education, not its core.

I have shown in this chapter how contracting can become a radical alternative form of governance for public education. Public schools would be operated by a variety of independent private and public organizations. Local school boards, which now act as monopoly providers of public schools, would no longer operate schools or directly supervise large public bureaucracies. They would become investors and contracting agencies, arranging for independent organizations to operate schools for all the children for whom the board is responsible. Every school would operate according to a specific contract that defined its mission, guarantee of public funding, and standards of accountability. Contracting separates responsibility for funding and establishing general policy for public schools (which remains in the hands of public education authorities) from the responsibility for operating public schools (which is put into private hands).

Each school would be an independent organization with its own staff, mission, and approach to instruction. In contrast, traditional public education systems regard schools as bureaus in a larger bureaucracy. Today's public school is not a legal entity or a cost center: it is a node at which a central administrative organization assembles a number of discrete instructional assets. Schools are put together out of the pool of personnel available to the whole public school system; they use curricula mandated for all schools. In-service training for teachers is chosen by central school system administrators.

Contracting could strengthen existing schools whose staffs and parents agree on goals and methods but are ensnared in public education's thicket of regulations, union contracts, and limitations on uses of funds. It is also likely to generate a large supply of new schools, also based on definite approaches to instruction, in place of the majority of existing public schools that are assembled out of spare parts and embody no specific intentions about instruction, staff collaboration, and student outcomes.

Localities in which good schools are scarce, like inner-city and rural areas of the United States, obviously need an alternative supply mechanism, and contracting is the most promising alternative. For state and civic leaders convinced that their public education bureaucracies have become lax and unproductive, whole-school contracting offers a workable alternative to the nearly hopeless task of changing institutions whose goals and procedures were established for another era.

4 Lessons in School Reform from the Edison Project

John E. Chubb

The public first learned of the Edison Project in May 1991, following a Washington, D.C., press conference that was attended by most broadcast networks and national publications. It was a fitting beginning for an enterprise that would never be far from the watchful eyes of journalists, policy makers, and education leaders.

Although the Edison Project was to be a private business venture, it held a lot of significance—at least potentially—for public education. When it was announced, the project proposed to open a national system of private schools, beginning with one hundred schools in 1996 and growing to perhaps one thousand in another ten years or so. The schools would share key features with public schools. They would accept all students, regardless of academic ability or record, and to further ensure representative enrollments, they would offer scholarships to students in need. The schools would operate for the same amount of money per pupil as public schools. By staying within public school budgets, Edison

schools could serve as models of educational innovation for public schools—
assuming, of course, that the new schools did a good job for students. And
doing a good job was essential. The project's core mission was to produce
world-class educational results—with public school resources and a cross-
section of American students.

Reaction to the project in Washington was skeptical. Nothing like this
had ever been attempted before. But few dismissed the plan, either. After
all, Edison was headed by Chris Whittle, a Knoxville, Tennessee, media
entrepreneur, who had a history of iconoclasm and remarkable financial
success. His largest and most recent triumph was Channel One, a daily news
broadcast for secondary schools paid for with commercial advertisements.
Public educators greeted Channel One with coolness, too. But within a few
years it had penetrated some twelve thousand secondary schools and was
viewed by eight million students daily. If Whittle could reach that many
students for ten minutes a day, people reasoned, perhaps he could reach
fifty thousand students—Edison's potential initial enrollment—all day.

The project gained additional credibility from its financial resources.
Whittle promised a multiyear research and development effort that would
cost $60 million. Although that effort was yet to be formally approved by
Whittle's investors, his company, Whittle Communications, was backed by
major corporations, including Time Warner, Incorporated, and was growing
rapidly. Compared with other efforts to "reinvent American schools" that
were also getting under way, the Edison Project seemed positively flush.

In 1991, the Bush administration was riding high in public opinion polls,
and Lamar Alexander—like Whittle, a Tennessean—had become the secretary of education. Both the president and the new secretary were advocates
of various market-oriented education reforms, including school vouchers
and their signature initiative, the New American Schools Development Corporation (NASDC). Funded by private contributions but promoted by the
White House, this federally sponsored nonprofit organization would underwrite major research and development projects aimed at creating "break-
the-mold" schools. These schools would then serve as models to help public
education reinvent itself as an institution that offered a range of excellent
choices. The Edison Project promised much the same benefit, except it
would be funded by for-profit investors—and it would have a lot more
money, perhaps as much as all of the NASDC projects put together.

During the year following the Washington announcement, the Edison

88 Project gained additional impetus. Whittle Communications added another major investor, Philips Electronics, and the Edison Project recruited a "core team" to lead the research and development effort. Among this prominent group were Chester E. Finn, Jr., former assistant secretary of education and a respected scholar who was critical of the public education establishment; Sylvia Peters, a celebrated inner-city principal from Chicago; Nancy Hechinger, a leading innovator in education technology from Apple Multimedia Labs; two prominent editors, Dominique Browning of *Newsweek* and Lee Eisenberg of *Esquire;* Daniel Biederman, president of the Grand Central Partnership and the 34th Street Partnership, the two largest business improvement districts in New York City; and myself, an education researcher from the Brookings Institution. At another Washington press conference (and in full-page ads in several national newspapers) the core team was introduced in February 1992.

The education world continued to be skeptical. But this was about to change. While the core team went quietly about its work, organizing for research and development, Whittle resumed his discreet effort to recruit a leader for the project. Over Memorial Day weekend of 1992, Benno C. Schmidt, Jr., announced he was resigning as president of Yale University to become president and chief executive officer of the Edison Project. Suddenly the project seemed a very serious endeavor. The national media gave it extensive attention. Doubts remained concerning how Edison would raise all the necessary capital, how schools could excel and make money on public school budgets, and whether advertising would be used to supplement school income—but no one seemed to doubt that the project was well worth watching.

Since 1991, the project has indeed made for good theater. Edison has been covered extensively in the press. Twice—in mid-1993 and in late 1994—the media speculated that Edison was about to go out of business.[1] Whittle Communications did go out of business, with Channel One sold (for a good return) to pay for bold ventures that did not pan out. Reported feuds between Whittle and Schmidt for control of Edison also attracted attention. Although Edison received favorable notice for its work in school design, the project was slammed in the media for failing to deliver on its bold promise of opening hundreds of private schools.[2] In early 1994, Edison announced that it would implement its design in public schools, operated in partnership with districts and states seeking innovative alternatives.

Despite the ups and downs, in early 1995 the Edison Project raised the capital required to open three waves of schools over a three-year span. In the summer of 1995 the first four Edison partnership schools—in Sherman, Texas; Wichita, Kansas; Mount Clemens, Michigan; and Boston—opened to more than two thousand elementary students. In the summer of 1996 eight more partnership schools opened: elementary schools in Colorado Springs; Dade County, Florida; Worcester, Massachusetts; and Lansing, Michigan, and middle or intermediate schools in each of the original four sites. Total enrollment in the 1996–1997 school year reached seven thousand. Two years into operation, the project was ahead of its original plan to begin opening schools in 1996, but behind on the number of schools planned: the first hundred schools will be at least several more years in coming. Nevertheless, Edison retains the core of its original mission—to establish a national system of schools offering first-rate education to a cross-section of students at public school costs.

The project also intends to be a successful business. From the start, this is the objective that has probably stimulated the most interest—and criticism. But if Edison is to succeed financially, it will need to succeed educationally. As we have moved from research and development into small-scale implementation and then into significant scaling up, we have had to learn important lessons in education as well as in management and finance. These lessons, often lost in the sensational reporting the project has attracted, are important not only to those in the business of education but to anyone interested in comprehensive school reform.

Lesson 1: School Design Is Harder Than It Looks

Read any recent book on school reform. Follow the latest innovations reported in *Education Week*. Attend a few sessions at one of the countless education conventions. Reformers, you could easily conclude, know what it takes to create a successful school: high academic standards, an orderly environment, a rich curriculum, a constructivist program of instruction, authentic assessment, site-based decision making, more technology. No list of recommendations will satisfy everyone, of course, but a fairly small number of major reform themes are widely embraced. It is often said in reform circles, "We know what works; let's just do it." Effective school design appears straightforward. It is not.

90   And so, during the spring of 1992 the core team began its work not with the task of school design, but with a series of questions: How should design work proceed? Should we begin with a vision of the well-educated child and plan backward? Should we ask what is wrong with today's schools and aim to design something fundamentally different? Should we survey the successful practices in existing schools and build a new school on those? Or is more basic research needed, perhaps focused on the latest findings in cognitive science? Values complicated these discussions. The core team was a diverse group politically, with differing views of the well-educated child—and just about everything else.

After many weeks of debate over how to proceed, Chris Whittle suggested a process to break the impasse. The core team would divide itself into several smaller design teams, with Whittle constituting a design team by himself. Each team would have four months to assemble a comprehensive school design, as complete as practicable in the time allotted. Each team would have a budget to expend as it chose, and each would have the help of several research assistants. The teams would work independently, except for one day a week, when the core team would convene to discuss topics of common interest or to meet with outside experts. Final designs would be presented in September.

Throughout the summer the teams worked independently—and competitively—reading, observing, consulting, and gathering information from diverse sources. With many professional backgrounds represented on the core team and among the research staff, the design work employed a variety of research strategies. Indeed, as each team followed its particular course, worry set in that the process was becoming divisive. How would the disparate ideas that the teams would soon present be integrated into a coherent design, and how would the participants embrace ideas that were chosen over their own? September arrived amid excitement and trepidation.

The design presentations, each lasting four hours and viewed by staff, core team members, other limited partners, Schmidt, and Whittle, were inspirational. Each expressed a vision of schooling that was powerful in its sense of purpose and possibility. Each design showed real creativity—something that I, as an empirical social scientist, found especially impressive. Yet each design had much in common with the others. After all the secretive labor, the proposed designs were more striking in their similarities than in their differences.

For example, in one way or another every design was rooted in core democratic values—the equal worth of every individual and the responsibility of the individual to the community. All of the designs also held high academic expectations for every child. Students were not to be tracked down different paths; all students were expected to work together for their own betterment and mutual growth. Each design endorsed the concept of a curriculum organized by clear standards. Each envisioned instruction to be more integrated and student-centered than is currently the norm, but direct instruction by teachers also received strong and specific endorsement. The projects and cooperative activities that would activate the classrooms were closely tied to standards and susceptible to rigorous assessment. Portfolios and performance assessments were expected to balance a respected place for traditional standardized tests and for the Advanced Placement Program.

Every design also paid a great deal of attention to school culture. Each offered promising proposals for strengthening school community: teachers working in multigrade teams, students working in multiage houses, teachers and students staying together for several years, and schools being divided into smaller schools-within-schools. Each design prescribed ethical behavior as an explicit part of the curriculum. Each also included attention to expanding the school community to include families and local citizens—a goal considered crucial to school improvement. Thus every design provided for regular parent conferences and volunteer work. Proposals also sought to make school as friendly as possible to parents. The schools all offered before- and after-school programs, adult education, and even weekend and evening accessibility. Technology was universally emphasized—though not as a teaching machine, as some have feared, but as a productivity tool facilitating writing, research, analysis, and communication for students, teachers, and parents. Furthermore, computers were proposed for home use to help students and to strengthen ties between families and schools. Technology was to be more than an instrument of learning; it was to be a force for equity, universally providing resources that now are available to far too few.

The proposals also showed wide concern about the hours of contemporary schooling. How can the high and growing expectations of society be met in schools that are open only six hours a day and 180 days per year? And what will happen to the students whose lives away from school are precarious if afternoons, evenings, and summers so far exceed the time spent in school? The proposals strongly endorsed a longer school day and year.

92   The designs also addressed the problems of professionalism that plague
many schools and school systems, and they reflected certain key assumptions. First, teachers need more control over their work. They need more
time during the day to observe one another, reflect, and plan as a team.
Teachers need more resources for seeking professional development, and
they need more opportunities to advance, to acquire new responsibilities, in
order to remain excited and fresh. They also need to take these strides
without leaving the school for a job in administration. Teachers, the designs proposed in various ways, should have a professional work environment. And they should be held accordingly responsible for student performance. Principals should have complete responsibility for building the
instructional team and should be held accountable for all aspects of school
performance. Smart principals would build a team of teachers with whom
to share responsibility.

Finally, the designs called for administration at the school level and outside to be cut to the bone. Only by cutting bureaucracy deeply and wisely
would systems be able to implement all of the other desired reforms and
stay within public school budgets. Only through extraordinary efficiency
would schools make money.

These highlights do not do justice to the thoughtfully specific proposals
that were contained in each design or to the unique proposals that distinguished each one. The familiarity of many of them may also suggest that
school design isn't so hard after all. In fact, the core team wondered exactly
that in the fall of 1992, when Paul Hill, a social scientist at the RAND Corporation who was heading the process of selecting the winning NASDC
school designs, visited the project in Knoxville. He shared with the core
team his view of the best proposals. The most striking thing about them, he
argued, was their similarity. Slowly, he listed the key features that the winning proposals had in common. As he proceeded, the core team members
experienced an odd mix of feelings—discouragement that careful research
and creative thinking had not produced more that was truly original, and
encouragement that a diversity of accomplished educators had many of the
same ideas.

But getting the fundamentals of the school design right was only the
beginning of the process. A unified design had to be worked out in detail.
And that process, which occupied us for the next year, taught us what
school design really looks—and feels—like.

Lesson 2: The Devil Is in the Details

Despite consensus about many of the fundamentals of quality schooling, actual progress in school improvement has not come easy. For behind the professional consensus are a lot of serious issues and disagreements about how precisely the fundamentals should be pursued. The Edison Project confronted these issues in the second phase of our research and development process. Our efforts to overcome them help explain why public education struggles to progress despite the apparent agreement on fundamentals.

Take the issue of academic standards. On the face of it the idea of high standards is appealing and noncontroversial. Schools should have high expectations for what students should know and be able to do. The expectations should be clearly expressed as standards—minimum acceptable levels of quality performance—so that teachers, students, and parents know what to expect from schooling. Education should be guided by these standards; it should focus not on what educators do but on what students actually learn. Like any organization, schools can lose sight of their most important goals, letting their routines take precedence over their results. Standards can help schools concentrate on what really matters—on students and their accomplishments.

A simple concept, yes, but standards have proven very difficult to put into practice. First there is the question of what students should know. Academic wars have been fought over the appropriate balance of Western and non-Western history and literature. E. D. Hirsch, an otherwise respected scholar, has been vilified for proposing a canon for "cultural literacy."[3]

The federal government endorsed the concept of voluntary national standards during the Bush administration and funded their development by various groups of subject-matter specialists from universities and schools. So far, the results have not been encouraging. Few efforts have escaped searing criticism, although some—science and foreign language standards, for example—are much less controversial than others.[4]

Matters have not been much more peaceful at the state and local levels. State standard setting has often degenerated into mushy generalities that garner political support but do little to change education. States have also ventured into nonacademic realms, where their efforts have sometimes sparked criticism from families concerned about overreaching and state-imposed values. So-called outcomes-based education was doomed by both

94 of these errors.⁵ And if all this were not enough, there is more than just the matter of what children should know. There is also the issue of which children should know it. If standards are for everyone, then won't they need to be low enough for every student to reach them? This question has prompted parents of successful students to oppose standards in various states and communities. In perhaps the ultimate irony, these parents oppose high standards because they doubt they really will be high.⁶

The Edison Project chose to build its curriculum around explicit standards despite all the difficulties the idea has encountered. The core team had become strongly committed to the concept, with Chester Finn, an influential player in the national-standards movement, providing crucial leadership. By this time I had become the project's director of curriculum. As a political scientist and participant observer of education battles in Washington and around the country, I was acutely aware of the challenge we faced. My first move was to hire a veteran of these fights who also understood the substantive education issues and who agreed with Edison philosophically. I was fortunate to persuade Francine Alexander to become deputy director of curriculum. A former teacher who had become a leader in education reform in California, she managed the development of that state's pathbreaking curriculum frameworks under State Superintendent Bill Honig. In 1991 she served another leader in the standards movement, working as deputy assistant secretary for Diane Ravitch at the U.S. Department of Education. In the spring of 1993 we launched an attack on the troublesome issues surrounding standards that would last eighteen months.

To begin, we addressed the issue of what our standards should be. For months, a staff of researchers collected and analyzed standards and (more often) draft standards from professional groups, state departments of education, and foreign countries. We debated these efforts internally, comparing them to the values and goals expressed in the Edison school design book, which was about to be published.⁷ Our discussions led to several key decisions.

First, we wanted to develop standards for traditional academic fields— reading, writing, speaking, listening, mathematics, history (not social studies), geography, economics, civics, and science. Although we believe in curriculum integration, we felt that standards that minimized traditional skill and knowledge objectives in favor of "higher order thinking" or other cross-curricular goals might encourage an inadvertent dilettantism or a coun-

terproductive disregard for fundamentals. We also realized that it is much
more difficult to be clear and objective about standards that are not an-
chored in disciplinary paradigms. And, we believed, standards that are not
clear and objective are not very useful.

To balance our disciplinary emphasis, however, we made another key
decision. We would develop standards for all fields simultaneously and organize and publish them in a chronological sequence of booklets describing
our expectations for students in each of Edison's six academies: Readiness,
Primary, Elementary, Junior, Senior, and Collegiate. Organized by academy,
the standards could ensure that the disparate fields—including not only the
"basics" listed above but also fine arts, practical skills, character and ethics,
world languages, and health and fitness—could constitute an integrated
whole for each phase of a student's education.

Next, we assembled advisory groups for each of the academic fields.
These groups comprised people from the classroom, school administration,
universities, think tanks, professional associations, business—wherever we
saw relevant expertise in standards development. Members were selected to
make each group representative of a diversity of viewpoints in the field. The
reading group, for example, included Pleasant Rowland, founder and president of the Pleasant Company; Eric Cooper, an associate professor at Teachers College at Columbia University and executive director of the National
Urban Alliance; Byron Dobell, former editor-in-chief of *American Heritage*
magazine; Linda Davis, deputy superintendent of the San Francisco Unified
School District; and Barbara Schmidt, a professor at California State University. Each group then met in New York to discuss how to conceptualize what
standards might look like and to brainstorm specific standards for each
academy. After the meetings, each group member was commissioned to
draft core standards for every academy. Edison's curriculum team then analyzed the drafts and distilled them into standards books, one for each of the
first four academies, which were published throughout 1994.[8]

This process was a difficult one, especially given the eighteen-month
time frame in which it had to be completed. We benefited enormously from
the work of an experienced education editor, Debra Martorelli, who left the
helm of *Instructor* magazine to become Edison's editor-in-chief, a capacity in
which she still performs. Even so, the advisory group members offered
widely varying points of view—nearly as wide as those represented by the
various official standards projects we had consulted. We were committed to

96   writing standards that were objective and assessable, so we couldn't gloss over disagreements with generalities. And we wanted the standards for the various disciplines to reinforce one another.

Yet we also had an important advantage: we were not trying to please everyone. We were not writing national standards or even state or district standards. We did not have to get our standards approved by a board of education for use in an entire district or an entire state. Yes, we knew that our standards would have to be acceptable eventually to political authorities who would be contracting with us. But they would be approving these standards for use in a school of choice, not for every school within their jurisdiction. We could develop standards that were true to a particular vision of world-class education. We could be true to ourselves instead of trying to please everyone.

We were thus able to produce comprehensive, useful (and perhaps even elegant) books of standards that now guide curriculum development and teaching in our schools. We were able to cut through the controversy, resolve issues in ways that were consistent with a core set of design principles, and put a powerful but problematic concept into practice. As it turns out, the decisions we made in this process have had wide appeal. The standards were well received by a range of reviewers and have fared well in marketing. Our vision is not esoteric.

Of course, Edison is not the only enterprise that is making good use of standards. But as Diane Ravitch has so thoroughly related, the concept of standards has lost power as it has been implemented through the current structure of public education, which must please everybody simultaneously.[9] Edison's experience suggests that the best hope for standards in public education may lie in the development of strong but different standards for implementation in different schools and communities. The competition among these ideas can weed out the weak and strengthen what remains. In other words, standards may require choice if they are to fulfill their obvious potential.

Lesson 3: Parents Are Not Enemies of Change

Advocates of major school reform often view parents as obstacles. Parents are almost notoriously complacent. When surveyed, they will agree that, yes, America's schools are mediocre. If asked to give the nation's schools a grade, parents (and nonparents) lately have been giving B's and C's more frequently than A's. But ask how their local schools are doing, and the responses are generally positive.[10] Apparently the public has been persuaded by the media coverage and political rhetoric of the last decade that the United States, somewhere and somehow, has a serious education problem. But the problem is not in their backyard.

When people do not see a problem hitting close to home, they are not likely to clamor for aggressive action or to support sweeping change that might disrupt their community. And so it has been with parents. They have not been in the vanguard of most of the national reform efforts aimed at education over the past ten or fifteen years. And they have often been difficult to persuade of the need for large-scale change.

Then there is the matter of what kinds of reform parents will support. Some of the most important reforms of the last generation have been about achieving social justice as much as education improvement: school desegregation, financial equalization, and special education. Over time, people have come to support the basic goals of these reforms. But parents especially have balked when their children and their communities have been asked to pay a price in the name of equity. Few parents want their children to attend a school that is perceived to be inferior or to see dollars drained from their local schools to improve someone else's school. Few parents are content to watch their children's classrooms grow unruly as behaviorally disordered students are returned to them.

Even the concept of school choice is said to generate little enthusiasm among parents, although they endorse the notion in principle. In fact, after reviewing a range of survey responses and actual experiences, the Carnegie Foundation for the Advancement of Teaching concluded that parents have relatively little use for school choice.[11] They don't want their children to travel any distance to school. Often they choose schools for the sake of convenience—for example, a school close to their place of work—and not for academic quality. And they would much prefer that reformers focus on improving neighborhood schools directly than to wait for choice and competition to spur improvement indirectly.

Of course, there are other ways to interpret the evidence of parental indifference toward choice—and toward wholesale education reform in general. Indeed, the Carnegie report has been accused of twisting the facts.[12] Nevertheless, we at the Edison Project were quite concerned that

98   our ambitious plans for wholesale reform, school choice, and the almost novel concept of for-profit schooling would be rejected by parents. We spent a great deal of time and money during the project's first year trying to understand parents better.

The research began in the fall of 1992, after the design teams had presented their plans, but before the integrated school design was completed. We began with a thorough examination of published work on parent attitudes and an original analysis of the parental attitudes and behaviors that were reflected in the National Educational Longitudinal Study, 1988, a federally sponsored survey of students, teachers, administrators, and parents in some two thousand secondary schools. This largely confirmed the conventional wisdom that parents seem fairly satisfied with their schools and not very eager for change. Unfortunately, these sources were not very illuminating. They provided few specifics about why parents were satisfied and little information about how and why parents choose schools. Yet these are the very data on which scholars and policy makers must rely if they want to draw informed conclusions about parental views.

We therefore decided to carry out our own field research, and we hired a nationally respected pollster to help us with the work. Paul Maslin had done polling for many leading Democratic candidates and market research for several major consumer product companies. He was recommended to Edison's core team by Hamilton Jordan, the former chief of staff for President Jimmy Carter and, in 1992, an executive with Whittle Communications. Jordan consulted with the project in late 1992 on political and marketing strategy.

Maslin recommended that we begin with a range of parent focus groups, representing different ethnic and socioeconomic groups across the nation. The purpose was to engage parents in conversations about different approaches to school improvement and about the possibility of choosing schools other than those traditionally offered in the neighborhood.

"Just the facts, Ma'am," is how Maslin summed up the first round of conversations. Recalling Sergeant Joe Friday's trademark plea to witnesses on the television classic *Dragnet,* Maslin said a key to reaching parents is straight talk and simplicity. Parents respond most positively when schools commit themselves to improving the basics—core skills and knowledge, schoolwide order and discipline—and when reform emphasizes traditional academic excellence. Parents quickly lose interest when the conversation

turns to topics that professional educators often value: higher-order thinking, integrated curricula, authentic assessment, heterogeneous grouping, or
the school as a social service center. Parents also showed relatively little
interest in school reform as an engine for national economic or social
change. They were interested in reform if it could improve the schools
available to their children.

This perspective on parents was distressingly familiar. It echoed the findings of survey research, and it threatened the viability of many of the ideas
that Edison thought held great promise for school improvement. (Interestingly, the same perspective on parent attitudes, recently corroborated in
a highly publicized Public Agenda survey and embraced by the American
Federation of Teachers, is spurring another back-to-basics campaign.[13]) But
this was just the first round of focus groups.

In round two we discovered that parents are not deeply conservative or
inherently suspicious of reform. They do not believe that schools were ideal
when they attended them and should return to the good old days. What we
discovered in this round is the importance of language, of the way in which
reform ideas are expressed and explained. Parents have legitimate concerns
that new ideas come with risks and problems. They need to see, for example, that cooperative learning can have individual accountability or that
computers and calculators can further thinking and not substitute for it.

In round two, then, parents began to respond positively to a range of
design ideas that they had greeted with suspicion or indifference in round
one. We also began to crack another important code. The ambivalence that
parents expressed toward school choice in previous research fell away when
they were presented with a concrete alternative of real quality. Parents
who, in our survey or in practice, show little interest in switching their
children's school may see little else to choose from. Perhaps the public
schools in their area are pretty much the same, and the private schools
represent someone else's religion. In such circumstances, what's the point
of choice? But if there is a solid, innovative alternative—which is what
Edison proposed to offer—choice becomes meaningful. Parents in our focus
groups, at any rate, seemed willing to consider a change.

To refine and test the ideas that grew out of the focus groups, we next
conducted a series of telephone surveys. Maslin and I designed a detailed
thirty-minute questionnaire to measure parent attitudes toward our school
design and parent willingness to switch to an Edison school. The survey was

100   administered to a national sample of approximately 1,000 parents and to samples of about 250 people in each of thirteen cities nationwide. We were interested in local variation as well as national averages.

What did we find? Like every other survey, we found seemingly satisfied parents. Although 39 percent expressed some dissatisfaction with schools nationally, only 10 percent were at all dissatisfied with their own children's schools, and only 2 percent were "very dissatisfied." This would seem a weak base on which to build support for changing schools. Yet these seemingly satisfied parents turned out to be surprisingly open to the idea.

The surveyors told parents that a new school, to be called an Edison school, might open in their vicinity. They were then asked to react to the school, element by element, as the school design was described to them over the phone. Specifically, they were asked whether each design element would make them much more likely or much less likely (or points in between) to send their children to an Edison school. The reactions were generally quite positive, and certain school improvements received overwhelmingly high ratings. Tops in our design: the pervasive use of technology, including computers in every home, and a career ladder for teachers that would promote the best to positions of greater responsibility and compensation and remove the weakest from the classroom. Interestingly, these are the two areas in which schools are probably most out of step with much of the world of work. Parents seem to recognize that schools do not use enough technology or reward teacher performance. Not bad for a group that supposedly doesn't understand what's going on in schools.

Beyond these top two elements, parents also gave strong support to progressive instructional reform. They were attracted to a promise of instruction that was varied and individualized and that got kids out of rows and away from traditional lectures. Parents were similarly enthusiastic about project-based instruction—but only when they were told that it meant real-world applications of academic knowledge and hands-on experience. These are decidedly not part of the back-to-the-basics rhetoric that supposedly holds such great appeal for parents. In fact, the one question on our survey that came closest to that traditional agenda, a reference to our core curriculum in the traditional disciplines, garnered less support than many more innovative proposals. Parents expect the basics, it seems, but they are looking for something more exciting and forward-looking than standard curricula and instructional strategies usually offer.

Parents are troubled by one forward-looking proposal, though. The least popular element of our school design turned out to be the longer school year—twenty-five additional days, leaving six weeks for summer vacation. Although a clear majority favored the idea, a little more than a quarter said the longer year would reduce their interest in the school. This corroborated what we learned in the focus groups, but it did not deter us. We continue to believe that the longer year is critical to academic progress, especially for disadvantaged groups, and it remains part of our school design. And, with everything else that the school design offers—and that parents endorse—the longer day has proved acceptable.

The survey provided a forecast of that acceptability. If the Edison school were a public school of choice, 86 percent of the parents surveyed nationally said they would consider sending their child: 53 percent said "definitely," and 33 percent said "probably." This support surfaced again in the separate city surveys, but with some variation. The South and West responded somewhat more positively to this opportunity to choose than did the Northeast and the Midwest. Stronger traditions of local school governance and neighborhood schooling in the latter regions may account for this rather minor difference.

Overall, our research and that of others revealed that parents are satisfied with their schools, but very open to the possibility of improvement. They seem to want something better for their children than they themselves experienced, and they are willing to choose something other than the neighborhood school if doing so will really make a difference. Parents are not wedded to a pedagogy of the past. Pollsters have missed much of what parents seem to be thinking because they have offered them nothing to think about. Edison has tried to offer parents a solid and progressive alternative. In our experience so far, parents have been mostly friends of change.

Lesson 4: Private Schooling Is a Potentially Large Market, But . . .

The Edison Project set out to build a national system of private schools that fulfilled the essential public school mission. Yet today Edison operates no private schools and has no plans to do so. Our first schools and our planned system of schools are entirely public. What happened, and what is to be learned from it?

In the media, Edison's switch from private schools to public schools was reported as a major defeat. At Edison, the experience seemed nothing of the kind. The media had defined Edison's mission rather narrowly, as the creation of a private, for-profit system of schools. Perhaps this was because a private system was the most novel, expensive (and audacious) part of Edison's mission. Whatever the reason for it, the media's view differed from Edison's own view of what it was trying to accomplish.

From the very beginning, the core team's work was guided by four objectives, each of which was extremely important to all of us. First, create a school that could deliver an absolutely first-rate education. Every member of the core team brought to the project a passionate belief in the power of certain kinds of school improvement. Every member had a vision of something different, something better, that he or she wanted to see realized in Edison schools. Second, and closely related, every member of the core team had a special desire to improve the opportunities available to disadvantaged children. Even though the instrument was planned to be private, we all thought that disadvantaged students were the key group to reach if we wanted the schools to make a contribution to the nation. We all were immodest enough to want to make such a difference.

Our third objective was to stay within public school budgets. We were trying to do a better job with the resources available to public educators. We hoped to provide a model that public educators could replicate. Fourth and finally, we had to be profitable.

These four objectives really drove the work of the core team during the design phase of our work. We never saw our essential mission to be the creation of private schools. Private schools were more the means to an end—four ends. When the core team began to come together in late 1991 (Whittle organized various brainstorming and recruitment meetings before the core team was chosen), we generally believed that public education would not permit for-profit organizations to operate schools on a sufficiently widespread basis, nor would the system reform itself enough to support the core objectives of the Edison Project. The team therefore agreed that private schools were the best way to begin building the system.

Yet days after Benno Schmidt joined the project on July 1, 1992, we began getting calls from prominent public officials—governors, mayors, superintendents—asking whether we would consider developing Edison schools for public school systems. Schmidt's presence added substantial credibility to the project's education mission and counterbalanced the project's image in the media as an enterprise concerned mainly with profits. Schmidt also brought to the project a firm belief that Edison would ultimately work with public education directly. This view was reinforced by a new member of the planning team, Mike Finnerty, who moved from Yale to Edison. Finnerty, who has since become Edison's chief financial officer, had fifteen years of public service in New York City and New York State—including service as budget director for Governors Carey and Cuomo—before joining Yale as vice president of finance and administration. Finnerty's experience gave the core team further reason to believe a public school relationship could prove workable.

By the fall of 1992, the core team was regularly debating the merits of a "public partnership" strategy. Several members of the core team—Finn, Biederman, and I—had considerable experience with the kind of reform that would make partnerships possible. Chester Finn and I had long been involved in the politics of school choice. Each of us believed that the public sector would continue to become more open to school choice as a systemic reform and to alternative schools as a concrete approach to improving education. Public school choice was already becoming commonplace, at least in weakened forms. Magnet schools were truly mainstream. The nascent idea of charter schools seemed likely to spread. Neither Finn nor I thought vouchers for private schools were likely to proliferate any time soon; but we did think that increasingly more powerful forms of school choice would.

It is important to note that the Edison Project was not founded on the hope that vouchers would make private schools an easier business. People sometimes presume that it was, because Edison was launched during the heyday of the Bush administration, and Lamar Alexander had been a (minor) investor in Whittle Communications. But the core team gave vouchers little prospect of being widely adopted. None of the school designs conceived over the summer of 1992, including the one crafted by Whittle himself, included any role for vouchers. Rather, we assumed that our private schools would be supported by tuition-paying parents, many of them receiving financial aid from the project.

The public school partnership idea got a boost from the view—advanced especially by Finn and me—that public education was becoming more and more open to market-oriented reforms, short of private school vouchers. The partnership strategy was also advanced by Biederman, who had a long and successful history of providing public services—maintenance, security,

104   social work—privately for New York City. Biederman, with his crucial expertise in "contracting out," argued that Edison should seriously consider the strategy.

Throughout the fall of 1992, the core team studied the financial, legal, and political feasibility of public school partnerships, while continuing to examine every element of the private school strategy. Finally, on December 21, 1992, the Edison Project presented its first integrated school design and business plan at a private meeting of limited partners. The school design was meant to work for both private schools and public schools. The business plan included a mix of both, with more public schools than private. These plans were laid six short months after Schmidt began meeting with public officials—and six months before the media reported our supposedly abrupt switch to public schools.[14] In fact, the "switch" had been a smooth and considered process that started on day one of the project.

Indeed, the process occupied much of the project's time and resources for the next six months. In early January we launched two major market research projects. One was aimed primarily at the potential private school market, the other at the market for public school partnerships. Chester Finn was put in charge of partnership research; I directed the private research. (This also marked the end of the work of the core team. With basic design work complete, Schmidt reorganized the project into operating divisions and assigned posts and responsibilities to core team members.)

Much of the research on the private school market was embedded in the focus group and survey work we had used to study our school design, as described earlier. Now we used those instruments to assess interest in private schools as an alternative to public education and to evaluate willingness to pay tuition. The results were quite encouraging. Even at a tuition level equal to national public school spending levels, 9 percent of the parents in the national survey said they would "definitely want to send" their child to an Edison school and 51 percent said they would "probably want to." In the local surveys, several cities had 10–18 percent saying "definitely."[15]

Of course, talk is cheap, and responses to a telephone survey must be interpreted carefully. But additional research tended to corroborate the strong survey results. In February of 1993, Benno Schmidt and several members of the original core team made test sales presentations to parents in four prospective markets around the country. The presentations described the design of an Edison school that might open in their community in the fall of 1996. Parents were surveyed on their reaction to the design and given the opportunity to register their children for the school, with guaranteed spots if the school actually opened. The results were even more encouraging in the face-to-face survey than over the phone. An average of 61 percent said they would definitely consider enrolling their child. And 40 percent of the parents who were in attendance actually signed up their children.

We also had evidence that these four test markets were representative of markets nationwide. Using detailed demographic data collected at the level of census tracts, we were able to identify every locale across the United States that contained enough families earning enough income (based on our survey research) to support an Edison school, assuming that a relatively small percentage of families would enroll their children. This research yielded several hundred promising markets. Finally, we dispatched a team of field researchers to the most promising markets. There they interviewed private and public school officials, private school placement consultants, local community and business leaders, realtors, and civic groups to see what the interest level in a new school might really be. Are people happy with the public schools? Are there waiting lists for private schools? Do good potential locations exist? After two weeks, the field researchers filed detailed reports. With this information and all that came before it, Edison was confident by the late spring of 1993 that there were excellent markets for at least one hundred private K–12 schools and acceptable markets for perhaps two hundred more.

While I was overseeing research on private schools, Chester Finn continued to evaluate the markets for public school partnerships. He organized a team of five to study the political, legal, financial, and educational climate for partnerships nationwide. They studied legislation, regulations, and case law. They canvassed governors, legislators, superintendents, and school board members. And they organized states and school districts into categories of prospects—an A list of top prospects, a B list of reasonable possibilities, and so forth. By the summer of 1993, Edison concluded that the market for a business in public school partnerships was strong.

During the fall of 1993, Edison continued to work on a dual strategy of public and private schools. But the momentum quickly shifted to the public school approach. Capital considerations, among other factors, pushed us in this direction. The capital required to launch a K–12 private school would have been four to five times the capital required to launch a partnership school. In the partnership context, the cost of the facility would already be paid for or amortized on the favorable terms of public debt. In the private context, the facility would have to be constructed or rehabilitated with expensive investment capital (or leased at market rents). With limited capital to launch a business that required multiple sites, the partnership strategy was more appealing. It offered the prospect of more schools up and running sooner than the private school strategy offered. Either strategy could make a nice business once it was off the ground. But in the partnership scenario, launch capital would go farther. Edison would be able to reach more students at an earlier date.

The public strategy also enabled Edison to focus its research and development budget—not to mention its organizational energy. Edison was never funded to pursue both strategies. And as development work got more intensive, the burden of two marketing and implementation forces became unworkable. By late 1993 the project simply had to make a choice.

By this time, Edison had recruited a top-notch team of partnership representatives, including Deborah McGriff, former Detroit superintendent; Stephen Tracy, former New Milford, Connecticut, superintendent and prominent school choice proponent; Walter McCaroll, former deputy commissioner of education in New Jersey and Florida; and several of the top education technology sales people in the country. In January of 1994, Edison decided to concentrate on the one strategy its funds and expertise would best support. It became a partnership project.

There are two general lessons to be drawn from this long process of research and consideration. The first is that private schools have a substantial potential to expand in this country. There is real interest in private schools that offer excellence without the baggage that often accompanies private education—religion, high cost, selectivity, even, sometimes, elitism. Especially if the tuition were relieved through a voucher program, such private schools could reach a large number of children. Second, there is a definite trend in public education away from the monolithic system model of the first half of this century. The country is increasingly open to market-oriented reforms of school governance. Different parts of the country will embrace this movement in different ways. But the days of the so-called "one best system" are clearly over.[16] The Edison Project would not have wagered its future on the public sector if it did not firmly believe that public education was more than ready for market-oriented change.

Lesson 5: Federalism Lives

Dead or dying—for most of the last century, the federal system looked like a goner. State and local governments steadily lost power, while the national government inexorably gained power. One after another, important issues were debated and solved in Washington. Not only did people stop looking to lower governments for solutions, they saw them as part of the problem.[17]

Poverty, unemployment, inadequate health care, malnutrition, inequality—these problems festered while states and cities did nothing or exacerbated the troubles with policies that favored the privileged. Instead of offering diverse and creative initiatives, the states differed mostly in their degree of inadequacy. Rich states like New York provided better services than poor states such as Mississippi. But the national government took responsibility from all of them. By the 1970s, the lower governments had become appendages of an extensive policy apparatus controlled and funded by Washington.

Education did not escape these powerful forces. Although education is a function historically and constitutionally left to the states, the system that evolved to provide it developed a remarkable sameness nationwide and came substantially under Washington's influence. By midcentury education was governed and administered by pretty much the same means in every community in the country. Students were assigned to schools based on their residence. First they attended an elementary school, then a junior high school, and finally a high school. As new schools were built, they grew steadily in size, more than doubling in average enrollment from 1920 to 1960.[18] Different forms of school organization—K–8 schools, one-room schoolhouses—all but disappeared.

Schools were organized into geographic districts governed by boards of education. Districts were administered by superintendents who headed (growing) central offices. Like schools, districts grew in size as tens of thousands of small districts were consolidated into larger ones. Over time, as the money to pay for schools came more and more from the state level, state departments of education grew to oversee the districts. By the 1960s, it was

108   fair to describe American education in terms of a single model, what the
historian David Tyack calls the "one best system."[19]

There are many reasons why so many communities arrived at the same
way of delivering education. One reason, which gained in importance over
time but did not assume real prominence until the 1960s, is the national
government. Through its efforts to promote school desegregation, to ensure
educational equity, and to pursue countless lesser goals that were not being
met by the states and school districts, the government in Washington became a major force in every school community in the country.[20] Federal
grant money and federal regulations spawned an intergovernmental bureaucracy that moved all schools in similar directions. In 1979, the importance of Washington was reinforced with the creation of the U.S. Department of Education. Throughout the 1980s, the department and the White
House regularly drew attention to the nation's educational health with
alarming studies and urgent pronouncements. Educational debate now
centered in Washington. State capitols seemed dead.

Yet by the 1980s things were not quite the way they seemed. Sluggish
economic growth and federal budget deficits had put a cap on federal aid to
education. As the dollars dried up, states demanded—and got—more flexibility in how they could use money. Meanwhile, state governments had
steadily become more professional. By the early 1980s, states saw education
as key to their own economic growth.[21]

Throughout that decade states aggressively sought to improve schools
themselves. Spending and teacher salaries increased. Tough academic requirements were imposed. Testing proliferated to hold schools more accountable. And in various ways, states and districts began to experiment.
States instituted various forms of school choice. Many states adopted charter school bills. Districts created alternative schools. Today it is far less accurate than it was a generation ago to describe the educational system as a
monolith.[22]

This change has been critical to Edison's success. The service that Edison
offers might never be delivered if it were up to the national government to
approve it. Too many constituencies with too much interest in maintaining
the systemic status quo would have had to be won over for Edison to be
politically feasible. This is why so many large school districts, in which the
structure of things is so extensive and so firmly established, find the sort of
fundamental change that Edison offers extremely difficult. Politics in these

places, as in Washington, tends to favor the well organized. And the best organized interests in education tend to be those who have jobs or programs in the existing system—and therefore a strong preference for reforms that do not seem to challenge the status quo.

But the politics of education is not everywhere so bound (or paralyzed) by tradition. Federalism is beginning to mean something again. The fifty states and their sixteen thousand school districts differ in ways that are more consistent with their number than ever in the recent past. Yes, their similarities are still impressive. But their differences have been vital to Edison.

During 1994, our first year of marketing, the Edison Project won acceptance from a wide range of communities in a variety of circumstances. Fifteen communities signed letters of intent to contract with Edison to open and operate some twenty-five "partnership" schools based on our school design. In Boston and Worcester, private boards of citizens elected to apply, with Edison, to the state of Massachusetts for approval (later granted) to open charter schools. In two large school districts, Dade County, Florida, and Wichita, Kansas, public boards of education voted to contract with Edison to launch new neighborhood schools of choice, something both districts were already leaders in offering. Several very small districts, among them Mount Clemens, Michigan, and Sherman and Wylie, Texas, signed up for partnership schools that would become the first choices for families in their communities. In Colorado Springs, the board of education voted to support Edison in the operation of a charter school independent of the district—and even competitive with it—to promote innovation. In Hawaii, where one board governs education for the entire state, six schools were tentatively approved, to be sited on the basis of petitions from communities throughout the islands.

The Edison Project fit comfortably into different reform plans in different communities: charters and contracts, big districts with a history of choice and small districts trying choice for the first time, state initiatives and local. The success that Edison has had in recruiting partners has less to do with shrewd marketing than with the opening of the education system to fundamentally different ways of providing education. These changes are not occurring everywhere, to be sure. They are not very evident in national policy making or in many large and institutionalized systems like New York City and Los Angeles. Perhaps the resistance to change in these centers of national media is why the far-flung reforms that make Edison possible are

110   not more clearly perceived or widely reported. Be that as it may, federalism lives, and through it, so has Edison.

Lesson 6: Not All of the Gorillas Weigh Eight Hundred Pounds

As much as education seems to be crippled by systemic rigidities, it can also appear paralyzed by powerful interest groups. On the left and the right, certain groups seem to carry the political weight of the proverbial eight-hundred-pound gorilla: they get anything they want—or at least, they stop anything they don't want. Teachers unions, for example, are said to wield so much influence that even such popular reforms as merit pay cannot be enacted over their objections. Or consider the so-called radical right: during the last decade, their opposition has meant near-certain death for such reforms as performance standards and authentic assessment. Any direction reformers turn, their path seems blocked by an immovable force.

Yet just as the federal system now admits considerable variation in school governance and administration, it sustains many differences in pressure politics. Groups that are all-powerful on a national scale do not enjoy the same measure of influence in every community. National organizations oppose major reforms while their state and local branches sometimes accommodate them. The Edison Project is all the more viable because of these growing differences. In our experience, the gorillas do not always weigh eight hundred pounds.

We were concerned, for example, that our school design would be opposed by the same (usually conservative) groups that killed outcomes-based education in so many places in the early 1990s. Our curriculum is explicitly standards based. Before we opened our first schools, among our main marketing tools were our standards books, which detailed our student outcomes. In each book, in addition to listing outcomes for traditional academic subjects, we've described our expectations for character and ethics, one of the five major domains of our curriculum, and a potential lightning rod for criticism of values education. The curriculum is extensively multicultural—a problem for some traditionalists. Moreover, we were marketing in parts of the country where opposition to outcomes-based education had been strong.

As 1994 progressed, Edison presented its plans in scores of community

meetings around the country. We answered thousands of probing questions
from cautious parents and community influentials. (We even amassed an
internal document accurately titled "Answers to 1,000 Questions" to help
our people in the field.) As we expected, there were many questions about
values education. Critics drew parallels between Edison and outcomes-
based education. More than a few communities wondered about the motives of an organization based, as Edison is, in New York City, a supposed
bastion of liberalism. But in the end, only one community rejected Edison
because of organized conservative opposition.

For the most part, we were able to distinguish our plans from those, such
as outcomes-based education, that communities had opposed. When potential opponents took time to read our standards, they found that they
were clear, objective, and based on traditional disciplines. They found that
our values were democratic and universal—not "political" or "personal."
When we wrote the standards books, we were careful to avoid the vague or
"transformational" language that got others into trouble.[23] Veterans of the
standards wars, such as Diane Ravitch and former U.S. Assistant Secretary
of Education Bruno Manno, vetted our draft standards. But the key to our
success has not been political sensitivity. Rather, it has been a philosophy of
education that values high expectations for all students, a rich liberal arts
curriculum, and strict accountability to families for clearly expressed academic goals. Understood in these terms, a standards-based curriculum becomes acceptable, even desirable, to groups that might otherwise oppose it.
Politics becomes less of a problem than generally anticipated.

One more example. Teachers unions have either opposed or offered only
limited support for school choice, charter schools, and contracting with
private providers of instruction. This presents a potential problem for Edison, for all of these concepts are important to our growth. In addition,
Edison must often work with local unions in forging partnerships in specific communities. So how have we been able to proceed? By developing a
school design and an implementation strategy that allow us to satisfy important union concerns and pursue our educational mission.

For example, our school design works hard to strengthen the professionalism of teachers. Relative to current circumstances, teachers in our system
are paid more (for more work). They have an opportunity to ascend a career
ladder that gives them more responsibility for leading the school. They have

112   more time off during the day for planning and working with their colleagues. They receive more training and more resources to seek professional development. They have more instructional resources, including a laptop computer that links them to Edison's nationwide network of educators.

Our implementation strategy ensures that teachers are not put at risk by district partnerships with us. We aim to operate no more than a few schools in any one district. (We really do believe in choice.) No teachers are laid off because of a partnership. Normal teacher attrition throughout the district is enough to ensure that if district teachers do not quite provide us with the necessary staff, we can hire sufficient new teachers without disruption. Teachers work in partnership schools, and under Edison's work rules, only if they volunteer to do so. Teachers who don't like the Edison experience or who don't work out are guaranteed their seniority and a position in the district. Edison maintains existing retirement benefits. In short, teachers are able to try out partnership schools with relatively little professional risk.

These measures have not transformed teachers unions into proponents of private contracting. But they have enabled Edison to build effective working relationships with unions in a number of local districts. Among our first four schools are two that required and received union blessing. In Wichita, the local affiliate of the American Federation of Teachers cooperated in planning for the Dodge-Edison elementary school, and in Mount Clemens the affiliate of the National Education Association supported the Martin Luther King, Jr., Academy, an Edison Partnership School. Among Edison's second wave of schools is one in Dade County, where one of the AFT's largest locals has worked very professionally with us.

Unions cooperate for various reasons. We like to think it is because our curriculum and school design are compelling, because our program offers concrete benefits for teachers, and because the risks of participation are fairly low. But unions also understand that reform must go forward, for the good of students and of teachers. They know that other groups—businesses, citizen activists—are paying more attention to education and gaining in influence. They recognize that power must be shared. They know that not every reform pursued will be their first preference.

The simple lesson here is that education politics is becoming more and more complex. Barriers that seem insurmountable on a national scale can be far less forbidding in America's varied communities. Edison has chosen to confront its obstacles on this smaller scale.

Lesson 7: Education and Profits Do Mix   113

Shortly after I joined the Edison Project, a member of the editorial board of
the *Philadelphia Inquirer* asked me whether Edison's pursuit of profits would
cause students to be shortchanged. Over the years since then, my colleagues
at Edison and I have been asked this question more than any other. Sometimes the question stems from objective interest: "Dollars that leave the
school and go to investors can't help educate children, it seems; so how can
a for-profit enterprise improve schooling?" Sometimes people ask the question in moral indignation with little interest in impartial answers: "Isn't it
wrong to make money off of public schools and their children?" Either way,
the question remains a major source of interest in the Edison Project.

In 1992, I told the *Inquirer* that "there's no magical way to make a profit
while providing lousy schools." The paper used that quotation in support of
its cautious endorsement of the Edison Project. The *Inquirer* editorial reasoned that a for-profit education enterprise would make money only if it
succeeded in providing schools that people valued—schools that work.
Schools that cut corners and shortchanged students in order to boost profits
would find themselves with few customers—and little profit.[24]

Of course, the issue is not quite so simple. Consumers are not always
good judges of quality, and they may not notice when profit taking compromises service. Consumers may not always insist on high quality, thereby
providing a market niche for a shoddy alternative. Education has had many
unhappy experiences with for-profit trade schools that take money or
vouchers from poor people and offer little in return. Critics of school choice
have long argued that ignorance and bias among some parents and community leaders could enable lousy schools to flourish.

All of these observations have merit; they represent well-known "market imperfections," as economists call them. In Edison's experience, however, the more basic observation—that the market tends to weed out inferior quality and to deny profits in the absence of value—is more telling.
There is indeed a tension between spending money in schools and returning
money to investors. But the tension can be a healthy one. In a number of
critical ways, the pressure to make profits has forced the Edison Project to
improve the service it offers communities, not compromise it.

Our near-death experience in the fall of 1994 is a prime example. At the
time, we knew that Edison's money for research and development would be

114   exhausted by year's end. We needed new funds to launch our first schools
and to keep Edison going. But investors were balking. We had a strong
product in our much-admired school design. We had a strong market, as the
many communities who had already signed up for partnership schools
proved. We also had a well-known problem: a connection to Whittle Communications, which had closed early in the year. But the capital markets
had another problem with us: they doubted our business plan.

To succeed—in education and in business—Edison spends more of each
education dollar on instruction at the school site than most school districts
do. More money for teachers, training, technology, and materials is part of
our formula for school improvement. Better schools, we assume, will in
turn mean more business. But for this simple formula to work, we must use
the money that is left after instructional expenditures very efficiently. We
have to provide accounting, reporting, purchasing, personnel, research and
development, facilities management, and the many other services that support schools but do not directly affect instruction, with less money than
school districts normally reserve for these purposes. This diminished sum
must also yield a profit.

In the fall of 1994, investors were not convinced that we had figured out
how to be so efficient. Our plans for support services at each site looked
promising, investors thought. But our plans for central office support did
not. We were criticized by investors in much the same way public school
systems are often attacked: we were accused of wanting to spend too much
money on central administration. We disagreed; our central costs were low
relative to the scope of the system we expected to develop. Investors responded that we were aiming to open too many schools a bit too soon.
Either we reduce central costs drastically or there would be no investment.

Our plan, investors thought, was putting the entire enterprise at unacceptable risk. The Edison Project depends on a cycle of investment and
returns on investment for its education model to succeed. We invest heavily
in the launch and development of a new school. We provide the capital to
give schools state-of-the-art technology, to put computers in every student's
home, to retrofit schools with instructional materials, and to offer teachers
extensive professional development. These are capital investments that
school districts cannot easily make on their own, and we believe they will
pay handsome educational dividends. But such investments can continue
only if the schools also pay financial dividends. Our investors, who have

risked a lot, have every right to have their capital repaid and to earn a return on their investment.

This virtuous cycle can benefit many, many schools—as long as it is not broken. In the eyes of investors, our business plan jeopardized the cycle by diverting too much money into central administration. Our financial projections worked on paper, but they did not make investors comfortable. In the end, investors insisted that Edison cut its central expenditures in half.[25] This was an extremely difficult demand to meet. But we literally had no choice. By the end of 1994, we figured out ways that we thought would enable us to succeed educationally despite the cuts. We then made a deal with our new investor, the Sprout Group, the venture capital affiliate of Donaldson, Lufkin, and Jenrette, to recapitalize the Edison Project and launch our first schools.

In retrospect, this painful experience was a useful lesson in simple market discipline. We would be in a precarious position today if we were trying to repay investors and cover high overhead costs simultaneously. With very lean administration, we have more room in our business plan to make unanticipated expenditures when unexpected problems arise. Yes, our administration is stressed and stretched. But it is still providing schools all essential services.

Have we compromised education or shortchanged students? We don't think so. The data are not yet in on student achievement gains in year one, and in any case substantial gains take time. But our customers have been satisfied. At each of our first four sites we were authorized to add an Edison Junior Academy in year two. And that brings me back to my initial observation: there's no way to make money by providing lousy schools.

Our customers are knowledgeable buyers. They include school board members, district administrators, and state education leaders. They have lots of hard data—standardized tests; performance assessments; surveys of parents, students, and staff; independent studies—to use in judging our performance. Our customers have the contractual right to terminate our partnership on short notice, and they take this accountability responsibility very seriously. As Wichita Superintendent Larry Vaughn put it, "Never has one educator promised to quit should I become dissatisfied with their work or productivity. Our current system of education is not equipped to provide such accountabilities."[26]

If, in our need to satisfy our investors, we compromise the education we provide to our customers, Larry Vaughn and his colleagues around the country will not fail to notice. They will not sit by idly. They will insist that we improve. They will cancel us if we do not. They will not accept lousy. It's as simple as that.

Lesson 8: Markets Can Be Equitable

By far the most common concern raised about market-oriented school reform (choice, charters, and contracting out) is that it will hurt the poor and disadvantaged. The poor are always hurt by markets, the argument goes. They have less to choose from. They have less money, less information, and less education to help them make good choices. Savvy and motivated parents will choose good schools for their children, while the most needy will be left behind, concentrated in bad schools.

The concerns are by now familiar—as are the responses: The poor are being hurt by the current system, in which supposedly protective bureaucracies fail to protect the disadvantaged from rotten schools. Choice is available today to anyone with the money to move to a better neighborhood and school system. A choice system could be structured to give preference to the disadvantaged. Competition would stimulate improvement among all schools, not just shuffle kids among unimproved schools. And so forth.

These arguments have raged since the early 1980s. And they will continue in full fury until there is more information to help resolve them. For the truth is that this country has only begun to implement market-oriented reform. Vouchers for private schools remain rare. Charter schools may be approved in a majority of the states, but the first schools are still young and not well understood. Contracting out is even newer. The early experience of the Edison Project can contribute information to an important education debate.

The Edison Project has always aimed to develop schools for the full range of families and students. All of the communities we serve know that we want our school populations to mirror the school population of the entire community. We also believe in school choice. We insist that all students attend our schools voluntarily—either by affirmative choice or by rejecting the choice of opting out (in cases where our school replaces the neighborhood school). These objectives could easily come into conflict. An open enrollment process might not provide a representative population. If critics

TABLE 4.1 Ethnic Composition of Edison Schools (percentages)   117

Ethnic Group	Boston		Mount Clemens		Sherman		Wichita	
	Dist.	Ed.	Dist.	Ed.	Dist.	Ed.	Dist.	Ed.
African-American	48	59	37	48	19	20	23	23
Asian	9	1	2	0	0	1	5	3
Hispanic	23	13	2	1	7	22	10	7
Native-American	1	2	0	0	0	0	2	1
Caucasian	19	23	59	51	73	56	61	66

of school choice are correct, our schools could easily underrepresent the disadvantaged.

So far, however, our student populations mirror the demographic characteristics of the district or larger community. If there are differences, they reflect a disproportionately large—not small—number of disadvantaged students enrolled in our schools. Table 4.1 shows the ethnic composition of our schools in comparison with that of the school district in which we operate.

In addition to the close matches on ethnicity, the schools attract representative enrollments of disadvantaged students. In all four schools a majority of the students are eligible for free or reduced lunch. All four schools qualify as "schoolwide projects" under new federal Title I regulations. In Wichita and Sherman, the partnership schools enroll a larger percentage of disadvantaged students than the district average. In Boston and Mount Clemens, the percentage is somewhat lower than the district average. Overall, the schools represent their communities closely.

How was all this accomplished? Through a combination of choice and design—but mostly through parental choice. In Sherman and Wichita, district authorities recommended schools in disadvantaged neighborhoods to become partners with Edison. We then had to meet with parent and community groups to present our plans, answer questions, and seek support. Once the school community agreed to participate, the children in the traditional attendance zone had first claim to seats in the school. Parents had the right to opt out—an option that we insisted upon, and that had to be granted anyway because our school day adds one hour and our school year adds twenty-five days to district requirements. But students in the attendance area were not automatically enrolled; they had to indicate their desire to

118 remain. Edison had to hold many parent information sessions to get families reenrolled. In the end, most families decided to remain—and enrollments reflected their known disadvantages.

But most of Edison's enrollments were not this simple to predict. Nearly half of the students in the Sherman and Wichita schools were chosen from districtwide application pools, using lotteries when applications exceeded openings. In Mount Clemens, the new Martin Luther King, Jr., Academy was filled through districtwide choice. And in Boston, where our Renaissance Charter School had no claim on students in Boston public schools, enrollments were determined by a lottery with rules determined by the state: no preferences could be given for race, disadvantage, or anything else. The only guarantee of a representative student body is representative recruiting—and this we did tirelessly.

By and large, our schools have the students they do because their families chose to send them. The schools have substantial disadvantaged populations and as much or more diversity than their surrounding communities because the schools have appealed to families that traditionally have had little—and little to choose from. With our advanced technology plan, extensive arts curriculum, and ambitious academic program, our schools could easily have been overwhelmed by applications from middle-class families or others with strong educational traditions. But this did not happen. Those families seem to be satisfied already with what their school system is providing them. Their children may already be succeeding. There is no compelling reason to choose to make a change. The families most inclined to choose, it appears, are those who are not already enjoying great opportunity or success.

It is possible that the disadvantaged students in our schools are somewhat unusual. They may have somewhat more motivated parents than is the norm. Or perhaps they are not as needy academically as their backgrounds would suggest. But none of this is much in evidence right now. The students in our schools have much ground to make up academically and require lots of extra help. Until test scores can be collected and compared to other scores in the districts, we won't know for sure how our students measure up. At this juncture it appears that they represent populations with great need. Given the opportunity to choose, disadvantaged populations have done so in great numbers. (All of our schools also have long and representative waiting lists. In Boston the waiting list is longer than the list

of enrollees.) In our first four communities, at least, the market—and Edison
—have increased educational equity, not diminished it.

Lesson 9: System Design Is the Hardest Part

In the fall of 1996 the Edison Project launched its second wave of schools. Eight new schools joined the four that had opened a year earlier. In the fall of 1997, the number of Edison schools could more than double again. Three years after beginning operation, Edison could be a system enrolling ten thousand to fifteen thousand students.

Whatever success the Edison Project has enjoyed to this point is due in large part to our school design. The design expressed a vision that inspired communities and educators to join us as partners, and it guided our planning for each school's opening day. Now, as the pieces of the design fall into place at school sites, students are beginning to reap some of the expected educational benefits. If our schools continue on their current course, each could become the special kind of place envisioned in Edison's school design.

But four, or twelve, or even a few more great schools is a far cry from a system of great schools. The United States already has hundreds of first-rate schools. And in those schools are many of the same structures and strategies found in Edison schools. Without taking anything away from those who have worked hard to create excellent schools, the major challenge in American education is not how to create a great school. School design may be harder than it looks, but we know more about what makes a great school than what makes a great school system. The hardest part of large-scale school improvement is not school design, it is system design.

Think about it. Successful schools are relatively easy to name. But name a system that can reliably create and sustain more of them. Or consider this: don't systems often seem anathema to individual greatness? In the public sector, excellent schools often emerge from the leadership of an iconoclastic principal. Successful school administrators frequently talk of the need to work around the system. The bureaucracy that plagues some of our larger school systems is not likely to stimulate widespread improvement among the schools under its control. The picture is not much brighter in the private sector. Private schools have resisted the formation of systems that would bind them together. America's elite independent schools jealously guard

120 their autonomy from one another and from government regulation. Indeed, schools may do better generally if they are free from strong external authority.[27] This is why school reform has embraced various decentralization strategies, such as school-based management and charter schools.

To be sure, some school districts in this country are doing a respectable job of trying to promote excellence systemically. A few of these districts are even quite large—for example, Charlotte-Mecklenberg under Superintendent John Murphy or Philadelphia under David Hornbeck. In addition, Catholic school systems manage to guide their schools without depriving them of the authority they need to succeed. But the fact remains, no system has demonstrated the ability to promote excellence consistently among its schools. System design is hard.

At the Edison Project, we have taken important steps toward building an effective system. First, we negotiate performance-based contracts with our customers that give us most of the freedom necessary to control the operation of partnership schools. We are able to select the principal (usually with the concurrence of the superintendent); and the principal, with our guidance, is able to choose instructional staff. The school can begin with a team of professionals who share a common vision. We are also able to implement our own compensation system, including a career ladder for teachers and merit pay, and our own performance appraisal system. We can reward educators for the contribution they make to the success of the school. We are able to establish our own standards for student performance. The academic goals of the school are clear and ambitious. Except for the need to satisfy certain federal and state regulations, we are largely free to organize the academic program as we see fit.

Our contract also holds us responsible for progress rather than process. Our partners give us the freedom to operate in exchange for strict performance accountability. If students make good academic progress, our partnership continues. If progress is unsatisfactory, our partners have the right to let us go. Our contracts provide us the firm foundation for building an effective system—the freedom to control our own destiny and the privilege to be judged by our results. All public schools should have the same opportunity.

But let us also be careful about what we wish. Opportunity is not without challenges—and Edison still faces many. For example, while every Edison school is free from conventional public authority, it is subject to the new authority of Edison. If we are to be successful, we must effect a delicate balance between autonomy and accountability with each of our schools. We have a school design that we believe in and that we believe will bring students success. Edison schools need to be faithful to that design. But educators must not be expected to follow that design slavishly. That is a recipe for irresponsibility and resentment, not professionalism and commitment. The Edison Project continues to work on getting this crucial balance right.

There is also the matter of training and professional development. There is no improving education without changing instruction. The standards that this nation wants children to meet in the future are standards that teachers often have not been prepared to meet themselves. Teachers need to know more about the demanding subjects they are increasingly called on to teach. They also need to know more about the many ways in which children learn. We are learning more all the time about learning.[28] But these understandings—admittedly, often abstract and debatable—are slow to influence classroom practice.

The Edison Project invests very heavily in training and professional development, both before schools open and on an ongoing basis. We work hard to build the capacity in each school for professional development needs to be assessed and met on site. All told, our schools are vested with five to ten times the resources of a typical school for staff development. Still, there is a lot to learn about first-rate systems of training and professional development. There are too few models in the world of education for anyone to believe that this is not a major challenge for Edison.

Finally, there is the matter of assessment. The Edison design promises a rich and challenging curriculum. And we have taken many measures to ensure that we provide one. Our teachers are excited about the possibilities, and our parents are thrilled about the opportunities. We have also been working with the Educational Testing Service to design a student assessment system that will allow students to demonstrate their growth in the many areas the program opens to them. A combination of common performance assessments and structured portfolios ensures that student work will be carefully evaluated.

But Edison schools will also be judged by standardized tests in basic skills. And although these tests measure only a fraction of what we hope our schools will accomplish, they take on enormous importance. Other schools in the district are judged by them. The media are familiar with standardized

122 tests and often trumpet their results. We are explicitly accountable to our customers for results on these tests—and our principals and teachers know this. The inflated importance of standardized tests makes our work more difficult. It is harder to direct a system of schools toward more ambitious goals when more basic goals command such attention. Of course, we want our schools to succeed in the basics—and we expect they will. It is difficult, however, to shift the focus forward when so much of the world is looking the other way.

All of this may sound like carping to public educators who struggle day in and day out against the very same obstacles. Perhaps it is. After all, the Edison Project has several advantages on its side—autonomy being the most important. Even so, the waters of system design are largely uncharted, and the sailing is never smooth. Our response to the challenges we face in this second phase of our work will determine our future. We're confident that we will succeed—but ever mindful that it won't be easy.

5 School Choice
in Milwaukee

Paul E. Peterson and Chad Noyes

The Wisconsin state legislature in 1995 enacted a large-scale voucher program that offered a choice among both religious and secular schools to thousands of Milwaukee children living in low-income families.[1] The program will not come into effect unless the state's supreme court rejects a challenge to its constitutionality. Until such time, low-income families seeking alternatives to the city's public schools must choose within the confines of a more limited plan set up in 1990.

This 1990 plan was but a "modest proposal."[2] It allowed approximately one thousand children a choice among several private secular schools in Milwaukee. Yet in concept it has posed a major challenge to defenders of the educational status quo, for it was the first publicly funded program offering central-city families the option of choosing between government-run and privately operated schools (a second now exists in Cleveland). As one early proponent put it, "The idea of this program was more than just to give vouchers to a few hundred students. It was to be the tail that wags the dog—the entire Milwaukee public school system."[3] Conceivably, the experiment might "wag" big-city education throughout the country.

Worried about the potential impact of the Milwaukee experiment,

124 choice critics nationwide have rushed to judge its worth. The Carnegie Foundation for the Advancement of Teaching, a longtime defender of public schools, claims that "Milwaukee's plan has failed to demonstrate that vouchers can . . . spark school improvement."[4] Albert Shanker, president of the American Federation of Teachers, declares that the "private schools [in the Milwaukee choice plan] are not outperforming public schools."[5] The Texas State Teachers Association, an affiliate of the National Education Association, avows that "the results [in Milwaukee] have been dismal—test scores have actually declined."[6] Harvard Professor Richard Elmore asserts that "thousands of children have participated in Milwaukee's public-private voucher experiment, . . . yet we see no discernible gains in learning."[7] The head of Wisconsin's leading teacher organization echoes these sentiments: "The bottom line ought to be whether kids learn more . . . and if you gauge it by that, it doesn't measure up."[8]

These claims have not gone unchallenged. Writing in the *Public Interest* in 1995, Daniel McGroarty points out that all critiques of Milwaukee's choice program depend upon questionable findings from a single evaluation, whose author has so far refused to release his data to the scholarly community. McGroarty goes on to note that, despite harsh national criticism, the choice schools are "well-liked by parents" and the number of students in attendance continues to grow.[9] The *Wall Street Journal* editorializes that the evaluation of the program, even if taken at face value, shows that choice schools do as well as public schools for half the cost.[10] Writing for a Texas audience, Professor John Pisciotta of Baylor reports that "the success of the Milwaukee School Choice Program indicates that Texas can be confident that school choice can be a valuable component of education reform."[11] George Mitchell, one of Milwaukee's best-informed choice advocates, flatly declares that "for most participating students, the program has been successful."[12]

Often lost in the charges and responses is the simple fact that Milwaukee's choice plan gave low-income families only a pitifully small approximation of what theorists have always regarded as essential for choice programs to succeed. Far from being a good test of the workability of a school choice program, the legislature placed it under nine restrictions. Not unlike Dante's *Inferno*, which subjected sinners to one of nine ever-narrowing circles of hell, each restriction was more wrenching than the preceding. As a consequence, the Milwaukee experiment can best be understood as a test of the durability of the concept of choice under extreme duress. When understood in these terms, it is a noteworthy success.

Choice is an extraordinarily elastic term. It can refer to choice among curricula within a school, choice among public schools, choice more or less hampered by rules and regulations, and choice that does or does not include religious schools. But if choice is to stimulate innovation, diversity, and responsiveness in American education, it must have the following basic characteristics: It must provide large enough vouchers so that families, especially poor families, can afford quality educational programs. It must allow families to supplement public funds with their own resources, if they wish. A viable plan must invite the participation of most existing schools and encourage new ones to form. Regulations must be modest and appropriate. Unless these basics are included in a choice plan, schools will not compete for students, and parents will not be able to choose among educational alternatives.[13]

That Milwaukee's choice program fell far short of these requirements was not chiefly the fault of Governor Tommy Thompson, its main sponsor. Thompson had originally sought to enact a more comprehensive choice plan that would have avoided many, if not all, of the limitations with which the program was burdened. Design failure is more appropriately attributed to legislative compromises necessary to soften the opposition of the Wisconsin Educational Association Committee (WEAC) and its allies in the state legislature.

The legislative search for compromise nearly ensured a stillborn program. But in spite of initial stumbling, Milwaukee's choice program has become an institutionalized component of the city's educational system. The program has grown steadily in size and scope. Parents, enthusiastic from the beginning, have remained loyal supporters. Reading and math scores of choice students in their third and fourth years were significantly higher than those of comparable public school students.

The Wisconsin state legislature felt confident enough in the program by the spring of 1995 to lift many of the restrictions on it. Although the expanded version of choice still must survive constitutional scrutiny by the Wisconsin judiciary, the very fact that the program continues to move toward the center of the state's educational agenda suggests the Milwaukee experiment might still "wag the dog."

The Milwaukee story is hardly a "best practice" tale that educators love to

126   relate. Its design has too many flaws to recommend it to other communities. But the story does suggest that even a flawed choice program, when compared with the education offered by many big-city school systems, constitutes a step forward.

The Legislative Politics of Choice

Legislatures often design new social programs in ways that place them at high risk of failure. The more dramatic the departure from the past, the more threatened groups will try to undermine its effectiveness. The nature of legislative processes is to facilitate compromise. Many participants, representing varied interests, exercise a veto at one legislative stage or another. To avoid defeat, proposals must be softened to mollify opponents. The typical result is a law that represents only a marginal departure from past practice, not a wholesale restructuring of it. At times, the compromises can be so extensive as to vitiate the innovative thrust of the program.

A generation or so ago education was one of the "apple pie" issues of state politics. The two major political parties generally fell over one another in their support for public education. Gubernatorial candidates could not hope to win statewide office without an educational plank. Teacher organizations and school board members backed Republican candidates at least as often as they favored Democrats.[14] Not until Jimmy Carter promised to create a Department of Education did the National Education Association endorse one presidential candidate over another.[15]

But in recent decades education issues have become politically divisive. Many Republican leaders have criticized public schools for falling standards, rising costs, and organizational rigidity imposed by collective bargaining contracts. They have called for a variety of educational reforms, ranging from national standards and merit pay to charter schools and voucher plans. Meanwhile, many Democratic leaders have formed close ties with teacher organizations. In 1994, NEA's political action committee gave 98.7 percent of its campaign contributions to Democratic candidates.[16]

Of all states, Wisconsin has been among the most educationally progressive. In 1989, Wisconsin spent more dollars per pupil on education than all but six other states; in per capita elementary and secondary education expenditures it ranked tenth. Its average eighth-grader scored higher on a

1990 mathematics test than the students of all but five other states.[17] In
spite of Wisconsin's history of educational emphasis, its curriculum in recent years has become more flabby, and student performance has begun to
slip.[18] The problems in Milwaukee have been particularly severe. Although
its per pupil expenditures in constant dollars increased by 82 percent between 1973 and 1993, its graduation rate dropped from 79 to 44 percent.[19]

The state's emerging education difficulties have helped fuel a new, more
partisan approach to educational reform. Using his item-veto power to considerable effect, Thompson, the popular Republican governor, has cham-
pioned a broad range of innovations. But the Democratic Party, in control of
the legislature until 1993, blocked many of Thompson's proposals, much to
the satisfaction of WEAC.

Thompson's initial voucher plan, proposed in 1987, included religious
schools, but WEAC and its Democratic allies buried the bill in legislative
committee. Although Thompson dropped religious schools from his proposal the following year, the revised bill was still stymied.[20] The next year,
Thompson and others pushed three different choice proposals, including
one that had the support of the Milwaukee school superintendent. Compared with the original proposal, these were so scaled back that some
thought they would, if enacted, prove "a disservice to the cause of broader
choice in education."[21] Yet all three bills went down to a defeat that Thompson and others chalked up to "strong lobbying" by WEAC. As one of the
plan's proponents observed, WEAC was "afraid that if choice starts in Milwaukee, it's going to take over the world."[22]

After all these battles, the voucher idea might have died altogether, had it
not dovetailed with the interests of several black leaders in Milwaukee, who
had been asking the legislature to carve an all-black public school system
out of a portion of the existing Milwaukee school district. When this sugges-
tion fell on deaf ears, Annette "Polly" Williams, a state representative from
an inner-city, African-American neighborhood of Milwaukee, proposed
school choice as an alternative.[23] Thus began an unusual alliance of conservative Republicans and minority Democrats, both of whom were frustrated
by WEAC's ability to stymie their reform objectives.

Williams's support for school choice changed the political dynamics of
the issue. WEAC had long argued that tuition vouchers would create a class-
based, racially segregated educational system, conveniently ignoring the

128 fact that the same characterization applied to the existing division of the Milwaukee metropolitan area into nearly all-white suburban districts and a central-city district serving a predominantly minority clientele. Because WEAC could ill afford to alienate black legislators—already angry at its rejection of their proposals for an all-black school district—it couched its antagonism to vouchers as a matter of egalitarian principle. At a late stage in the legislative process, WEAC agreed to withdraw its opposition to a Milwaukee choice plan if the governor agreed not to use his item veto to remove a variety of restrictions included in the bill.

Legislation Designed to Fail

The end result was a program designed to fail. Written by a legislature controlled by Democrats, the bill gave only enough choice to satisfy Williams's most urgent demands. Limiting participation to low-income families was the least—and the most justifiable—of the restrictions imposed. Nine additional limitations narrowed the program's scope and made failure more likely. In the candid words of one participant in the choice debates, the program did not "amount . . . to a good-sized flea on the tail of a dog."[24] To show how choice was limited, we can best begin, as did Dante's guide, Virgil, with the least serious restriction, then proceed to the more severe.

REFUSE STUDENTS PREVIOUSLY ENROLLED IN PRIVATE SCHOOL

Dante discovered in limbo, Hell's first circle, the good people whose only fault was to have been born before the coming of Christ.

The Milwaukee choice plan created a limbo of its own by excluding from participation all students who were currently enrolled in private schools. A student could not get a voucher unless he or she had been attending a public school or had been younger than school age. One parent tried to escape limbo by enrolling his child in a public school for the last two weeks of the public school year (after the choice school's academic year had come to an end). The ruse did not work.

Creation of limboland had the advantage of minimizing the initial cost to the state. The size of the voucher was pegged to the amount of per pupil aid

Milwaukee received from the state. If a student left the public schools to go to a choice school, the state aid simply followed the student. Had students already enrolled in private schools been entitled to vouchers, immediate costs would have been much higher.[25]

This limit on choice was difficult for the program's supporters to swallow. Some of the people who had worked the hardest to secure passage of the legislation were specifically denied the right to benefit from its provisions. But the restrictive impact of this rule decayed with time because every small child yet to attend school had a chance to receive a voucher.

RANDOM ASSIGNMENT

As Virgil and Dante descended to the second level, they encountered Paolo and Francesca, two lovers who by chance were forced to endure the Inferno's never-ending winds. Had Paolo's father picked Francesca as Paolo's wife and not his brother's, the two would have sung the sweet songs of Paradise.

Within the interstices of the Milwaukee choice plan, the goddess Fortuna can still be found. Whenever the number of applicants for participation in a choice school exceeds the number of places available, the school must select students at random. As a result, applicants cannot be assured of a school, and schools cannot select the children who seem most likely to benefit from their program.

Still, the costs of this restriction on choice were not excessive. The number of applicants have not greatly exceeded the number of seats available. And random assignment has helped the choice program avoid the accusation that only the more able and more self-disciplined students are selected.

LIMITED SIZE

At Hell's third circle, Dante met the Gluttons.

The legislature helped preserve corpulence in public education by limiting the size of the choice program to 1 percent of the city's public school enrollment (with an increase to 1.5 percent in 1994). The action was taken because "we didn't want [the public schools] to take a significant financial loss." In other words, the plan was designed explicitly to minimize the

130   competition between public and private schools that choice theory says is critically important.

Though restrictive in the long run, the impact of the rule during its first five years was more limited than one might presume. The other restrictions on the program proved so potent that enrollment never attained the numerical limit set by the legislature.

LIMITED FUNDING

> In Dante's fourth circle battle endlessly the Miserly, who learned too late that "all the gold that is or ever was beneath the moon won't buy a moment's rest."

To overcome pecuniary objections to choice, the legislature designed the plan to be, in the words of the governor's aide, "revenue neutral." Choice schools were given the same amount of state aid per pupil as was granted to the Milwaukee public school system (approximately $2,500 in 1990, $3,000 in 1994). This arrangement had the political virtue of imposing few additional costs on the Wisconsin taxpayer. The provision also allowed Milwaukee public schools to concentrate local tax revenues on the reduced number of students remaining in public school, thereby increasing its per pupil expenditure. It was a win-win situation for both Milwaukee public school officials and Wisconsin taxpayers.

Of course, the very feature of the compromise that made it politically attractive increased the likelihood the choice experiment would fail. As state aid accounted for less than half the cost of public education in Milwaukee, the voucher amounted to less than half the per pupil cost of Milwaukee's public schools.[26] Some tried to defend this miserly treatment of choice schools on the grounds that private schools could "waive the difference" between the voucher and their tuition.[27] But only a school with a large endowment or a substantial amount of nontuition income can absorb half the cost of educating any more than a token number of its students.

Several schools found the tuition voucher too small to attract their participation. One private school administrator said it would have admitted as many as half of its students under the choice program had the voucher been more generous. Another said his school "would participate further if we did not lose so much money per student accepted."[28]

As the ancient boatman Phlegyas steered Dante through the swamp constituting Hell's fifth circle, he heard the slothful weeping in the slime beneath him.

The architects of Milwaukee's choice program cheerfully sought to crowd this sad slough by denying parents the opportunity to assist in the education of their children. The ostensible purpose of the ban was to keep school choice from becoming elitist, but this goal was already assured by the rule that no money could go to families with income substantially above the poverty line. The ban was also defended by one participant on the grounds it guaranteed that parents would not "have to pay anything." Dante would have regarded the person a fit candidate for the slough of sloth.

This restriction on parental contributions placed serious limits on school choice. When combined with the small size of the tuition voucher, it guaranteed that most choice students would attend fiscally constrained institutions with limited facilities and poorly paid teachers. It also made more difficult the establishment of a financial tie between home and school that many private school officials think key to educational success.

NO RELIGIOUS SCHOOLS

Hell's sixth circle was reserved for heretics who challenged the dogma of the faithful.

Just as dogmatically, the Wisconsin legislature came up with its own definition of heresy by forbidding parents from using vouchers to send children to any other than secular schools. Religion was banned from the choice plan, even though Milwaukee's skyline is well embroidered by the steeples and domes of churches and cathedrals built by tens of thousands of Germans, Poles, and Scandinavians who settled a century ago. These noble structures, now blackened by decades of industrial soot, still testify to the religious faith and ethnic identity of the communities out of which they rose. Adjacent to most stands a building that in many cases still serves as a parish school. In 1994 nearly twenty thousand students (or nearly 18 percent of all Milwaukee students) attended one of more than a hundred schools with a religious affiliation—most of them Catholic, but also many

132 Lutheran schools, as well as a Jewish yeshiva, a Muslim school, and two Christian Pentecostal schools.

Most of the religious schools were ready and eager to enroll more students. When the choice program was expanded to include religious schools in 1995, approximately one hundred schools agreed to participate, and places for more than 6,200 additional students were found within Milwaukee's religiously affiliated schools.[29] By denying parents the opportunity to choose a school with a religious affiliation, the Wisconsin state legislature denied families access to 90 percent of the private school capacity available in Milwaukee.

Because religious schools could not participate, high school students had no mainstream educational options available outside the public school system. A few alternative high schools did participate in the choice program, but they offered highly specialized services for pregnant teenagers and other at-risk students. However appropriate these schools may have been for some students, they could have little influence on the Milwaukee public schools. As one analyst has observed, the experiment is "more accurately labeled the Milwaukee *Elementary* School Choice Program."[30]

SCHOOLS MUST HAVE NONCHOICE STUDENTS

> As Dante and Virgil descended closer to the center of the earth, they were forced to mount the centaur Nessus to make their way through the river of blood that boiled those souls who had acted violently toward their neighbors.

No restriction more directly violated the concept of choice than the legal requirement that half of a choice school's enrollment had to comprise students outside the voucher plan. If choice is to enhance educational quality, it must do so in part by encouraging the creation of new schools with new technologies, new approaches, and new systems of management. Establishing a new school is extremely challenging. At a minimum, it involves finding a location, obtaining financing, recruiting students, and assembling a staff. It would be no easy task to start a new school even if all incoming students could receive a voucher.

By requiring that more than half the students be fee payers (in 1994, the requirement was reduced to one third), the Milwaukee plan greatly increased the barrier to forming a new school. In addition to all other tasks, a new school would have to recruit tuition-paying students to sit next to those receiving a voucher. As a result, not a single new school was formed.

EVALUATION

> In the holes of Hell's eighth circle, Dante found—stuffed upside-down,
> fire sliding from heel to toe—the practitioners of deceit and fraud. Fraud
> was severely punished, because in earthly life, deceit, if practiced
> effectively, can be difficult to discern.

Although the evaluation of the Milwaukee choice plan suffered not from fraud but only from the mistakes, limitations, and misjudgments that often plague social science research, an acrid stench surrounds the manner in which the evaluator was selected. Responsibility for overseeing the evaluation was given by the legislature to the superintendent of public instruction, Herbert Grover, no friend of school choice. Acting decisively, Grover appointed an evaluator on September 9, 1990, just days after the first choice students began going to school.

A choice critic like Grover had good reason to move expeditiously. The early years are times when experimental programs are most fragile, most prone to error. Nothing poses as great a danger to an innovative governmental program as an immediate, apparently rigorous evaluation of its effects.

Evaluations are complicated undertakings in which a number of major research organizations have specialized, including such well-known entities as ABT Associates, Mathematica, NORC, RAND, and the Manpower Development Research Corporation. If Grover had followed standard practice, he would have solicited competitive bids and selected the most cost-effective proposal submitted by one of these research organizations. Instead, he gave the assignment to John Witte, a political science professor at the University of Wisconsin with only limited experience in conducting large-scale evaluations.

Witte was known to have doubts about the advantages of private education. He had just finished editing a book on school choice in which he predicted that "singular adherence to [choice] will have us in ten years looking backward on . . . choice as simply another set of failed reforms."[31] He had also written a paper, well received in union circles, criticizing studies that had

134   found private schools outperforming public schools.[32] Witte later became a
       public opponent of the expansion of the Milwaukee choice program in
       1995.[33] Choice critics have relied heavily on the results of Witte's evaluation.

HOSTILE IMPLEMENTATION

> Locked in Lucifer's jaws at the very core of the Inferno squirm the three
> archtraitors of antiquity, Brutus, Cassius, and Judas Iscariot.

Had Lucifer but one more jaw, it would close over the legislator who be-
trayed Milwaukee's choice plan by delivering its implementation into Superintendent Herbert Grover's arms. Wisconsin's superintendent of public
instruction is elected for a four-year term in low-visibility elections held in
odd-numbered years. During the 1980s, the turnout for superintendent
elections averaged 21 percent of the electorate (compared with a 43 percent
turnout rate in gubernatorial races held during this period).[34] With light
voter interest, WEAC was in a stronger position to dominate the outcome.

Grover was first elected state school superintendent with the support of
WEAC in 1981, and he received its strong support in three subsequent
elections. In return, Grover criticized all "reforms which might displease
WEAC." When Governor Thompson proposed that local school boards be
allowed to circumvent inflexible hiring procedures by contracting out for
practice teachers, WEAC opposed the bill. So did Herbert Grover. When
Governor Thompson wanted to reward schools exhibiting superior performance, WEAC fought the idea. So did Herbert Grover. When the governor
recommended that students be allowed to take college courses for high
school credit, WEAC insisted the courses could be counted only if not offered in the high schools. So did Herbert Grover.[35] In 1990 Grover's legislative liaison was the former president of WEAC.

Grover made little secret of his hostility to school choice. Even after the
legislation had been enacted, Grover attacked it. In July of 1990 he said the
choice idea "could ruin public schools."[36] In August he said, "It's a disgrace. . . . Has the citizenry in Wisconsin lost its sense?"[37] When a choice
school was forced to close, Grover issued a public statement that the closure
"proved the program wouldn't work."[38]

Minimal Publicity Given Grover's hostility, the Department of Public Instruction (DPI) did only the legal minimum required to implement the program.

The choice plan was enacted in March of 1990, to begin the following September. Although required by law to ensure that Milwaukee parents were
adequately informed about the availability of school choice, Grover chose to
wait until May 29 to issue a press release telling schools that, in order to participate, they had to apply within two weeks. In mid-June, DPI gave parents
two weeks to apply. Only seven schools expressed an interest in participating, and space was made available for only 341 students out of the 577 who
applied. DPI followed similar procedures in subsequent years.[39]

Excessive Regulation Grover also threatened the choice schools with a host of
regulatory burdens, which schools managed to avoid only by securing a
court order invalidating them. Grover also gave his support to a legal effort
to challenge the constitutionality of the plan. Although the program's constitutionality was eventually upheld, legal uncertainties cast a shadow over
the choice plan well into the program's second year.

Defining Secular Although the statute forbade participation by schools that
had a "pervasively religious" orientation, Messmer High, a private high
school serving a largely African-American, inner-city population, sought
eligibility.[40] The school had once been a Catholic parish school, but in 1985
the archdiocese decided it could no longer afford to keep the school in
operation. Its neighborhood no longer middle class, the school's enrollment
had fallen markedly. But under the leadership of a dedicated, energetic,
African-American principal, the school was re-creating itself as a community school. It purchased the building from the archdiocese, raised funds
from alumni, and appealed to local foundations and the business community. Given its independence from the archdiocese, school officials felt their
educational program was not so pervasively religious as to be excluded from
the choice plan. DPI initially admitted Messmer to the program.

Yet the school did not deny its Catholic heritage. Students were still
expected to take classes in religion, the principal wore a clerical collar, and a
sharp observer could occasionally spy a cross or religious portrait when
walking the corridors or visiting the principal's office. The Milwaukee news
media cried foul. After a full investigation and a public inquiry (at which
the Messmer principal was asked whether he took his orders from the
pope), DPI revised its earlier judgment and concluded the school was, indeed, pervasively religious and could not participate in the choice program.

However one judges the merit of the reversal by DPI, its ultimate consequence was that Grover succeeded in virtually eliminating access to high
schools via the choice program.

An Experiment That Nearly Failed

> When inducted into Hell, there is no easy route out. Even with Virgil to
> guide him, Dante had to endure the long travails of Purgatory before
> reaching Paradise.

It should come as no surprise that the travails endured by choice schools
were not much easier than Dante's. New programs almost always experience a troubled beginning, marked by uncertainty, confusion, overreaction,
and overscrutiny. Both personnel and operating procedures are poorly
suited to the new tasks. An innovative program, especially if it is designed to
fail, can often trip before it learns to walk.

Few events were as calamitous for the choice program as the closing of
Juanita Virgil Academy a few months after the program began. Although
the school had existed as a private school for a number of years, Juanita
Academy was eager to admit sixty-three choice students in order to alleviate
its enrollment and financial difficulties. Even with the addition of the choice
students, the school's problems persisted. The school had to drop its Bible
classes to meet DPI standards. Parents complained about food service, overcrowded classrooms, a shortage of books and materials, and a lack of cleanli-
ness and discipline. A new principal, who had been hired away from the
public schools, had to be relieved of her responsibilities two months into the
school year. The school withdrew from the choice program the next semes-
ter, giving as its reason the desire to "reinstate religious training in the
school." A few weeks later the school closed altogether.

Given the design of the Milwaukee choice program, more Juanita Academies might have been expected. After all, the program was set up so that
only schools facing serious financial difficulties were likely to participate.
Consider the calculation that any school had to make before joining the
choice program. It had to give up any religious identification it might have
had. It could charge choice students only $2,500 in tuition. Students had to
come from poor families. Students had to be accepted at random, without

regard to their academic abilities or sociability. The courts might shut the program down at any moment.

Only a secular school serving a low-income community desperately in need of additional students would want to admit large numbers of choice students under these conditions. Such a community school would almost certainly have limited facilities, poorly paid teachers, falling enrollments, fiscal difficulties, and no more than a modest reputation. Admittedly, this characterization does not apply to all the schools initially participating in the program. A Montessori school serving a middle-class constituency admitted three students the first year and four the next, even though it seemed under no financial imperative to do so. School administrators said they wished to diversify its student body. Woodlands School, formerly a laboratory school for a local Catholic college, also served a middle-class clientele. But since its break with the college, the school's financial condition had become precarious, a factor that helped explain its enrollment of twenty to forty choice students each year.

But three community schools, which together with Juanita Academy admitted 84 percent of the 1990 choice students (table 5.1), looked more like the dying Juanita than either the Montessori school or Woodlands. Bruce Guadalupe, for one, nearly suffered the same fate as Juanita Academy. Established in 1969, it sought to preserve Latino culture and teach children respect for both the English and Spanish tongues. Many teachers had once taught in Central American schools. Instruction was bilingual, often more in Spanish than in English.

In spite of its distinctive educational mission, the school had difficulty making ends meet. Even finding an adequate school building seemed a never-ending problem; the school moved on several occasions during its first two decades. By January 1990 things had become so desperate that the school was on "the verge of closing." But enactment of the choice program gave the school "new hope for the future," a hope that "otherwise had been snuffed out."[41] A tuition voucher of $2,500 was a boon to a school that had trouble collecting $650 from participating families.

The first choice students arrived in the fall of 1990, but the school, still in financial distress, was forced to cut its teaching staff by a third. The school's difficulties were fully reported in the *Milwaukee Journal*: "Two staff aides were fired, the seventh and eighth grades were combined, the second grade

TABLE 5.1 Enrollment in Choice Schools

	1990–91		1991–92		1992–93	1993–94		1994–95	
					September of School Year				
Community Elementary Schools									
Juanita Academy	63								
Bruce Guadalupe	44		111			162		188	
Urban Day	101		195			212		259	
Harambee	83		154			186		217	
Subtotal	291	(84%)	460	(86%)		560	(76%)	664	(80%)
Middle-Class Elementary Schools									
Woodlands	25		33			44		33	
Montessori									
Downtown						9		3	
Highland						14		19	
Lakeshore	3		4			11		7	
Milwaukee						9		13	
Waldorf						7		11	
Subtotal	28	(8%)	37	(7%)		94	(13%)	86	(10%)
Alternative High Schools									
Exito						19		37	
Learning Enterprise						40		32	
SER Benito	26		37			20		11	
Subtotal	26	(8%)	37	(7%)		79	(11%)	80	(10%)
Total	345		534		608	733		830	

Sources: State Department of Public Instruction, as reported in "Court Time on Choice Extended," *Milwaukee Journal*, October 3, 1991; Legislative Audit Bureau, *An Evaluation of Milwaukee Parental Choice Program*, February 1995, table 2, p. 22; table 3, p. 23.
Note: Enrollment by school not available for 1992–93.

was eliminated with children put into the first or third grade, and the bilingual Spanish program was cut. . . . Two teachers were transferred. . . . The former eighth grade teacher is now teaching fourth grade. . . . Overall, the teaching staff was reduced from 14 to 9."[42] The school's principal described staff morale as low.

The two other community schools with large choice enrollments, Harambee Community School and Urban Day, had better reputations but still suffered from serious financial difficulties.[43] Like Bruce Guadalupe, they catered almost exclusively to a low-income minority population. Established in the sixties in former Catholic parish schools, they tried to survive as secular institutions after the archdiocese had abandoned them. Named for the Swahili word meaning "pulling together," Harambee presented itself as "an African American–owned school emphasizing the basics through creative instructional programs, coupled with a strong cultural foundation."[44] Urban Day was said to place "a heavy emphasis on African history and culture."[45]

Like Bruce Guadalupe, they could ask families to pay only a very modest tuition. Although they set their annual rates at somewhere between $650 and $800, only a few families attending the school actually paid full tuition. Scholarships were the norm, not an exceptional privilege. However, parents were expected to participate in fund-raising activities.

Teacher salaries were much lower than those paid by the Milwaukee public schools. As one principal observed, "The teachers who stay here for a long time are either very dedicated or can afford to stay on what we pay."[46] The quality of the physical plant provided a visible sign of the school's modest financial resources: "Recess and physical education facilities were relatively poor in the schools. One school had easy access to a city park for recess, one relied on a blocked off street, two others asphalt playgrounds with some wood chips and playground equipment. All the schools had some indoor space for physical education, but it often served multiple purposes."[47] One of its hardest-working supporters was asked what she would most wish for the school. "I'd like to see the school financially self-sufficient," she said.[48]

Both schools had discovered that strong political connections were essential to survival. In fact, it was their institutional needs that had helped prompt Representative Williams to throw her support behind the choice program. To win its passage, parents and teachers from these schools designed legislation, wrote letters, and testified before state legislative hearings. When the legislation passed, they worked hard to enroll additional students within DPI's two-week deadline.

Yet the choice plan initially proved to be a mixed blessing for the two schools. The schools had survived for two decades on the dedicated efforts of families who had dug out their last dollars to send their children to a private

140   school. All of a sudden, new students walked through the door with tuition vouchers in hand. Combining new students with old traditions proved a taxing experience for principals, teachers, and parents. Entry of large numbers of former public school students disrupted a school environment that emphasized order, discipline, and personal responsibility. To school administrators it seemed that the choice students who enrolled were among the public school's least proficient educationally and most maladjusted socially.[49] One administrator who had for years played a key role at one of the schools found the transition so difficult she had to resign her position.

In Spite of Everything, Choice Survives

> Dante discovered that if Purgatory's travails are well endured, one can finally glimpse the Gates of Paradise.

If programs can overcome initial challenges, an experiment may succeed, provided basic premises are sound. Uncertainties are gradually reduced, obvious weaknesses eliminated, routines established, appropriate personnel recruited, and acceptance finally achieved. Sometimes even programs designed to fail can succeed.[50]

CHANGES AT THE DEPARTMENT OF PUBLIC INSTRUCTION

It certainly did not hurt the choice program that Superintendent Grover did not seek reelection in 1993. Although his successor did not favor choice, neither did he attempt to frustrate its operation.[51] DPI could have closely monitored the schools to make sure that all waiting lists were constructed randomly. Instead, it seems to have taken school administrators at their word. DPI could have assigned responsibility for administration of the program to an antagonist of choice; instead, the job was given to a sympathetic administrator whose own child attended private school.

    DPI also generously interpreted the statute forbidding parents to supplement the tuition voucher. Most choice schools asked parents both to pay registration, book, and other fees and to make a "voluntary" contribution to the school's fund-raising program. The total of all fees and contributions typically amounted to between $300 and $550, a supplemental contribution to the school of as much as 22 percent of the tuition voucher. A severe interpretation of the statute might well rule such supplemental payments illegal; indeed, one parent threatened to sue one of the schools for demanding supplemental payments. But for several years DPI turned a blind eye to the issue, though very recently it has given some indication that it might restrict the fees the schools can require.

RELATIONS WITH MILWAUKEE PUBLIC SCHOOLS

Relations between choice schools and the Milwaukee public school district also improved. In 1992 the Milwaukee School Board asked Howard Fuller to become school superintendent. Fuller had favored the establishment of an all-black school district, and he had joined Williams in her campaign for a choice program. While superintendent, he quietly helped the choice schools. By means of a contractual agreement, the city school system paid for the education of 132 preschool children at Harambee. It paid for bilingual instruction for sixty students at Bruce Guadalupe. It continued to contract for the education of students attending alternative high schools, despite their heavy involvement in the choice program.

The importance of these contracts to many of the choice schools should not be underestimated. Students attending choice schools under these contractual arrangements helped constitute the nonchoice enrollment against which choice students had to be matched. Had the school superintendent not been so cooperative, growth of the choice plan would have been much more limited.[52]

CHOICE SCHOOLS FIVE YEARS LATER

As it was, the number of students participating in the choice program more than doubled over the first five years of the program (table 5.2). Eighty percent of the choice students in 1994 were still enrolled in the three community elementary schools (table 5.1). But the number of participating schools increased from seven to twelve, giving parents somewhat greater choice. Furthermore, the three community schools were all "in better financial condition today—and without exception, their facilities [had] improved."[53]

The most visible change occurred at Bruce Guadalupe. Once located in a run-down, hopelessly cramped building, the school has become a core component of the United Community Center, a $2.4 million structure that is the pride of Milwaukee's Latino community.[54] It features beautiful modern

142   **TABLE 5.2** Increasing Participation in Milwaukee Choice Program

School Year	Schools	Applicants	Enrolled
1990–91	7	577	345
1991–92	6	689	534
1992–93	11	998	608
1993–94	12	1,049	733
1994–95	12	1,046	830

Sources: For 1990–1991 and 1991–1992 enrollment, State Department of Public Instruction, as reported in "Court Time on Choice Extended," *Milwaukee Journal,* October 3, 1991; for all other information, Legislative Audit Bureau, *An Evaluation of Milwaukee Parental Choice Program,* February 1995, table 2, p. 22; table 3, p. 23.

classrooms, a handsome gymnasium, a spacious dining facility, and even a nursery (with a viewing window) for preschool children of teachers and other staff members. Aided by its new building, Bruce Guadalupe has also been able to entice out of retirement a well-respected principal from one of Milwaukee's public schools. Under the new principal's direction, teachers have committed themselves to a coordinated curriculum that has the goal of achieving full reading and speaking competence in English. Morale at Bruce Guadalupe in 1994 could hardly have been higher.

Harambee and Urban Day have also recovered from the difficulties they initially encountered. As their financial situation has improved, they have been able to become more selective in admitting students. Although they are still required to admit students randomly by grade level, they now concentrate their recruitment on preschool and first- and second-grade students, who can be more quickly socialized into the norms of the schools. In 1994 more than half of all choice students in all schools were either in kindergarten or in first or second grade.[55] The administrator who resigned has come back to her old school now that it has restored much of its traditional character and quality. In an in-depth review of the community schools in 1994, one careful reporter observed, "Classes here are highly structured and yet free of regimentation; there is a sense of order, yet order itself is not the point. The activities are purposeful; the students enthusiastic participants."[56] But a seventh-grader made the most convincing case for choice. Having come from a public school where merely staying out of fights required much of her energy—"You really can't avoid it," she said. "They'll think you're scared"—she praised the learning environment in her new school: "As soon as I came here it was a big change. Here, teachers care about you. . . . [In public school] the teachers were too busy to help."[57]

STUDENT TURNOVER RATES

Student retention within any one school is an extraordinary problem in Milwaukee, in good part because of the residential mobility of low-income, welfare-dependent populations. For central-city, female-headed house-holds with children between the ages of six and seventeen (77 percent of the choice student population), the annual residential mobility rate is 30 percent for African Americans and 35 percent for Latinos. Not every change in residence dictates a change in school attendance, but in Milwaukee's public elementary schools, nearly 20 percent leave even before the end of the school year in June.[58] Come the following fall, 35 percent of the students are no longer in attendance at the same public elementary school as one year before.

The choice schools substantially reduced this migration from one school setting to another. All but 23 percent of the choice students returned to the same elementary school the following fall. Within the school year itself, the percentage leaving choice elementary schools was as little as 4 percent in 1993 and just 6 percent in 1994.[59]

PARENTAL SATISFACTION

The higher retention rates in choice schools than public schools could well be due to the higher parental satisfaction with choice schools. Seventy-five percent of choice parents gave their child's school a grade of either A or B, 10 percent more than gave such grades to public schools. Choice parents expressed substantially greater satisfaction than did public school parents with every aspect of their children's education: the amount their children learned, teacher performance, programs of instruction, discipline in the schools, opportunities for parental involvement, textbooks, and location of schools (table 5.3). Some critics doubt whether low-income parents can truly evaluate school effectiveness, but as a reporter, after visiting the schools, commented: "Participating parents . . . very much like the plan. And to suggest that this is not a legitimate gauge [of school success]—that parents lack the wherewithal to judge their children's schools—is to engage in the sort of condescension that drove many parents from the public schools in the first place."[60]

TABLE 5.3 Parental Satisfaction

| | Percentage of Parents Very Satisfied with Child's School, by Element of Education | | | |
| | Choice Schools | | Public Schools | Prior Public School |
	1991	'92–'93	1991	'90–'92
Amount Child Learned	64	50	36	33
Teacher Performance	67	51	40	36
Instructional Program	62	43	33	30
Discipline in School	52	41	27	27
Parental Involvement	62	50	36	33
Principal Performance	55	47	37	31
Textbooks	54	40	29	27
School Location	57	44	41	35
N (8-Question Average)	103 (59)	465 (46)	1,539 (35)	401 (32)

Source: Witte reports, as summarized in Paul E. Peterson, "A Critique of the Witte Evaluation of Milwaukee's School Choice Program," Center for American Political Studies, Harvard University, Occasional Paper 95-2, February 1995.
Note: Figures for prior public school are for parents of students who have moved to choice schools.

TEST SCORES

In spite of these manifold signs of stability and progress, critics have concluded that choice has not been effective in Milwaukee. Their conclusions depend on the findings reported in the Witte evaluation commissioned by Herbert Grover. Witte reports that choice student performances on standardized reading and math tests do not differ significantly from those of public school students."[61]

Witte's study suffers from numerous methodological deficiencies. His analysis depends upon a data set in which 81 percent of the cases are missing for his test group and 91 percent of the cases are missing for his control group. Even worse, his test and control groups differ markedly in almost every respect—pretest score, race, income, household structure, and educational attainment. In all but one respect, choice students are the disadvantaged group. Their pretest math scores (taken before entering the choice program) were 9 percentile points lower than the group with which they were compared. Their pretest reading scores were 8 percentile points lower. Only 3 percent of the choice students were neither African American nor Hispanic; 40 percent of the comparison group were of neither minority background. The percentage of choice students living in two-parent families was 24 percent, compared with 47 percent of the comparison group. The percentage of the choice group receiving welfare benefits was 58 percent, compared with 40 percent of the comparison group. Quite simply, Witte compared apples to oranges.

A second analysis of the Milwaukee data compared choice students to those who had applied but had not been admitted for lack of space.[62] Inasmuch as choice students had been accepted into the program at random, this study compared two groups of essentially similar students. Their pretest scores in math and reading were almost exactly the same, as were their demographic characteristics. Upon entering the choice program, the selected students scored, on average, at the 39th percentile of the math test; those not selected scored at the 40th. On the reading test, the selected scored at the 38th; the non-selected scored at the 39th. The income of the selected families was $11,250, the nonselected $11,500. The selected students had slightly better educated mothers, but when this difference was controlled, the results remained essentially the same.

Enrollment in a choice school did not affect performance on standardized tests during a student's first two years in the program. But in years three and four, choice students made substantial gains. On the math test, choice students' scores were, on average, 5 percentile points higher than nonselected students in year three and more than 11 points higher in year four. On the reading test, choice students' average scores were 3 percentile points higher after three years than those not selected into the program; after four years their scores were nearly 5 percentile points higher. Statistical tests suggest that these results are significant. Substantively, the findings are impressive. If duplicated nationwide, they would reduce the current difference between white and minority test score performance by at least one third and perhaps by more than one half.

That the improved performance does not appear until the third and fourth years is consistent with a commonsense understanding of the educational process. Choice schools are not magic bullets that transform children overnight. It takes time to adjust to a new teaching and learning

146   environment. The disruption of switching schools and adjusting to new routines and expectations may hinder improvement in test scores in the first year or two. Educational benefits accumulate and multiply with the passage of time.

Some may think the strong results in years three and four are due to the retention in the choice schools of the better-performing students. But at the end of the second year, the test performance of students who remained in choice schools did not differ significantly from those who left. Others may claim that the results are affected by the distress experienced by families who applied to the choice schools but were not admitted. But if that were the case, the differential success rate should have been the greatest in the first year, when no differences between the two groups could be observed.

Because test scores were not available for all students, we cannot draw conclusions with complete certainty. But an appropriate statistical analysis of data from a natural randomized experiment indicates that the Milwaukee choice program, for all the compromises and problems it endured, has proven successful after all.

6 Catholic

Lessons for

Public Schools

Valerie E. Lee

There is much to be learned from the study of Catholic schools in the United States.[1] At least four factors motivating such study come to mind: their rich intellectual and social history; the predominant numerical position they have held among U.S. private schools; the spare structure that guides their internal operations; and the favorable outcomes that contemporary Catholic schools appear to engender among the students and families who choose them. The historical story of Catholic schools in the United States deserves to be told, in that it reflects one vehicle for social mobility for successive waves of immigrants. Americans are among the most admittedly religious residents of the industrialized world. Thus, schools organized around religious values have always constituted an important educational sector in this country.

Almost one quarter of Americans claim to be Catholic, and the Catholic Church in the United States at one time urged "every Catholic student in a Catholic school." Although this never occurred, the schools historically have occupied an important position within U.S. Catholicism.[2]

To a very large extent, Catholic schools are located in America's cities

148   rather than the suburbs or rural areas. Historically this occurred because Catholic immigrants settled, by and large, in cities. Urban Catholic schools experienced some extremely serious pressures during the late 1960s and 1970s, and many of those pressures endure. Americans (many of them Catholic) embarked on the "white flight" from the cities to the suburbs. Forced busing in cities increased interest in Catholic schools among ethnic whites who remained. Simultaneously, large numbers of religious order members, who had provided the bulk of low-paid faculty for these schools since their inception, were abandoning both their religious and their teaching vocations. The result has been that between 1965 and 1990, enrollment in Catholic schools dropped by half.[3]

The response of the Catholic Church to this crisis and the intellectual milieu in which this response was crafted have largely shaped the nature of Catholic schools today. In the mid-1960s the Catholic Church and its schools experienced enormous changes as a result of the Second Vatican Council. A major thrust of Vatican II was the Church's commitment to social justice as an explicit aim. First, after serious self-examination (and often over objections from its members), the Church decided to aggressively and firmly resist the tide of racially motivated enrollments during this period. Second, it sought to redress racial injustice directly. Rather than following their clientele to the suburbs, inner-city schools either closed, consolidated, or opened their doors to large numbers of racial minorities, most of whom were not Catholic. Third, it decided to hire laypersons as faculty to replace the religious order members who had departed. These decisions—to remain in the inner city, to enroll many students from low-income families, and to pay faculty salaries for what used to be largely contributed services—have combined to create severe and substantial financial difficulties for the Catholic educational sector. Constrained tuitions, salary pressures, decreasing Church subsidies, and a continuing decline in enrollment plague contemporary Catholic schools in every U.S. city.

The most obvious purpose of including a chapter on Catholic schools in a book about reforming urban schools focuses on the fact that this is where the schools *are*. However, my own purpose is somewhat different. I return to the last of the four motivations I listed earlier: to explore some explanations for why contemporary Catholic schools appear to engender favorable outcomes among the students and families who choose to attend them. I

want to be quite clear here. I am assuming that only a few readers are
familiar with, or even interested in, Catholic schools for their own sake. The
vast majority of American children attend *public* schools, and the nation
now sees those schools in trouble. This chapter focuses on my primary
motivation for studying Catholic high schools: what their story has to say
about urban *public* schools.

How My Work with Catholic Schools Started

I am not a Catholic, nor did I attend or send my children to Catholic schools.
I would not even describe myself as conventionally religious. So why would
I have become so deeply involved in work on this topic? After more than a
decade as a classroom teacher in several schools in various localities, I returned to school in 1981 in a doctoral program at the Harvard Graduate
School of Education. Two experiences in that first year were seminal. First,
that fall I enrolled in a required integrated qualitative/quantitative course
in research methods. I'd never taken a statistics course in my life, and I was
ignorant about social science research. But I got hooked by this course,
especially the numbers part. I decided that I had found my calling right
there, and the person blowing the trumpet was Tony Bryk, who taught the
quantitative part of the course.

The other revelation came when I read a newly released report by James
Coleman, Tom Hoffer, and Sally Kilgore, "Public and Private Schools." They
had been commissioned by the U.S. Department of Education to conduct
the first analyses of the department's new longitudinal study "High School
and Beyond" (HS&B). Coleman's team chose to focus on comparing the
achievement of American high school students attending public, Catholic,
and other private schools. They concluded that students in Catholic high
schools "did better." Another finding, somewhat obscured in the furor
surrounding the report, was what Coleman and his colleagues called "the
common school effect": not only was students' achievement higher if
they attended Catholic rather than public secondary schools (taking into
account many other factors that influence selection into the two types of
schools), but achievement *differences* between affluent and poor students, or
minority and white students, were less in Catholic than in public schools.
Not only were Catholic schools found to be more effective, but they were

150 also found to be more equitable. Because U.S. public schools had begun almost two centuries earlier under this "common school" premise—that students from all backgrounds would learn together through a series of common academic experiences—the claim that in the late twentieth century some private schools seemed to be doing this better than public schools was provocative.

Several factors made me especially interested in this report. Almost all of my teaching had been in private schools, as I moved with my family to many cities in the United States and abroad. My own children had attended private schools, and the last school I had taught in before coming to graduate school, Marymount School of Paris, was Catholic. Under Bryk's tutelage, and with the commitment of a new convert—to statistics, not Catholicism—I became instantly passionate about quantitative research. Here was an issue into which I could sink both my teeth and my computing fingers.

Marymount was a fine place, but I hardly considered it a typical Catholic school. In fact, I held a low opinion of Catholic schools in general. Like the large majority of readers of the Coleman report, I was skeptical about its findings. As a neophyte researcher, I was eager to try out my new statistical skills on these new data to prove the report wrong. Most of the November 1981 issue of the *Harvard Educational Review* was devoted to comments on Coleman's report, including a critical article by Tony Bryk. At almost the same time, Tony and Peter Holland, then a second-year doctoral student and a Catholic religious order member, received a modest grant from the National Catholic Education Association to study Catholic secondary schools, both with the new HS&B data and also through some field work in a few Catholic high schools. Because of my familiarity with and interest in private schools, Tony offered me a place on the research team to do the HS&B analyses.

I hesitated, for I wasn't interested in singing the praises of Catholic schools, but I overcame my misgivings. Tony became my dissertation adviser, and we have worked together since that time. Peter and Tony were products of Catholic schools from infancy through college. My not being Catholic has been an advantage—I've been the "resident skeptic"—and perhaps that is one reason that I was invited to write this chapter. I have given quite a few talks about this work during the last decade, and it has always been important to say, "But I'm not Catholic." The point is, I came to this research *without* any inclination to find in favor of "the pope's schools."

Quite simply, the data alone have convinced me that something important
is going on in Catholic schools. As I said, I'm most eager to identify practices
that make the schools effective, particularly for disadvantaged children, in
order to translate these practices to public schools.

The Focus of Our Inquiry

Our book, *Catholic Schools and the Common Good*, opens with a case study of a
Catholic girls' school in south central Los Angeles. We compare the school in
1955 and the early 1980s, when we visited it as part of our research. Because
the Catholic Church and its schools experienced the seismic event of Vatican
II in the mid-1960s, the case study may be seen as a study of the effects of the
council on one Catholic school. In the 1950s, St. Madeline's enrolled about
one thousand white girls of mostly Irish extraction, virtually all of whom
were Catholic. The faculty were all nuns; the curriculum was conservative
and offered almost no elective choices; uniforms were obligatory. The
school's religious focus was on the lessons of Catholicism and the students'
obligations to follow the Church's teachings and to become good Catholic
wives and mothers. In the 1980s St. Madeline's enrolled about half as many
girls. All were still in uniform, but all were African-American and almost
none were Catholic. The faculty were entirely laypersons (but mostly Catholic), the curriculum was still very constrained, but the religion courses were
now ecumenical. The school's tone was much less otherworldly. The focus
was on academic learning, social justice, and the empowerment of these
young black women to take their rightful places in a professional world.

We chose the St. Madeline's case to illustrate several major themes:
changes in Catholic schools as a result of Vatican II; the severe decline of
enrollments over the period; the "evaporation" of religious order members
as teachers; the change in enrollment to large numbers of minority students, most of whom were not Catholic; the increased focus on social justice
as a motivating force; and a changing role for women. It should be noted,
however, that some things had not changed: the curriculum had continued
to be mostly academic in nature, few choices about courses were afforded to
students, and the school had continued to enroll only girls. This study of a
single school and its changes suggests the developing nature of Catholic
secondary schools.

Our cooperative research on Catholic schools began with a shared interest in testing the validity of the early findings of Coleman and his colleagues. Those findings focused both on higher achievement in Catholic schools than in public and on what we have come to call a more equitable social distribution of that achievement in Catholic than in public schools. The findings about social equity were of special interest to me. Because the original Coleman findings had been based on cross-sectional data from the first wave of HS&B, the follow-up data (and the ability to make stronger causal inferences) were anxiously awaited by the research community. Many of them expected that the initially favorable findings for Catholic schools would disappear when analyses used longitudinal data. They didn't. The majority of Coleman's early skeptics were forced to admit that he was right again.[4]

We wanted to avoid the controversy that had surrounded Coleman's work and to avoid duplicating it as well. Instead, we took his findings as given and used them as our base. We defined our own task as a search for explanations for why Catholic schools (compared with public schools) were able to induce higher achievement in their students and create social equity in educational outcomes. These were important findings, taken as a set. Much of public discourse about excellence and equity has supposed that these two outcomes were antithetical.

THREE-PRONGED APPROACH

Our inquiry was constructed with three interlocking objectives. One approach involved analyzing nationally representative data of the largest sample of students in public and Catholic high schools ever collected (from the first two waves of HS&B). The second approach involved trying to learn more about the internal operations of Catholic schools. To do this, we collected extensive field data in a sample of seven "good" Catholic high schools across the nation. We observed classes; interviewed students, teachers, and parents; wrote extensive field notes; and collected some survey information to provide descriptive information. The field schools were selected for their variability: affluent and impoverished schools, small and relatively large schools, single-sex and coeducational schools, relatively new schools and schools with a long tradition, schools with mostly white and entirely minority clienteles, and at least one ethnic Catholic school. We embarked on the third approach several years into study, when we recognized our inability to really make sense of our findings until we understood the schools' intellectual and social history (including the content and effects of Vatican II). Although all of us were at Harvard during the study's first three years, we scattered thereafter: Tony to the University of Chicago, I to the Educational Testing Service for two years and then to the University of Michigan. Peter left his religious order and entered public school administration in Massachusetts. After the results were all in, Tony and I spent nearly a decade bringing the book to publication.

Our major purpose for the book is also the focus of the research and findings about Catholic schools described in this chapter. Beyond providing a description of how contemporary Catholic high schools operate, we tried to identify and understand the organizational characteristics and qualities of Catholic high schools that helped explain the findings of Coleman and his colleagues. How are these schools able to create two favorable outcomes simultaneously: high average achievement and an equitable distribution of that achievement among students from different social class, racial, and ethnic backgrounds? We also wanted to explain positive effects for students and teachers in the affective domain. Catholic school students are more engaged: they cut class less frequently, have fewer unexplained absences and fewer behavioral problems, and are more interested in academics than students in public schools. Teachers in Catholic schools are also more committed than their public school counterparts: they see themselves as more efficacious, enjoy their work more, have higher morale, and are absent less frequently. Thus, our inquiry also pursued organizational explanations for the unusual engagement of students and commitment of teachers in Catholic schools. The search for explanatory factors assumed comparisons with students and teachers from public schools.

The Major Findings

Catholic schools enroll about 5 percent of America's secondary school population and about three-quarters of all students in U.S. private high schools.[5] Between 1970 and 1990 the proportion of minority students enrolled in Catholic schools grew from less than 10 to more than 20 percent, and non-Catholic enrollment quadrupled. In schools like St. Madeline's, East

154   Catholic High School in Detroit, and other inner-city Catholic schools in many of the nation's largest cities, these proportions are much, much higher. Catholic high schools are still mostly found in cities, with only a modest proportion in the suburbs. Even fewer are in rural areas.

Compared with other types of private schools, most Catholic schools do not enroll an elite clientele. Historically, Catholic schools have served a dual role of Americanization and social mobility for the children of Catholic immigrants from Ireland, Germany, and southern and eastern Europe. They still serve this role for recent immigrants from Latin America. The family income of Catholic school students in the 1980s exceeded that of their public school counterparts by about $6,000, and the average parent had one more year of education.[6] A somewhat smaller proportion of blacks and a higher proportion of Hispanics attend Catholic than public schools. Children in Catholic schools come from slightly larger families and are somewhat less likely to live in families headed by single parents. Over the past decade or two, tuitions have risen sharply. Catholic high schools are somewhat more selective than elementary schools, and their tuitions are higher (averaging around $3,000, with a wide range). School-financed scholarships are uncommon.

Although Catholic schools enroll somewhat more advantaged children than do public schools, the social differences are modest. They have often been called "the poor man's private school." To this day, many Catholic school parents have working-class backgrounds, and many have not attended college. Thus the major difference between students in the two sectors is one of self-selection: families who send their children to Catholic schools choose and pay to do so. Many parents sustain considerable financial sacrifice to pay the required tuitions. Although the majority of students in Catholic schools are still Catholic, which explains a major motivation for choosing this type of education, increasing proportions of families who choose Catholic education for their children do so *despite* the religious orientation, not because of it. In terms of the social characteristics of their clientele, Catholic schools are much more similar to public than to non-Catholic private schools.

WHAT EXPLAINS CATHOLIC SCHOOLS' SPECIAL EFFECTIVENESS?

Four foundational elements appear to explain why Catholic schools engender favorable outcomes for their students and teachers: a delimited tech-

nical core, a communal school organization, decentralized governance, and
an inspirational ideology.

A Delimited Technical Core The academic program of Catholic high schools is
organized as a core curriculum. Almost the same program of study is followed by virtually all students, regardless of their family background, academic preparation, or future educational plans. The structure of this curriculum is predicated on a proactive view among faculty and administrators
about what all students can and should learn. These views connect to long-
standing traditions in the Church about the capacities and proper aims of
human beings and about what constitutes a proper education. Required
courses predominate in any student's course of study, with elective courses
limited in content and number. Catholic schools, like public schools, must
accommodate some diversity in the intellectual preparation of their students, but such accommodation is accomplished quite differently. In Catholic schools the same basic academic goals apply to all students, whereas in
public schools students with different levels of preparation are offered substantially different courses of study.[7] Compared with public schools, the
amount of tracking in a Catholic high school is modest, constrained in both
scope and level. Whatever programmatic differentiation exists does not produce the invidious consequences found in public schools, in part because
explicit school policies allocate more of the schools' limited fiscal and human resources to the students who need them most—at the lower end of the
academic spectrum. A fundamental institutional purpose is at work here:
the aim of a common education of mind and spirit for all. This purpose
integrates the schools' academic structure and policies.

The consequences for students of this constrained academic organization
are profound. When all students follow an academic curriculum and all
have common academic experiences, it is not surprising that they all learn
more. The academic organization of Catholic high schools goes a long way
toward explaining the higher levels, and more equitable distribution, of
academic achievement in Catholic schools. This organizational form also
makes efficient use of the limited fiscal and human resources that typify
many Catholic high schools. This type of curriculum cultivates a relatively
informal relation between organization and individuals, allowing for positive personal and social consequences for teachers and students. Furthermore, the small size of Catholic high schools reinforces their constrained

156   academic structure. Although there is no reason why large schools necessarily offer more differentiated academic and social experiences to their
students, it is more logical and much easier to do so when there are more
students to accommodate.

Communal School Organization The academic structure of Catholic high
schools is embedded in a communal organization. In other writings, Tony
Bryk and I have contrasted two forms of school organization: communal
and bureaucratic.[8] Three features typify the core idea of communal organization in Catholic schools. First is an extensive array of school activities
whose purpose is to provide frequent opportunities for face-to-face interactions and shared experiences among school members, both adults and students. These activities include the common curriculum, as well as the numerous school events that promote high levels of participation and more
informal interactions: athletics, drama, musical events, and some religious
activities (such as retreats or masses). Other well-established traditions and
rituals allow current students to share experiences with former members of
the community, also important dimensions of these communities.

A second component enables the community to function. This component of communal organization focuses on the role of teachers. These roles
are more extended or diffuse than those of their public school counterparts.
Rather than defining themselves as subject-matter specialists whose "space"
is delineated by their classroom walls, teachers in Catholic high schools see
their responsibilities as extending to any encounters with students: in hall-
ways, the school grounds, the school neighborhood, and sometimes into
their homes.[9] These teachers often define their professions in explicitly
moral terms: as shapers of character as well as developers of skills. Collegiality among teachers in communally organized schools is common, extending to personal as well as professional contact. In such contexts, school
decision making is less conflictual and more often characterized by high
levels of mutual trust and respect. Just as it influences academic organization, small school size provides an advantage in facilitating a more personalized role for teachers, as well as in community building as a whole.

A third component important to fostering community in Catholic
schools is a set of shared beliefs, not so much about the tenets of Catholicism, but rather about what students *should* learn, about proper norms for
instruction, and about how people should relate to one another. Moreover,

the expression of these beliefs is facilitated in an environment defined by a general set of moral understandings about the dignity of each person, a commitment to genuine dialogue, and a commitment to work toward an ethos of caring that defines the schools' social encounters. The idea of community was spelled out in Vatican II documents about Catholic education. Both the language and living of a community defined in this way is evident in Catholic schools.

Decentralized Governance The administrative layer within any school is very thin, with most administrative responsibilities held by staff members who also teach. The principal has considerable control over daily operations, a tradition that likely flows from the formerly strong religious order governance of almost all Catholic high schools. Even now, if a religious order is represented at a school, the principal is likely to be a member of that order (61 percent of principals in 1988 were religious order members). Even with the expansion of a lay principalship, deference to the principal's authority is common. Principals are often selected from the faculty, rather than from a professional cadre of administrators. Compared with public schools, Catholic school principals are seldom motivated to assume a leadership role for personal gain—to advance their professional careers, to improve their salaries, or "move to a plum job downtown" (which do not exist in this context). Rather, the decision to seek or accept an administrative role is often motivated by the opportunity to help the school. Individuals often move in and out of the principal's role from the faculty.

Catholic schools are linked to one another only very loosely. Virtually all important decisions are made at the school site, with diocesan education offices offering only very limited guidance or support (fiscal or moral). Current reform efforts in public schools toward decentralization are modest in comparison with the level of school-site autonomy among Catholic schools. The substantial autonomy at the school site typical in the Catholic sector (and among other private schools) has been used to argue in favor of parental choice of schools. In an important study of school choice, John Chubb and Terry Moe focused on the importance of decentralized governance for school effectiveness (defined by student achievement). Also using data from HS&B, they concluded that the absence of what they called "bureaucratic influence" is a crucial factor in school organizational effectiveness.[10] The most important explanation for bureaucratic influence in their analyses was

158 whether a high school was public or private. They used these findings, which to a large extent relied on their findings about the importance of school sector, to support their arguments in favor of parental choice of schools. An underlying theme in Chubb and Moe's work, important to consider in writing about any schools where families and students enroll by choice, is that such schools are educational markets.

Like all private schools, Catholic schools are subject to market forces. Because few Catholic schools have waiting lists and many are underenrolled, there is a strong institutional interest in holding students in order to balance budgets. These forces may also contribute to the schools' relatively low dropout and expulsion rates. However, the control structure in these schools embodies considerably more than market responsiveness to client pressure as suggested in the Chubb and Moe model. Market forces cannot explain the broadly shared institutional purpose of advancing social equity, nor can they account for the efforts of Catholic educators to maintain inner-city schools (with large non-Catholic enrollments) in the face of mounting fiscal woes. Market forces cannot account for the differential allotment of resources within schools in a compensatory manner in order to provide a solid academic education for every student, nor can they explain the norms of community that characterize daily life in these schools. Thus we reject the market forces argument that is offered by school choice advocates as a major element explaining the effectiveness of Catholic schools.

An Inspirational Ideology The ideological thrust from Vatican II that energized Catholic education is a topic both too broad and too narrow to discuss in any detail here. However, two inspirational ideas that shape life in the schools deserve some mention: *personalism* and *subsidiarity*. Personalism underlies the attention Catholic schools pay to the importance of the numerous small social encounters in shaping school life. It motivates the extended role that encourages teachers to care about the kind of people their students become, as well as about the knowledge and skills they acquire. It drives teachers to model behaviors that are held out as ideals for students. Under personalism, social behavior is seen in moral terms, behaviors that are practices within a just community. Personalism makes claims on humans to act beyond their own individual interests, toward the common good.

The principle of *subsidiarity* holds that human meaning derives from voluntary associations around small institutions that act as buffers between the individual and an impersonal and bureaucratic society. This principle motivates the organization of Catholic schools in that they provide a public place for acting on moral norms. Instrumental considerations about such issues as work efficiency and subject-matter specialization—so common in the bureaucratically organized public comprehensive high school—are mediated in Catholic schools by an overarching concern for human dignity. School decentralization, seen through the lens of subsidiarity, is advanced less because it provides a client-sensitive environment or more efficient operation but rather because personal dignity and human respect are advanced when work is organized in small communities where collegiality may flourish. The social solidarity that flourishes in these small group associations literally gives meaning to the lives of school members—teachers and students.

Clearly, the inspirational ideology underlying the organization of Catholic schools binds their members into a functioning whole. It would be hard to deny that this ideology was connected to the basic religious philosophy that binds the schools together or that it was energized by Vatican II, a fundamental force of change in the Catholic Church worldwide. On the other hand, the "religiousness" of this ideology is not crucial to the effects that accrue from it. Although the ideology derives from religious understandings either actively engaged or at least accepted as a condition of school membership, the ideas underlying these understandings are not antithetical to basic democratic ideals.

What Are the Lessons for Public Schools?

LESSON 1: A CORE CURRICULUM

Why are Catholic schools able to induce high achievement in their students —all their students? What makes the most difference to students' learning, reassuringly, is the courses they take. With few exceptions, we have found that all Catholic high school students follow a narrow academic curriculum, which concentrates on courses that would normally define the college preparatory track. Students have few choices in their courses of study, and those choices they do have are constrained. That is, they have choices *among* other academic offerings. Regardless of students' academic or social background,

160   irrespective of their plans or aspirations for their post–high school futures, Catholic schools direct their students to academic undertakings that the schools define as appropriate intellectual preparation for all students.

These findings, although perhaps not terribly surprising, have considerable relevance for public schools. Responding to individual differences in ability or background, offering a smorgasbord of courses for students to choose from, and then asking those students who made poor choices to suffer a lifetime of responsibility for them is a policy that has introduced social stratification into the educational process in the United States. Because poor and minority students are most frequently the ones who "choose" (or have chosen for them) low-track and undemanding courses, these findings have particular importance for schools that enroll large numbers of disadvantaged students. How our public high schools became such differentiating institutions, and how they may be changed, are important issues, though not the subject of this chapter. But the direction that curricular change should take seems clear. Catholic schools, particularly those in the inner city and those that enroll large proportions of disadvantaged students, serve both as good models and as evidence of the effects of these models. They represent lighthouses that guide the direction for curriculum change.

LESSON 2: THE SCHOOL AS A COMMUNITY

It should be clear by now that there are profound organizational differences between Catholic and public high schools. I've tried to point out some benefits that accrue to students and teachers in schools organized as communities. The differentiated environment of the average public high school acts against the formation of high levels of personal interaction. Several school reforms in recent years have focused on trying to engage students with their education. A common claim is that greater engagement can be developed by offering students more choices within a diverse curriculum taught in a more stimulating fashion. A related argument holds that teachers will expend more effort when they teach classes and subjects in which they have a high degree of personal interest. Still other reforms aimed at accountability offer extrinsic rewards to students for simply staying in school: promised jobs or college tuition upon graduation. Related ideas threaten students with sanctions for dropping out: canceled drivers licenses, cuts in parents' welfare payments. Merit pay proposals represent a complementary reward initiative for teachers who would be recognized for special performance in comparison with their colleagues.

Our findings on Catholic schools challenge the premise of such reforms and argue against their efficacy. These initiatives draw on basic tenets of individualism. As a group, they represent appeals to personal interest or to the utilitarian calculus of the "carrot and stick" to encourage good behavior and discourage bad. Catholic schools direct their attention to the *social* rather than the *individual* basis of human engagement. We have considerable evidence that daily life in these schools represents a source of considerable meaning for members. The results of our work on school communal organization provide considerable evidence that schools organized around the social principles I have described have much power to engage their participants.

LESSON 3: EDUCATION AS A CULTURAL AND MORAL ENTERPRISE

Enculturation occurs in all schools, public as well as Catholic. Although the former do not have religious classes or direct and deliberate efforts toward forming a coherent social life, today's public high schools convey a distinct vision of society: one in which individuals strive for personal success while pursuing their own self-interest. Accounts of contemporary public high schools by Cusick and Wheeler, Gerald Grant, Mary Metz, or Sara Lawrence Lightfoot describe institutional norms that are competitive, individualistic, and materialistic. These norms are embedded in the differentiated curriculum, the tracking structure, and teacher assignments whereby good teachers are often rewarded with classes filled with the most able students. These norms are also embedded in the routine social encounters that are regulated by explicit codes of conduct that specify prohibited behaviors and elaborate individual rights. In his account of Hamilton High, Grant described how its students had learned "how to manipulate the rule system to advance their self-interests," to replace "doing the right thing" with "doing the procedurally correct thing."[11] Over the last half century, aggregated self-interest has come to replace the common good as the social milieu to which students are directed. We argue that the common good is distinct from what is best for most individuals.

I am talking here about aims and visions, which may not typify every occurrence in every high school. The Catholic school vision stands in direct

162   contrast to the type of enculturation I've just described. It is grounded in quite a different belief system from the one that typifies today's culture: a belief in the dignity of each human being and in every person's responsibility to advance the goals of peace, justice, and human welfare. Because Catholic schools define education in terms of forming the conscience of all students toward an awareness of what they share in common, according to this definition a proper education cannot be affectively neutral.

Our vision of the common good is open to challenge and clarification. But active pursuit of the common good is what education is all about (or at least it should be). The traditional academic program, complemented by a communal life rich in symbols and a set of norms that makes quite clear how the school expects people to behave toward one another—these elements of Catholic schools afford opportunities for students to ponder questions about how we should live together, not just in school but throughout life. Such schools stand in stark contrast with the secular high schools described in recent years by Grant and other writers, schools that rarely catalyze a sense of moral obligation on the part of teachers or students toward any enterprise beyond the individual. Such schools neither make demands on the human conscience nor help members discern which commitments are worth holding, beyond a reasoned self-interest.

Some philosophy of education drives every school. Embracing democracy depends on developing a broadly shared dialogue about the nature of individual and group interests, on fostering a civic conscience that makes moral claims on citizens to act in accordance with this balance. Education for democratic citizenship requires sustained encounters that pose questions for students about the nature of persons and society and about appropriate and worthy personal and social aims. Although such encounters may be simpler to foster in small educational environments that are explicitly formed around a moral core, a democratic education—not training but true education—requires more. Besides imparting technical knowledge and skills to negotiate a complex secular world, students must be pushed to develop a moral vision toward which those skills should be pointed and a conscience that encourages them to pursue that vision. In this sense, education is fundamentally a moral enterprise.

In our book Bryk, Holland, and I argue that Catholic schools that operate with very constrained fiscal and human resources and that serve a broad cross-section of our society offer these (and other) lessons to ponder when considering educational reform. These lessons are particularly appropriate when considering the reform of urban schools. The purposes served by public education are currently under intense scrutiny and criticism. Many have argued that the existing system of public education has lost its position as an agent of the common good. The old arguments about common schools ring hollow when measured against the reality of schools that afford unparalleled opportunities for some while simultaneously undereducating large segments of our society and denying basic human dignity to the most disadvantaged.

It seems clear that although the public schools alone have not created the extreme social inequities in our society, they are organized in ways that more frequently magnify than diminish inequities effected by family income, race, or ethnicity. I certainly do not intend to demean the efforts and motivations of individual public school teachers, principals, and administrators. Rather, we have used a comparative framework, public vs. Catholic schools, to highlight the difficult organizational conditions under which most public educators work. My colleagues and I are convinced that the work of these educators and their students could be more effective and more personally rewarding if it were performed in environments similar to those we have seen in Catholic high schools.

7 Chicago
School Reform

Anthony S. Bryk, David Kerbow,

and Sharon Rollow

A tragic story unfolded in a series of articles in the *Chicago Tribune* throughout the spring of 1988. The Chicago Public School system was failing the students and parents that it was intended to serve and was placing at risk the future economic and social vitality of the city. Students, parents, and local schools were portrayed as victims to the interests of career bureaucrats in the central office, politicians in the city council and state legislature (many of whom send their own children to private schools), and a teachers union that saw its role as protecting the jobs and benefits of its aging membership. The *Tribune* concurred with a pronouncement from then–U.S. Secretary of Education William Bennett: this was the "worst school system in America."[1]

This newspaper series galvanized public opinion against the status quo. The *Tribune*'s analysis reaffirmed what many Chicago school reform activists had concluded some time ago. Unless the basic governance arrangements of schools changed, reformers doubted that wide-scale improvement would occur. While many principals, teachers, parents, and interested citizens might work hard to promote better schools, the larger institutional system in which they had to work would continue to frustrate their best efforts.[2] The highly centralized governance of schools was fundamentally incompatible with wide-scale improvement.[3]

Mobilizing for Reform

For years advocacy groups had been reporting on the failings of the CPS. A 1985 study by the Chicago Panel on School Policy exposed shockingly high dropout rates for the Chicago Public Schools.[4] Previous school system reports had seriously underestimated the severity of the problem by counting only those students whose official records explicitly marked them as dropouts. Many actual dropouts were mislabeled as transfers, pregnant, or "enlisted in the military." Using more accurate methods, the Chicago Panel found that the systemwide dropout rate for the years from 1978 to 1984 was about 43 percent, but the rate was as high as 63 percent in some racially isolated high schools. Almost one in every two Hispanic and African-American students in Chicago dropped out of school.

A report from Designs for Change in 1985 amplified these themes.[5] These researchers found that nearly half of the children who entered the city's eighteen most economically disadvantaged high schools in 1984 dropped out before graduation. And even among those who did manage to graduate, more than half were reading below the ninth-grade level.

The case for change also appeared in annual school system statistics about student achievement. In the fall of 1987, for example, the CPS reported median percentile rankings on reading comprehension from the Iowa Tests of Basic Skill (ITBS) ranging from a high of the 47th percentile in the first grade to a low of the 33d percentile in grade 4. Mathematics scores ranged from a high of the 47th percentile in grade 8 to a low of the 38th percentile for first-graders. Moreover, these results were from a test form that had been in continuous use for almost ten years, and they were based on norms from 1978, which were among the easiest in recent memory. In fact, the full dimensions of the problem did not become apparent until 1990 when Chicago finally changed forms of the ITBS and reported results in terms of more recent norms (from 1988). When this shift was made, school system statistics in reading and math plummeted even further. Percentile statistics in the low thirties appeared across many grade levels.

These reports confirmed a growing sense among the city's elite that major

166   changes were needed. Alarmed by the poor skills of entry-level workers, the
business community had approached Mayor Harold Washington immediately following his reelection in 1986.[6] They asked him to convene an education summit that would begin to tackle some of the problems of public education in Chicago. The summit was first conceived as a limited partnership
between the Chicago business community and the public high schools. The
intent was to replicate the so-called Boston Compact, which had sought to
motivate that city's high school students to stay in school with the promise of
an entry-level job in a local business upon graduation. The Chicago plan
died, however, when then–Superintendent of Schools Manford Byrd refused even to consider first steps without a major commitment of new funds.

The next catalyzing event was the teachers strike in the fall of 1987. The
CPS and the Chicago Teachers' Union were again locked in a battle over
wages and work rules. The 1987 strike, the longest in Chicago's history, was
the ninth in eighteen years. The press decried both the board of education
and the union for their "stranglehold" on the system.[7] Parents were frustrated by the strike as well. They complained that neither the system nor the
union seemed interested in the fact that the schools were failing children.

In the aftermath of this strike, Mayor Washington initiated a populist
strategy for school reform. He organized an all-day open meeting that was
attended by thousands, and from it the mayor appointed a Parent Community Council, which became the centerpiece of a new education summit.
Ten evening forums were eventually held across the city, and additional
hearings were scheduled for school advocacy groups to present their proposals to the council on weekends. These measures were intended to assure
that reform was accessible to poor and working parents. Efforts to engage
professional educators, however, were more limited, and neither the central office nor the union took the effort seriously.

A power vacuum was created when Harold Washington died of a heart
attack on the eve of the first forum. This paved the way for numerous
advocacy organizations and community-based groups, working in alliance
with business leadership, to increase their influence. When the action
moved to the state legislature's spring session, several groups came forward
with competing drafts of legislation.[8] The formal legislative process spanned
two sessions. It was marred by leadership conflict between Democrats and
Republicans, while competing groups lobbied to influence specific reform

provisions. After much debate and politicking, a compromise bill passed in December 1988. A sharp departure from efforts under way elsewhere, PA 85-1418 shocked the reform world and was immediately hailed as "radical . . . an historic change . . . the most fundamental restructuring [of an urban system] since the early part of the twentieth century."[9]

Chicago's reform, however, was not without its critics. Suspicion simmered within the city about the "real motivations" behind the reform. A number of the city's African-American leaders were skeptical.[10] They argued that parents wanted good schools for their children, but they did not wish to run them nor did they necessarily have the expertise to do so. They feared that this reform was designed to fail in order to achieve the real aim of some within the political and business communities—the replacement of the CPS with vouchers and an educational market. In addition, these critics were suspicious of a radical decentralization that had swept over the school system just as African Americans assumed leadership of the central administration and teachers union. Chicago's reform was also criticized in some quarters as antiprofessional because the legislation stripped tenure away from principals and granted teachers only a minority role in the new local school governance arrangements at the heart of the reform.[11]

Expanded Local Democratic Participation as the Antidote

Ironically, just as major critiques of democratic control of schools were taking shape, school reformers in Chicago embraced expanded local democratic participation as a lever for change.[12] Chicago's reformers analyzed the core problem, however, not as the success of democratic governance per se but rather as the dysfunctioning of centralized bureaucracy. They argued that a commitment to democratic control was essential to public education but that much more of it should be exercised at the local school-building level. For this to occur, the influence of the central bureaucracy had to be substantially curtailed. More specifically, Chicago reformers agreed that control centralized in the superintendent, central office, and board of education had to be weakened. Similarly, they concurred that both resources and authority should be devolved to local school communities, predicated on a belief that local communities can effectively solve local problems.

School-based professionals, however, were also seen as part of the

168   problem. Don Moore, an author of the school reform legislation and director of one of the city's school advocacy groups, argued that "the power of
urban school professionals must be curtailed because professional judgment
has repeatedly been used as an excuse for practices that are harmful to
children."[13] Similarly, in a series of community forums held across the city
in an effort to mobilize for reform, principals and teachers were sharply
criticized by parents and community members for a perceived lack of concern and effort. If schools were ever to become more responsive to their
local communities and to the parents and children that they were intended
to serve, it was argued that a fundamental rebalancing of power from these
professionals toward parents and community members was necessary.

In response, political leaders in Chicago took a unique tack. Drawing on a
a well-established network of community-based organizations, they opted
for an unparalleled level of parent and community control. In essence, they
chose to shift from centralized democratic control, exercised through a bureaucracy, to expanded local democratic control, exercised through a school
council. Chicago cast off a centralized system of education and banked instead upon principles of citizen participation, community control, and local
flexibility. These commitments are captured in the idea of democratic localism.[14]

At base, Chicago reformers sought to create new institutions in each
community that would engage the sustained participation of parents, community members, and school professionals around issues of school improvement. The reformers believed that this heightened local participation
would not only promote more effective solutions to local problems than
could be formulated by a central bureaucracy but also foment a broad sense
of urgency among the adults in each school community to work together on
the children's behalf. In this way, local democratic practice would also create a social movement, necessary to sustain structural change, around the
education and welfare of children. The authors of Chicago's reform were
confident that, with parents and community members more engaged in the
conversation, decision-making activities would refocus around the interests
of children rather than those of distant bureaucrats and vested interests.

It is important to distinguish the elements of the Chicago reform from the
earlier movement for community control of schools in New York City during the 1960s. In both instances, community activists argued that the sys-

tem was failing poor and minority children and that a greater voice had to be given to their needs and concerns.[15] In this sense Chicago's reform looked back to New York for inspiration, but with a critical difference: Chicago pushed much further toward a democratic localism than was the case in New York City. The New York community boards are as large as many midsized urban districts. In contrast, the primary governance unit in Chicago is the individual school. Thus in Chicago the distance between the site of political activity and its consequences was radically reduced. Individual political accountability is now personal, immediate, and sharply drawn.

We also note that, unlike other current efforts to restructure large urban school systems, the commitment to democratic localism was seen, by at least some advocates for reform, as a part of a larger strategy at urban community building.[16] The loss of local institutions of all kinds—social, economic, and religious—has denuded urban community life and undermined the viability of these very communities. Any effort to stem the current destruction and to re-create these communities requires a massive commitment to local institution building. Key in this regard are expanded opportunities for citizen participation and community education about local affairs. With sustained social engagement and some external supports, activists argue that even poor citizens can take control of their circumstances and improve them. From this perspective, Chicago school reform can be viewed as part of a larger movement to renew urban life through revitalizing the public sphere.

Key Features of the 1988 Reform

The Chicago School Reform Act, PA 85-1418, attacked the failures of the Chicago school system from two directions. At the school community level, it encouraged expanded participation among parents and community members, teachers, and the principal by devolving to these local actors significant formal authority and new resources to solve their local problems. Complementing this local focus was a mandate for districtwide objectives that encouraged new programmatic innovation and set explicit goals for improving student achievement. The act directed the board of education to create a new accountability process and to report annually on the improvement of each school. The system was also directed to create its own

TABLE 7.1 Primer on Chicago School Reform

Establish local school councils (LSC)
  Membership
    6 elected parents
    2 elected community members
    2 teachers
    principal
    1 elected student member (high school LSCs only)
  Key responsibilities
    Evaluate, hire/fire school principal
    Help principal develop and approve budget and School Improvement Plan
      (SIP)
    Monitor implementation of SIP and develop other local initiatives
  Aim
    Parents and community members gain formal authority with respect to
      their neighborhood school

Reshape principalship
  Remove tenure; four-year performance contracts subject to LSC review
  Authority to recruit and hire new teachers
  More discretionary money to spend and more freedom regarding its use
  More control over physical plant and ancillary personnel
  Some effort to shorten process for removal of incompetent teachers
  Aims
    Increase principal's authority over building and staff
    Change basic system of sanctions and incentives shaping principal's work

Expand influence for teachers
  Voice in selecting/retaining the principal through two votes on LSC
  Advisory role regarding school curriculum, instruction, and budget through
    a Professional Personnel Advisory Committee (PPAC)
  Aim
    Increase teachers' role and influence in school decision making

Redirect school fiscal resources
  Cap on central office administrative expenses
  Implement a school-based budgeting process
  Requirement for an equitable allocation of base funds to individual schools
  Increased discretionary revenues to schools with high percentages of
    disadvantaged students
  Aims
    Greater revenue equity across the system
    New discretionary resources at the school level to foster restructuring

TABLE 7.1 *Continued*   171

Reduce or eliminate line authority of the central office
    Eliminate board authority to name principals
    Restrict central control over curriculum
    Eliminate line control over regular school operations
    Aim
        Assure that authority remains decentralized

A central pull toward academic improvement
    Systemwide goals established for student learning and objectives for school
        improvement
    Schools required to develop and annually update the three-year SIP
    System must report annually on progress
    Escalating levels of sanctions and external intervention for nonimproving
        schools by the district
    Aim
        Focus local schools' efforts on substantially improving student learning

strategic plan to better support local needs. Thus, taken together, PA 85-1418 sought to create an overall environment in the CPS that would promote school change.[17]

More specifically, the act created local school councils comprising six elected parents, two elected community members, two appointed teachers, and the principal.[18] The chair of the council must be a parent member. Elections occur every two years, and terms are not staggered. The LSC was given a key power—to hire and fire the school principal. It must also approve the annual school budget and a three-year school improvement plan (SIP).

The preponderance of parents and community members on Chicago's LSCs—as well as their power to hire and fire the principal—distinguishes Chicago school reform from other efforts that mandate parent involvement in school governance. Reform activists in Chicago were aware of the limited success in these past attempts to empower local constituencies, when parents typically constituted only a minority faction on local councils whose role was often only advisory.[19] Reformers sought to assure that parents and community members would be a legitimate site of power in school affairs.

Chicago's reform also substantially reshaped the sanctions and incentives affecting principals' work. Guidance for this initiative came from several

172   directions. Research advocacy groups drew on findings from the effective schools literature about the importance of principal leadership.[20] Another powerful force was the business community. The involved business leaders spoke frequently about how principals should be the "chief executive officers" of their schools. At base here was an image of good schools with strong leaders who had significant vision, autonomy, resources, and powers. The act sought to get rid of "deadwood" and bring in "new blood" that would stimulate innovation and leverage leadership for change.

Specifically, principals were made more accountable to local constituencies by being placed on four-year performance contracts subject to LSC review. So that they could better lead change in their school communities, principals gained new powers over their budgets, physical plant, and personnel. To expedite the removal of incompetent teachers, the remediation process was shortened from one year to forty-five days. (Only after an unsuccessful remediation process can an incompetent teacher be removed from the classroom.)[21] Principals were also given a voice in hiring and evaluating new janitorial and food service personnel, and they now have a set of building keys. (Prior to reform, civil service and ancillary staff were accountable to their supervisors only, and principals held keys only at the discretion of the school engineer.)

The reform's treatment of teachers was much more subtle. Unlike principals, teachers were not politically vulnerable. In fact, any reform that was likely to pass the legislature had to be acceptable to union leadership.[22] Thus, the act took a compromise position with regard to teachers. They were given advisory authority on school curriculum and instruction decisions through a professional personnel advisory committee (PPAC). Teachers also gained a direct voice in principal selection and retention through their two votes on the LSC.

To be sure, this aspect of the reform looks meager in comparison to then-emerging plans in other urban districts, such as Rochester and Cincinnati, that emphasized greater teacher professionalism. On balance, however, we note that the provision for teachers to have a direct influence over principal selection and retention was actually quite radical compared with existing practices in most districts. It significantly recast the traditional power relations between principals and their faculties.[23] Thus, although direct changes in teachers' work was not a major focus of the reform, the act did introduce some very important changes here, too.

Balancing the emphasis on local empowerment were legislative provisions that sought to pull all schools toward educational improvement. These consisted of explicit educational goals for children (for example, 50 percent of the students in each school were to be at national norms in five years) and an extended set of school objectives (enhanced teacher professionalism, multicultural curriculum, and greater parent involvement). The act also mandated elements of strategic planning in an attempt to rationalize local school decision making. Schools are required to develop three-year improvement plans, which must be evaluated and updated annually to assure progress toward both local and legislatively mandated goals. As part of this process, the school system must report annually on each school's movement toward these goals. Schools that fail to improve are subject to a variety of increasingly severe sanctions that may culminate in termination of the principal's contract, removal of the LSC, and placement of the school under the receivership of the system's board of education.[24]

New resources also became available to support local school improvements. PA 85-1418 changed how state compensatory education funds (state Chapter 1 funds) were to be used. Previously the district had received these monies as general aid; now they must be allocated directly to local school budgets based on the number of disadvantaged students enrolled. As a result, schools with primarily low-income populations received substantial increases in discretionary dollars and greater freedom regarding how they could be spent. In 1993, for example, the per-pupil allocation under Chapter 1 was $734. In larger elementary schools with very disadvantaged student populations, the total allocation of this new state aid could approach one million dollars.[25]

Moving beyond the formal legislative provisions, PA 85-1418 also catalyzed a dramatic expansion around the city of institutional activity focused on educational improvement. Over the first five years of reform, new associations among the city's business and professional leaders united with existing ones to provide technical and financial assistance to individual schools and to advocate for them.[26] Education maintained a sustained focus of activity among existing civic groups and community-based organizations (CBOs).[27] The local philanthropic community committed substantial new funds.[28] Individual faculty members from colleges and universities in the metropolitan area became more active in Chicago's schools, and several new research, development, and professional education centers emerged. These

174   activities have generated extensive support for local school efforts and extended conversations throughout the city about school improvement.

The Logic of Our Analysis

A process of institutional change can be divided into several components. First is an initiating or catalyst phase, in which a dysfunctional status quo is challenged. This period is often marked by conflict about new directions and ambiguity about day-to-day routines. This melds with a second, sustaining phase, in which individual roles, rules, and responsibilities are fundamentally reshaped under a reordered authority structure. During this second phase, basic changes crystallize in the organization of work, in the school's relations to its parents and local environment, and in actual classroom practices. Finally, in the third phase the organization begins to resettle. New routines have clearly emerged that mark a restructured and more productive school organization.

We know from past research that individual urban school improvement of this sort can take five or more years to develop fully. Typically, measurable changes in student achievement do not occur until relatively late in the process.[29] To be sure, substantial transformations are occurring during the first two to three years, and there is a clear logic to these developments, but the "bottom line of student achievement" is one of the last improvements seen. No empirical evidence exists against which to establish benchmarks for adequate progress for an effort to transform an entire urban school system. It seems reasonable to assume, however, that if successful individual school change can take five years, districtwide changes are likely to take longer.

We argue by analogy that evaluating Chicago's school reform is much like trying to assess the effectiveness of a major corporate restructuring, which can take ten years or more to unfold fully. Short-term profitability (in our case, changes in test scores) is not an adequate standpoint from which to assess productivity.[30] In fact, short-term profits might plummet as losses are incurred in the process of reshaping the organization's basic mission and operating procedures. Thus, while the long-term standpoint for judging school reform properly emphasizes substantial improvements in student learning, in the short term we need to focus instead on the actual organizational rearrangements that are under way. Are the changes envisioned under the Chicago School Reform Act in fact occurring? Where and how often have they taken place, and when they have occurred, is the implied logic of school change actually operating as hoped?

A summary of developments during the first four years of reform is a highly varied story of 550 school communities that make up the Chicago Public School system. In many schools, serious challenges have been raised to the prereform status quo, and sustained efforts are under way to restructure operations. Other schools are attempting to move in this direction but are struggling; still others we describe as "left behind by reform." There are few signs of any meaningful changes occurring in this latter group. In general terms, system-level developments during this first period of reform may be characterized as "a third moving forward, a third struggling, and a third left behind."

Evaluating the Early Developments Under Chicago School Reform, 1989–1993

Our emphasis in analyzing the first phase of Chicago school reform was on early indicators of whether reform was "on track or not."[31] That is, was reform developing across the system in ways that might conceivably lead to substantial improvements in student learning? Specifically, as noted above, reformers argued that the new governance structures and roles established by the Chicago School Reform Act would create a political force for improvement in school communities. They maintained that such politics could leverage the organizational changes needed to make schools more responsive to the communities, families, and students they now serve. Further, this local engagement of all participants in the school's work would sustain attention and provide substantial support for the significant changes in classroom instruction and ultimately in student learning. This basic logic of democratic localism as a lever for school change is summarized in figure 7.1.

The Consortium of Chicago School Research has organized a long-term research agenda to probe the validity of this logic in operation.[32] Our inquiry seeks to scrutinize the core premise of the reform—is democratic localism a viable lever for revitalizing local public schools? We view the first four-year period as a systemwide initiating phase for fundamental school

176

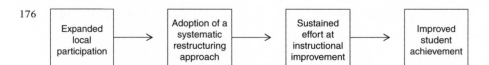

FIG. 7.1 Basic logic-in-operation of Chicago school reform

restructuring. Thus for this phase of the reform, we asked, "Was Chicago school reform mobilizing initiative in school communities to promote fundamental change in the ways schools operated?"

Specifically, we concentrated our attention on the first three boxes in figure 7.1. How were the new governance arrangements functioning in Chicago schools? Were schools using their newfound authority and resources to restructure their core operations or just making marginal changes? Was there any evidence of sustained attention toward improving teaching and strengthening instructional programs? Finally, what connections exist, if any, between the evolution of local school governance, the types of organizational changes occurring and instructional improvement efforts? That is, at the core of testing the logic of Chicago school reform during its first phase is the query: "Where expanded local participation has emerged, is there any evidence that it provides an effective lever for organizational change and instructional improvement?"

We note that from the outset we expected reform to proceed at varied rates. Some schools, especially those with talented faculties and a history of cooperative work relations with their local communities, were likely to move quickly to take advantage of the opportunities provided by reform. In other schools, however, where the base condition consists of weak faculties marred by distrust, negative community relationships, and serious problems of safety and disorder, restructuring would be more difficult to initiate and take longer to effect measurable changes. These arguments implied that we should examine the variability in outcomes among schools and that the school community (rather than the school system) should be the central unit of analysis.

Along the way, we made a couple of critical decisions that bounded our inquiry. First, we decided to limit attention only to elementary schools. On the practical side, we had assembled an extensive array of survey data and field observations for elementary schools, but the information on high schools was much more sparse. Moreover, for a variety of theoretical reasons, including the fact that high schools are larger, more complex organizations and are harder to change, a full assessment of their reform efforts might well be a very different story.[33] Second, we chose to focus primarily on those elementary schools whose average achievement levels were substantially below national norms when reform began in 1989.[34] These elementary schools, which make up 86 percent of the system, were the primary target of the school reform legislation. If this reform was of any merit, these were the places where significant changes would have to occur.

Methods and Evidence

The diverse and emergent character of Chicago school reform posed considerable problems in framing our study. Given the uniqueness of the reform, there were no extant studies of closely related phenomena that could help guide our inquiry. Thus, one key demand on the research design was for an empirically grounded framework, based on experiences in Chicago, to help conceptualize the overall investigation. Fortunately, two independent studies of the implementation of school reform had been carefully documenting the political activity and organizational changes occurring in Chicago elementary schools.[35] Through a synthesis of data from these multisite case studies, we were able to build a conceptual framework to organize our work.

Answering our research questions, however, demanded more than just a description of the main types of governance and organizational change that have occurred, as could be accomplished through a case study synthesis. We also needed to know about the frequency of each activity type and how they were related to one another. This necessitated systemwide data. For this purpose, we collected original survey information from principals and teachers and drew on extant administrative records from the school system. This allowed us to create a set of indicators of the various activities in each school and provided a basis for addressing questions about the prevalence of various reform efforts.

Third, to understand more fully the actual change processes precipitated by PA 85-1418, we need some in-depth studies of school communities that had taken advantage of the opportunities provided by reform to move

178   forward. Because these phenomena were emergent, however, no one could
tell at the outset of the reform precisely where this would occur. Thus
retrospective accounts of some of the most successful restructuring school
sites became the major third strand in our investigation.

Capsule Summary of Findings: Local School Governance

Our field studies identified four distinct patterns of political activity that had
emerged in Chicago schools during the first four years of reform. Using a set
of school indicators developed from survey information and administrative
records, we were also able to develop range estimates of the likely percentages of schools in each category.[36]

Consolidated principal power occurred when neither the faculty nor the
parents and community became active in school affairs. In essence, the local
governance structures created by PA 85-1418 were not really functional in
these schools. Thus, by default, power consolidates in the principal, who
now has considerably more authority and autonomy than before reform.
We estimated that four years into reform between 37 and 44 percent of the
elementary schools were in this category.

Adversarial politics typified school communities that were factionalized
and continuously at war about control and power. These fights tended to
have little substantive content; they were instead about personalities and
allegiances. Stalled by the struggle for power, these schools were often unable to make even very basic decisions. Between 4 and 9 percent of the
schools were of this type.

Strong democracy, in contrast, characterized school communities where
there was sustained debate about school goals, standards, and activities.
Various committees, teams, cadres, and other structures had been created
that expanded opportunities for engagement in school decision making, and
a broad base of participation was evident. Through sustained discussion, a
collaborative spirit had emerged among different interests that focused on
promoting fundamental school change. This form of school politics was the
aim of the Chicago reform. Four years into the process, this type of political
activity had clearly emerged in between 28 and 34 percent of the schools.

Maintenance politics and other mixed forms characterized the remainder of
the schools. Included in this group of between 13 and 26 percent of the

schools were contexts that could not easily be classified in terms of one of the first three types above. Some of these schools exhibited a mixture of these types; others were instances of maintenance politics.[37] In general, the prevalence of a politics focusing on maintenance of the status quo appeared very low. We interpret this as a reflection of both the widespread dissatisfaction with Chicago schools and of the more general normative character of low-income school communities—communities that are more accustomed to the paternal direction consistent with consolidated principal power than to the pluralist bargaining that is more commonplace in liberal democratic settings.

In general, the incidence of these four types of school community politics was not strongly related to schools' student composition. Strong democracy schools exist in virtually every neighborhood across the city. Adversarial politics was somewhat more likely, though, in predominantly minority schools with mixed racial and ethnic populations. Similarly, strong democratic practices occurred more frequently in small schools and in schools with more than 85 percent Hispanic students.

Capsule Summary of Findings: Organizational Restructuring

The second aspect of our analysis focused on the basic organizational changes that have occurred. Our field studies identified four distinctively different patterns here as well.

Environmental order issues took precedence in schools where safety and security posed serious problems. At the start of reform, many Chicago schools worked to develop new discipline and attendance programs. They also used their discretionary funds to buy basic supplies and to repair their building and grounds. Taking control of the physical and social environment was the main theme in these schools.

Peripheral academic changes have occurred in schools where, four years into reform, no clear academic improvement plans had emerged. New programs and personnel had been added haphazardly, without any obvious strategy and often without even considering the specific needs of students and community. Little attention had been paid to changing classroom practices in such core subjects as language arts and mathematics. Instead, allocation of discretionary resources emphasized more add-on programs.

180   *"Christmas tree" schools* were similar to peripheral academic change schools, but they have done more. These schools "looked good" because they had added numerous programs and resources, some of which might have good reputations. These additions, however, were often ill implemented and did not necessarily fit well with preexisting programs. Moreover, there was little attention to improving the overall functioning of the school as a self-guided organization—developing a capacity to plan, budget, evaluate, and analyze its own operations. As a result, although staffs were working hard, student learning did not appear to be improving.

Emergent restructuring schools, in contrast, had taken a more systemic approach to school improvement. Basic operations were changing and dysfunctional norms were being contested. Four years into reform, many teachers acknowledged that their classroom practices must change. A facilitative principal actively fostered more positive relationships with parents and community. A sense of professional community was emerging among at least some of the teachers, and new ideas were entering the school through extensive contacts with outside organizations. Although many aspects of these schools were changing at the same time, there was a sense of purpose and plan at work.

During the first year or two of reform, many schools focused on environmental order and improving the social relations in the school. Eventually, most schools moved on into one of the other three approaches. For our analysis purposes, the major distinction was between emergent restructuring, which is a systemic approach to improvement, and the two other unfocused alternatives.

Our indicator analyses found that 31 to 39 percent of Chicago's public elementary schools were pursuing unfocused school improvements. On the other hand, between 35 and 41 percent of schools had developed a systemic approach to reform. Of the remaining schools between 20 and 35 percent showed some features of both approaches. These schools appeared to be lurching toward systemic change but were not as far along.

Here, too, we encountered a very equitable pattern of distribution. Systemic restructuring can be found in both the poorest and the more advantaged schools in the city. As with strong democratic practice, both small schools and predominantly Hispanic schools were more likely to be pursuing a systemic approach. Schools with racially mixed populations were also more likely to have an unfocused approach.

Capsule Summary of Findings: Instructional Improvements

Our first phase of inquiry also explored whether schools were attending to instructional improvement. We focused on the introduction of innovations aimed at fostering higher-order thinking skills and more active forms of student learning. As reform began, only limited attention was paid to these elements in the vast majority of schools. According to principal reports, most were engaged in adding computers to the school and using more small group work, but not much else. A major upsurge of activity, however, occurred in the ensuing four years. By 1993, the majority of principals reported moderate to extensive emphasis on "authentic learning experiences" for children.[38] Students were more likely than before to encounter learning tasks emphasizing deep exposure to at least a few ideas rather than only broad superficial knowledge. They were also now more likely to engage in situations requiring them to actively inquire rather than just reproduce extant knowledge. Whereas in the past, schools have emphasized work sheets, drill, and practice, now more time was being spent on personal writing, sustained classroom discussions about ideas, and group-based projects where students were responsible for developing their own plans and carrying them through.

We also note that these positive reports about instructional innovation since reform were especially prevalent in the schools that we had identified as pursuing a systemic approach to organizational restructuring. In such schools, principals were, for example, much more likely to report a recent introduction of writing across the curriculum, literature-based reading, and efforts to introduce hands-on math and science. Again, we found a very equitable pattern of distribution across the city. No strong differences emerged with regard to racial/ethnic or income composition.

Testing the Causal Logic: Expanded Local Participation as a Lever for Systemic Change

Of primary concern in our first phase of research on Chicago school reform was the linkage question: where expanded local participation has emerged, is there any evidence that it provides an effective lever for organizational change and instructional improvement? We developed a path analysis to reflect hypothesized links from strong democratic practice to systemic

182   restructuring to instructional innovation.[39] To test this model we used our database of survey and administrative information to form a set of indicators that revealed for each school the extent to which its local governance arrangements were "strong democratic" and its organizational change could be characterized as "systemic," as well as whether by 1993 a strong emphasis on instructional innovation was present. We also entered controls into the analysis for a wide range of school context and key structural features (for example, school size), as well as for retrospective reports about restructuring activity in each school prior to reform.

As we have seen, the progress of reform in Chicago has not been strongly influenced by school context. The path analysis further confirms these findings. The overall pattern of association is quite weak between basic school characteristics and the three central elements in the logic of the reform. One can literally find a school in almost every neighborhood of the city where broad local participation has sustained attention to fundamental organizational changes, including instructional improvement. In this regard, the effects of Chicago's reform have been quite equitable.

Not surprisingly, the level of restructuring activity in schools prior to reform is positively related to strong democratic practice, systemic restructuring, and particularly instructional innovation. Schools that had begun to adopt more authentic learning experiences prior to reform have expanded and deepened these experiences during the reform process.

Even after adjusting for these differences, however, the results of our path analysis firmly support the primacy of the central connections of interest-school politics, organizational change, and instructional improvement. The statistical link between strong democracy and systemic restructuring is especially strong. Activist school politics appears to be key to adoption of a more focused approach toward improvement. Similarly, schools that approached organizational change in a systemic fashion were more likely to have introduced classroom practices that placed students as active participants in the learning process.

We note that no direct statistical connection between strong democracy and instructional improvement was evident. The actual impact of strong democratic politics on instructional change appears to depend upon the development of a systemic restructuring that includes such key features as strategic planning, greater teacher involvement in an emerging professional community, and stronger school-community ties. Absent such organizational developments, strong democratic practice does not by itself stimulate greater instructional innovation.

What Role Did Local Democratic Enablement Really Play?

The statistical evidence summarized above links the emergence of a strong local democratic practice, sustained attention on school restructuring, and instructional innovation. We know that these processes are interconnected, but through what mechanisms does this occur? Our in-depth field studies of actively restructuring Chicago schools provided insights.

It is important to recognize that Chicago's reform was a complex piece of legislation. It included a number of provisions to directly promote school improvement in addition to establishing local school governance arrangements. Some of these school-improvement provisions may also have had the effect of expanding local participation. In this sense, one might be tempted to reverse the causal arrow in the logic of Chicago of school reform detailed above—that is, an improving organization might actually promote more participation. In at least three important ways, however, democratic localism acted as a critical catalyst for change.

RECASTING THE PRINCIPALSHIP TO PROMOTE ENTREPRENEURIAL BEHAVIOR

In order to vitalize local control (and to curtail substantially the direct administrative control of the central office), reform sought to make principals locally accountable. It advanced this goal by eliminating principals' tenure and placing them on four-year performance contracts subject to LSC review. The reshaping of the principalship that ensued from this policy initiative was a key factor in fostering systemic change. In actively restructuring schools, the principal was the direct and immediate link through which the expanded local participation influenced school activity. The beliefs and actions of these persons provided a powerful conduit for the school community's political activity to enter the formal school organization and redirect its efforts.

In most general terms, making principals accountable to local constituents—not only parents and community members but also teachers—fundamentally altered the system of sanctions and incentives affecting the

184 principalship. Principals have become local entrepreneurs of values, ideas, and money.[40] This behavior is now publicly endorsed both in school communities and more generally around the city.

SOCIAL SUPPORT FOR FUNDAMENTAL CHANGE

In schools with strong democratic politics, we found sustained discussion among local participants about the need for fundamental change. Actions by principals and other school professionals toward these ends were encouraged and supported. In the past, school professionals might have taken refuge behind some central office mandate or rule, even if it was dysfunctional. Now they were more likely to challenge such external constraints in the interest of moving their schools forward.

In short, reform expanded the moral authority of local professionals to act in the school community's interests. It created processes and structures that encouraged interactions among parents, community members, and local professionals, all of whom had been silenced previously by a highly centralized bureaucracy. To the extent that these groups were able to sustain a positive engagement around shared concerns, the reform tapped a powerful mobilizing agent that resides in such public conversations. At base here is the moral force of a social movement.[41] As local professionals engaged other local constituents, they recognized that they were not alone. In conversations with parents and community members, a nucleus of school leaders emerged who shared a deep dissatisfaction with current affairs. In this collective solidarity, they found strength to act.

OPENING UP THE FLOW OF IDEAS

A major tenet of the school restructuring movement is that schools must become learning organizations. By weakening central office control over schools and legitimizing the participation of parents, community, and local professionals in school-based decision making, reform opened up these organizational learning processes. The embrace of democratic localism promoted an expanded equality whereby teachers, parents, and community members brought improvement plans to the table. As a result, the number of channels by which new ideas enter schools has increased substantially.

In addition to legitimizing an expanded access to ideas, reform also created numerous forums, such as the LSC, PPAC, and other derivative com-

mittees, where ideas could be publicly discussed and might eventually come
to be collectively endorsed. In the past, individual teachers might introduce
notions about innovation in their own classrooms and might even collaborate with a few close colleagues, but there were few structured opportunities for these initiatives to diffuse more broadly through the organization.
Contexts for meaningful cooperation of local professionals with parents and
community members were even less common. These discussion contexts
have expanded substantially.

Thus the two major components of organizational learning—access to
outside ideas and internal structures that facilitate their diffusion through
the school community—have both been significantly influenced by Chicago's embrace of democratic localism. A major strength of the Chicago
reform is that it legitimized this activity and created at least some initial
structures through which it might develop, accompanied with a strong ex-
hortation for local actors to "get involved."

Developments Under Chicago School Reform, 1993–1996

The Chicago School Reform Act of 1988 sought a complete reorganization
of our nation's third-largest school system. By 1993 parents, community
leaders, teachers, and principals had joined together in many communities
to take advantage of the resources and the opportunities offered by school
reform in order to institute broad and deep changes that aim to revitalize
their schools. In other places, however, the progress of reform had been a bit
slower and more uneven. And in still others there was little sense that
schools were moving forward.

We estimate that in the elementary schools where student assessments
were below national norms prior to reform, about one third developed
strong democratic participation within the school community that focused
on a systemic approach to school improvement. Another third or slightly
more had some of these characteristics but were not as far along in the process. At least a quarter of the schools in the system, however, still appeared
"dead in the water" four years into reform. Although these schools welcomed the additional authority and discretionary resources, there were no
indications of extended local participation or any strategic use of the opportunities provided by reform to advance significant local improvements.

186 Moreover, there was little reason to believe that most of these schools would improve if left to their own devices. These schools appeared to be left behind by reform.

Efforts to Transform the System Center, 1994

A major conclusion of the consortium's 1993 report, *A View from the Elementary Schools: The State of Reform in Chicago,* was that Chicago had probably already realized as much impact from the 1988 legislation as was likely to occur without genuine reform at "Pershing Road"—the system's central office. Although PA 85-1418 had mandated a range of central initiatives to complement local empowerment, the central office had been slow to take up these responsibilities during the first four years of reform. School personnel continued to complain, often bitterly, about central office obstruction to local improvement efforts. Although the Pershing Road office was officially rechristened Central Support Services, its organization in 1993 was not fundamentally different from that prior to reform. There were fewer employees at Pershing Road, but they continued to function as if they were the control center of a large bureaucracy, and most still thought about themselves in these terms. In addition, a complex pluralist politics among board members, outside interests, and long-term senior staff continued to frustrate the policy development that was necessary to support the decentralization.

In addition, even in the schools that we had documented as moving forward under reform, most local participants felt that student achievement was not what it should be.[42] Much greater systemwide commitment and support were needed for professional development, more time had to be created for this activity (without subtracting from instruction), and a new infrastructure had to emerge to support such development in what was increasingly becoming a more diverse system of schools. Similarly, an accountability system had to be built. The CPS had no capacity to identify the schools left behind by reform or to intervene in these communities to catalyze change. More generally, the entire system of collective bargaining agreements, school code, and system policy needed to be reexamined with an eye toward building incentives and removing barriers for school development. The role of sanctions in system policy also needed to be reassessed. A dysfunctional local school could hide behind a mantle of local autonomy even when no viable local governance had emerged and no serious improvement efforts were being attempted. Grossly incompetent teachers also remained well protected by their union, while the central office asserted little leadership to change the state of affairs.

Our 1993 report on the state of school reform was released just as a new superintendent, Argie Johnson, took office. This change of leadership, coupled with the message of our report, opened the door for business activists and community advocacy groups to renew the push for structural change at the system center. With substantial local foundation support, a restructuring of the central office was initiated. A major corporate reengineering firm, CSC Index, was selected to guide this effort.[43] CSC organized what was originally intended as a multiyear process involving extensive stakeholder consultation to fundamentally redesign both the business and education sides of the Central Service Center. This work, however, was overtaken by political events. Republicans took control of both houses of the state legislature in the fall of 1994. Encouraged by the Republican governor, this legislative leadership quickly proclaimed its own "one hundred–day agenda," of which further Chicago school reform was a major element. Suddenly, initiative had again shifted away from Chicago to Springfield, but now the key political actors had changed in very significant ways. Reforming the system center had been the unfinished business of 1988, and the time was right to move. In addition, the unions, which had been protected by Democratic leadership in 1988, became a vulnerable point of attack.

The Chicago School Reform Act of 1995: "Reform II"

In the spring of 1995 the Illinois State Legislature passed a second major Chicago school reform bill, which rivaled the original 1988 legislation in both size and complexity. The 1995 act described a "school system in crisis," unable to solve its own policy and budget problems. The governance and managerial layers at the top of the system needed overhaul, and strong medicine was prescribed. Tantamount to the imposition of a bureaucratic martial law, the act ceded vast powers and responsibilities to the mayor for control over the Chicago school system, including direct appointment of all board members. It created a new administrative structure that vested

188   substantial powers in a chief executive officer, who was directly appointed
by the mayor and replaced the superintendent.[44] The complex maintenance
politics that had strangled past central office reform initiatives was suddenly
replaced by a seemingly unitary voice. To be sure, the diverse political interest groups that pressed on the old board of education have not disappeared.
Much of the decision making now occurs, however, in close consultation
with the mayor's office. Moreover, once a policy initiative is formulated by
the chief executive officer, it tends to move very quickly into implementation. New policy activity at Pershing Road proliferated rapidly during the
first nine months after Reform II.

The 1995 act also extended budget and accounting flexibility to the
school system, in essence setting aside many of the stringent provisions
established by the School Finance Authority in its watchdog role over system affairs.[45] In addition, it struck down numerous restrictions on collective
bargaining that had previously been preserved in state law through the
efforts of various unions. The legislation granted substantial new degrees of
freedom for policy activity by the new board and chief executive officer.

It also substantially extended central authority to identify and intervene
in nonimproving schools. Under the 1988 law, central office action could be
initiated only through a cumbersome "bubble-up process" involving subdistrict councils. These subdistrict councils, and the subdistrict superintendents whom they in turn selected, were eliminated by the new legislation.
Specific provisions were incorporated to permit school reconstitution; for
cause, the chief executive officer can vacate an LSC, terminate a principal's
contract, and revoke teacher tenure in these schools. A governance mechanism for a new accountability council was also established and charged with
developing and implementing a plan of periodic review of all CPS schools.
In this regard, the legislature made a second attempt at structuring a viable
accountability process for a decentralized system of schools.

In October 1996, just weeks after the opening of the new school year, the
president and the chief executive officer of the school system announced
that 109 of the 557 public schools in Chicago were being placed on probation because of poor academic performance. Under its new statutory powers
the board of education could implement a range of corrective actions from
removing staff to shutting down institutions entirely if improvements were
not realized within a year. Another 25 schools were identified for a less
aggressive form of oversight referred to as remediation.[46]

From one perspective, the developments described above might be char- acterized as a recentralization of the system. Clearly central authority was reframed and, in some situations, like the authority to intervene in failing schools, substantially extended. On the other hand, the democratic localism, at the heart of PA 85-1418, was also sustained by the new legislation and strengthened in several important ways. Efforts were made, for example, to improve LSC function by assuring training for new LSC members. (This had been required under PA 85-1418 but was never implemented.) Principals' powers were extended to include supervisory and personnel evaluation responsibility over all school site staff. A cumbersome process for removing incompetent staff, which had been a major complaint of principals, was also further streamlined. Schools were also assured that their primary source of discretionary funds, state Chapter I dollars, could not be cut in order to balance the system budget.

In sum, the 1995 legislation sought both to redress some problems in local school governance that had emerged since 1988 and to create a more productive policy-making and administrative support structure at the top of the system. Although many reform activists continue to worry about the long-term consequences of the extraordinary concentration of power in the mayor's office, the local media have offered consistently positive articles and editorials about recent central initiatives. In general, the implementation of this legislation is still just beginning, and it is too early to tell how its various aspects will ultimately unfold. See table 7.2 for additional details about the 1995 legislation.

The Ultimate Benchmark: A Status Report on Student Achievement

Aggregate trends in student achievement are the "thirty-second sound bite" of any school reform. As noted earlier, such trends are not very informative during the early stages of a systemwide decentralization effort. Deep structural changes in individual schools are likely to take several years to unfold, and it is not until such developments occur on a wide scale that we might expect to see a positive signal in aggregate systemwide trends. Moreover, the first four years of Chicago's reform were marred by central office resistance, chronic budget crises, delayed school openings, and threats of teachers strikes. Often schools did not know how much discretionary money they would actually be allowed to spend until well after the school year

TABLE 7.2 Primer on Chicago School Reform II

Turnaround management and governance structure mandated for four years
   Eliminates existing school board, board nominating committee,
      superintendent, subdistrict councils, and subdistrict superintendents
   Suspends the financial and administrative oversight of School Finance
      Authority
   In the year 2000, system reverts back to board and superintendent structure,
      with oversight by the School Finance Authority

New central office modeled on corporation
   Mayor-appointed five-member Reform Board of Trustees
   Mayor-appointed corporate-style management team
      Chief executive officer
      Chief financial officer
      Chief operating officer
      Chief educational officer
      Chief purchasing officer

Clarifies the authority of the chief executive officer to determine and enforce
accountability in schools in crisis
   Extends authority to chief executive officer and chief educational officer to
      fire, lay off, or reassign employees (including disbanding of the local school
      council) at schools determined to be in crisis and requiring intervention
   Sets aside 5% of an intervention school's state Chapter 1 funds as an
      employee incentive fund
   Authorizes chief executive officer to conduct an annual evaluation of all
      principals in consultation with the LSC; those found unsatisfactory may be
      terminated
   Authorizes chief executive officer to supervise inspector general, who
      investigates waste, fraud, financial mismanagement of LSC members,
      contractors, and central office (inspector general previously employee of SFA)

Establishes a new school accountability mechanism for the CPS
   Creates Academic Accountability Council—appointed by trustees in
      consultation with State Board of Education—to develop and implement
      a regular system for review, evaluation, and analysis of all schools'
      performance, and to determine a course of action for nonimproving
      schools
   Evaluations made by the Academic Accountability Council may recommend
      future school improvement and plan initiation of remediation, probation,
      intervention, or closure of schools not meeting academic standards

Support for school-site decision making and principal authority strengthened
   Changes service of local school council members from two-year terms to
      four-year staggered terms

TABLE 7.2 *Continued*

Mandates three days of university-provided training for all LSC members within six months of taking office

Authorizes LSCs to approve school hours, schedule staff and facilities use, and approve expenditures and receipts, in accordance with board rules and policies

Freezes state Chapter 1 funds to local school councils at 1995 levels

Authorizes principals to evaluate and discipline all school employees, including engineers and food service managers, and recommend them to trustees for employment, discharge, or layoff

Grants board of trustees expanded flexibility in use of system funds

Consolidates 7 separate school property tax levies into single operating levy

Consolidates 25 state categorical funding streams into two block grants with broad flexibility to spend them (bilingual, transportation, free lunch, preschool, special education, summer school, service centers, and administrator's academy all continue to be required by state, but all others may be eliminated or expanded)

Chicago Board of Education allowed to carry unfunded liabilities for the teachers' pension fund from now until 2045

Privatization encouraged

Allows any and all functions (central and school-based) to be outsourced in contracts up to five years in length

Decision of the board or an LSC to privatize is not subject to collective bargaining

Allows employees to be dismissed within 14 days if privatization makes their work redundant

Eliminates all previous statutes that restrict privatization

Collective Bargaining Limited

Prohibits strikes for 18 months

Eliminates reserve teacher clause; teachers found redundant by a school are no longer guaranteed employment by the CPS

Removes 13 educational issues from collective bargaining table, including class size, assignments, academic calendar, layoff or staff reduction decisions, charter school, contract and pilot program decisions

Authorizes schools to waive any collective bargaining agreement by a vote of 51% of the school's faculty

Sources: Illinois 89th General Assembly Conference Committee Report on House Bill 206 (1995); Lawyers' School Reform Advisory Project (1995), "Description of 'The Governor's Plan' (summary of House Bill 206)," Lawyers' School Reform Advisory Project, Chicago; Paul Williams, Memo/summary on House Bill 206, Paul L. Williams Law Offices, Chicago, 1995.

192   began. These were far from ideal environments for launching a major reform. Nonetheless, no reporting of the Chicago reform would be complete
without at least a cursory look at these data.

The Illinois Goals Assessment Program (IGAP) tests elementary and high
school students in a variety of subject areas. Trend data exist at grades 3, 6,
and 8 for reading since 1988, for mathematics since 1989, and for writing
since 1990 (see figures 7.2, 7.3, and 7.4).[47] Chicago has observed systemwide increases in mathematics at all three elementary levels over the past
three years. Similarly, writing scores have been trending up across all three
grades since the inception of this assessment.

How to interpret these positive trends, however, is unclear. These two
subject areas have been the focus of considerable externally organized professional development.[48] These activities have operated largely independent of the CPS and have been funded with a combination of external
resources and some discretionary dollars from individual school budgets.
Although this local school allocation can be viewed as a reform effect—
because reform gave schools the necessary authority—others might argue
that these gains could have been accomplished without the democratic
localism at the heart of the Chicago reform. In general, without a more
detailed analysis of which schools are actually improving and the factors
contributing to their improvement, it is unclear to whom or to what we
should attribute these positive trends.

Counterbalancing these positive reports in math and writing are negative
trends in reading on the IGAP, especially at grade 3. The latter represents
about a half–standard deviation drop systemwide between 1990 and 1994.
This general decline in reading scores across the elementary grades would
be alarming if it were mirrored in the citywide assessments based on the
Iowa Tests of Basic Skills, ITBS. But figure 7.5, which displays ITBS trends
from 1990 through 1995, shows the same bump up after 1993 as observed
in math on both the IGAP and ITBS.

Moreover, the reading test score decline is statewide, leading Illinois
Board of Education officials to commission an independent evaluation and
audit of the IGAP reading assessment program. We should also note that the
ITBS and IGAP reading tests have a mutual correlation of about .8, depending upon the particular grade in question. Thus this is not a case of two tests

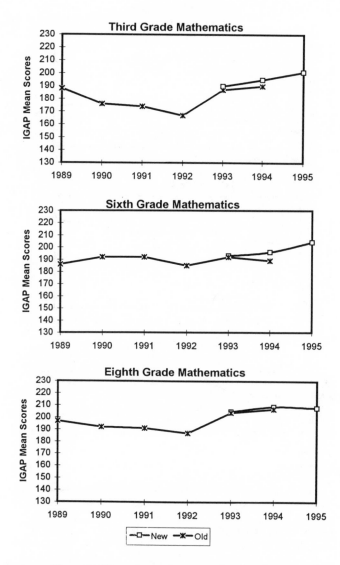

FIG. 7.2 Mean IGAP mathematics scores for the Chicago Public Schools

Note: In 1993 the equating procedure used to calculate IGAP scores was changed. As the new scores are not directly comparable with the old, both sets of scores are presented here.

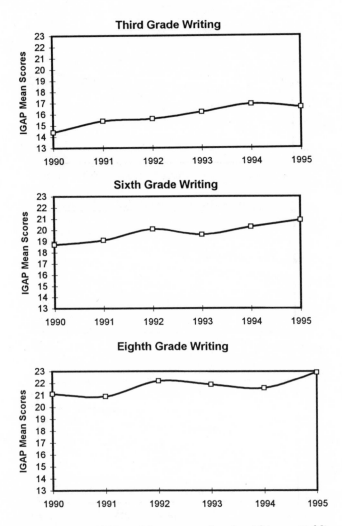

FIG. 7.3 Mean IGAP writing scores for the Chicago Public Schools

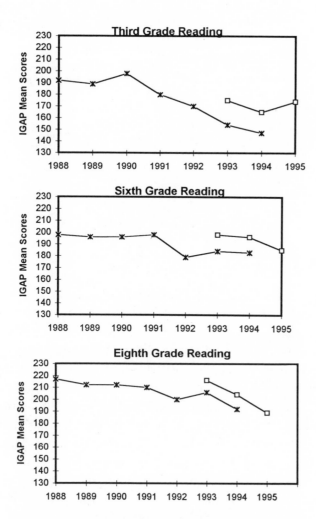

FIG. 7.4 Mean IGAP reading scores for the Chicago Public Schools

Note: In 1993 the equating procedure used to calculate IGAP scores was changed. As the new scores are not directly comparable with the old, both sets of scores are presented here.

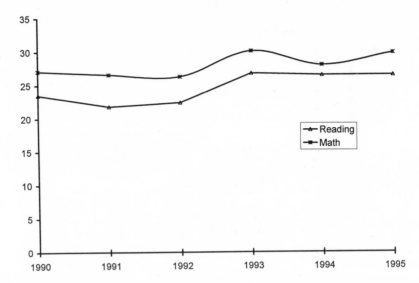

FIG. 7.5 ITBS reading and math, 1990–1995: percentage of third- through eighth-grade Chicago Public School students at or above national norms

measuring something fundamentally different. Rather, this anomaly appears to be a function of a variety of such factors as execution of the across-level and across-form equations, changing subject matter content over time in the reading tests, and changing directions of test administration directions.

Embedded in this experience is a very important lesson. Trends in test scores are often not the stable baselines for marking progress that the public has been led to believe. Idiosyncratic cross-time variation is intrinsic in the nature of these testing programs. At this point, the only clear conclusion that can be drawn is that the data conflict, the causes of the conflict are unclear, and interpretation of trends is uncertain.

MOVING BEYOND AGGREGATE TRENDS

A basic question still remains. What is appropriate evidence for making early judgments about the impact of a decentralization reform on student learning in a system of schools? As we have shown, trends in system-average test scores are a very blunt indicator of progress in a reform that is predicated on changing schools "one at a time." Especially in the first stages of reform, we expect variability in improvement in student learning as a corollary of the variability in school progress with restructuring. At a mini-

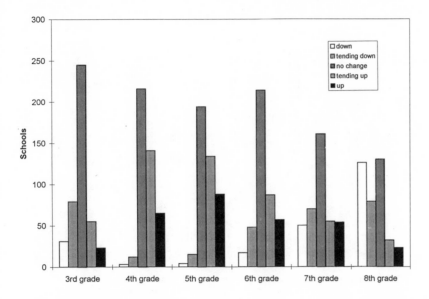

FIG. 7.6 ITBS reading, school trends

mum, then, trends in student achievement should be disaggregated by school. In addition, overall student achievement is unlikely to improve suddenly. Rather, initial improvements are likely to be limited to selected grade levels and subject matters. That is, all teachers cannot change all of their instruction at once, and even if they could, few schools have the resources to simultaneously support both acquisition of new textbooks and instructional materials and intensive professional developments across all grades and subject matters. This suggests that we have to further disaggregate trends by subject matter and grade.

Figures 7.6 and 7.7 present such data for reading and mathematics achievement for all Chicago public elementary schools from 1990 to 1995. For each grade (3 through 8) in each school, the grade level trend over this five-year period is classified as "up" (or "down") if it has achieved, on average, a 0.1 grade equivalent improvement (or a 0.1 grade equivalent decline) per year. This is tantamount to about a 50 percent increase (or decrease) in student achievement in that grade over the five years.[49] Similarly, a grade level in a given school is classified as "tending up" or "tending down" if at least a 25 percent change in productivity has been recorded. All others are classified as "no change."

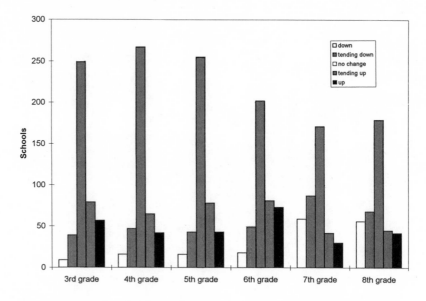

FIG. 7.7 ITBS math, school trends

In general, the no-change category is most prevalent for all grade levels in reading and math. The percentage of schools in this group ranges from a high of about 60 percent in fourth-grade math to a low of 30 percent for eighth-grade reading. For most of the grades and subjects, about 50 percent of the schools are in this category. On the positive side, there are considerably more schools trending up than down in both reading and math up through grade 6. Somewhat counterbalancing, however, is a larger number of downward trends in grades 7 and 8.

Again, the issue of how to properly interpret these results leaves us in a bit of a quandary. Proponents of reform might reasonably argue that these data are consistent with the idea of growing reform not only "one school at a time" but also growing it up from the primary through the middle into the upper elementary grades. From this perspective, we just have not given reform long enough for the kick up in grades 7 and 8 to emerge. Again, however, without much more information about the actual reform activities occurring in each school, we are left uncertain.

Further, even with more school-level data, the picture would still remain clouded. In addition to the onset of reform, many other factors have changed coterminous with reform and must also be taken into account in our anal-

ysis. For example, the student population in the CPS has become more disadvantaged over the past ten years. (Maintaining a constant level of aggregate
achievement in the face of such an impediment implies that school productivity is actually increasing.[50]) We also know that the school system retention
policy changed during this period, with many students who formerly would
have been retained in grade now being promoted. Also, a new policy went
into effect on the testing of bilingual children. As a result, many of these
children who were not tested prior to reform are now included. Clearly these
factors have an impact on both the aggregate and school-grade levels.

Finally and most problematic of all is the issue of student mobility. In a
typical Chicago elementary school, only 75 percent of the children tested in
a given school in a particular year were tested in the same school the previous spring.[51] In some schools, this stability rate is less than 50 percent.
Trends in average student achievement, even when disaggregated by school
and grade level, can be highly misleading under these circumstances. A
school may be adding a lot to student learning, but if the school has a
continuous influx of weak students (as do schools in "port of entry neighborhoods" in Chicago), we are likely to miss these positive effects. That is,
the learning of students who are under instruction in a school may be
improving, but these gains can be obscured by student mobility. Even when
schools are succeeding, average test scores can decline.[52]

In general, in order to make a valid inference about the performance of a
school, we need to assess how much children are learning while enrolled in
the school, how much the school has contributed to this development, and
whether this "value added" is increasing over time. This means assessing the
gain in student learning rather than in achievement status, adjusting these
gains in turn for changes over time in the various confounding factors.[53]

In sum, the casual examination of test scores, as often occurs in media
accounts of school reform, is more likely to misinform than enlighten. We
are currently in the midst of an analysis of value-added trends for the
CPS that attempts to take seriously both the various psychometric problems
and confounding factors. Our experiences to date with these efforts, however, leave us far from sanguine about the potential of these data to mean-
ingfully inform.

The Chicago School Reform Act of 1988 launched an undertaking of
enormous scope that is still in the process of unfolding. Only time will tell

200 how much of the improvement that we have observed to date will eventually be institutionalized in restructured operations and a new organizational culture, which taken together mark an effective institution that is responsive to its community.

As for the early phase, however, the record appears clear. We have amassed considerable evidence that supports the basic premise of the reform. Our analyses strongly support the conclusion that weakening central office control and promoting local democratic enablement is an effective lever for catalyzing basic organizational change. Moreover, the content of this conversation is evolving and these changing understandings are influencing policy. In 1990 attention focused almost exclusively on the formation and training of LSCs. Now discourse has shifted to the kinds of additional resources and institutional supports needed by local schools to effect substantive changes in classrooms. It is a dynamic conversation that has the feel and form of a social movement.[54] Moreover, like a social movement, its character is fluid and its course can be fully discerned only in hindsight. The process is still very much unfolding, and its final form has yet to emerge. In a very real sense, "Reform II" was an outgrowth of this process.

Although we still cannot know whether this will translate into widespread improvements in student learning, these first steps must be viewed as productive developments. Against a historical backdrop on which urban schools have often seemed impervious to reform, we judge the success of democratic localism in catalyzing basic organizational changes at the school-building level as a significant accomplishment.[55]

8

Successful
School-Based
Management:
A Lesson for
Restructuring
Urban Schools

Priscilla Wohlstetter, Susan Albers Mohrman,

and Peter J. Robertson

School systems, bureaucratically structured to emphasize productivity and efficiency, are failing to meet the educational needs of our youth. They have failed to adequately prepare large numbers of students, particularly those in the inner city, to become productive, gainfully employed members of society. The educational model using standardized approaches to teaching and learning has not dealt effectively with the diversity of students that our urban schools confront. Many students are not developing adequate basic skills, let alone the complex cognitive reasoning capabilities increasingly required in today's and tomorrow's society.

Answers to this challenge have not been forthcoming from the remote and impersonal bureaucracies in which schools are embedded. There has been a loud cry for reform, and many reform plans have called for returning

202   control of the schools to local school communities. Among the major approaches to restructuring is school-based management (SBM), which features a change in the governance system of a school district by decentralizing decision-making authority from the district's central administration to local schools as a means for stimulating school improvement.[1] SBM programs aim to give school constituents—administrators, teachers, parents, and other community members—more control over what happens in schools. The ultimate goal of most SBM programs is to enhance school performance and the quality of education provided to students.

SBM has become a popular reform in public school districts across the country. In recent years, thousands of districts across the United States have experimented with some form of SBM. By 1993, more than 95 percent of the fifty largest urban school districts in the United States had SBM programs in at least some of their schools.[2] Similar efforts have been adopted in Australia, Canada, France, Japan, New Zealand, and the United Kingdom. Some measure of local school control is included in a number of models of high-performance schools, including Ronald Edmonds's Effective Schools Model, Henry Levin's Accelerated Schools, James Comer's School Development Program, and Theodore Sizer's Essential Schools.[3]

Across school districts, SBM appears in many different forms; its impetus, structure, and substance vary considerably. In some districts, like Milwaukee; Jefferson County, Kentucky; and Prince William County, Virginia, SBM was initiated by the superintendent as part of a districtwide improvement strategy. In other districts—Dade County, Florida, and Los Angeles, for example—SBM came through the collective bargaining process, as an agreement between the teachers union and the district in an implicit power-for-dollars trade-off. Finally, the impetus for SBM in some cities came from outside the district, either mandated by the governor, as in Denver, or the state legislature, as in Illinois and Texas. SBM programs also differ in the extent to which there are formal constraints on local schools concerning the form that SBM should take. In some cases there are contractual or governmentally determined parameters and restrictions on such issues as when schools adopt SBM and who at the school site has decision-making authority. In other cases, schools are allowed to make such decisions within broad guidelines.

Although SBM programs typically include the establishment of a site council, the council is constituted differently in different districts. In Chicago, for example, community members are the predominant force on the council, holding a majority of seats. In other districts, like Jefferson County and Rochester, New York, teachers constitute the majority and community members are minimally represented. Schools in Edmonton, Alberta, and Prince William County have principal-based management. In such districts, although councils are not required, principals usually are encouraged to get input from a variety of community and teacher task teams; in general councils exist at these principal-based SBM schools also, at least in an advisory capacity. In high schools, students are often included on school-site councils.

Across school districts, there are various representation and selection schema for site council members in SBM schools. In some cases, teachers are elected to the council to represent different segments of the teaching staff, such as a department in a high school or a grade level in an elementary school. In other cases, teachers are elected at large and expected to take a schoolwide perspective on issues. Likewise, parents and students are sometimes elected and sometimes appointed—either to represent a particular constituency (for example, parents involved in Title I programs or students of the senior class) or to speak for parents or students as a whole.

The level and domains of authority transferred to individual schools also vary considerably.[4] The most comprehensive SBM programs allow schools to decide how money is spent and who works at the school, in addition to educational decisions related to the curriculum. However, even the most ambitious of these plans are constrained by collective bargaining contracts. In addition, often curricular directions and broad instructional goals are determined outside the school by the district or by the state through curriculum frameworks and student assessment systems. Thus, with regard to educational decisions, SBM schools have considerable authority over how the curriculum is delivered but comparatively little over the content. Many SBM programs also feature deregulation provisions, whereby schools can expand their scope of authority by applying for waivers from district or state requirements.

Although specifics of SBM programs vary considerably, a common set of beliefs about the efficacy of SBM as an approach to school improvement usually underpins the decision to implement such a program. Proponents of SBM suggest that transferring decision-making authority to schools carries several benefits: (1) SBM enables the school to tailor decisions to the community it serves, thus promoting a more effective application of limited resources than is possible when a centralized bureaucracy makes

204 systemwide decisions; (2) SBM involves more perspectives in decision making, thus leading to better decisions; and (3) SBM empowers school-level participants, thereby creating ownership and commitment to decisions and generating energy for school improvement.

SBM has been so widely adopted that if transferring decisions to the local school were all it takes to improve schools, widespread improvement would be well under way in many districts. Yet the few published studies of SBM have found little impact on school outcomes.[5] One interpretation is that as schools gain more experience with SBM, they will be better able to use school-based processes to improve school performance.[6] Another perspective on the disappointing record of SBM is that the transfer of decision making to the local school, while an important component of school reform, is not sufficient to lead to the adoption of new approaches to educating youth. Developing the context for school improvement also requires the development of school capacity for improvement as well as building an incentive structure for the hard work of innovation and continuous improvement.[7] Thus, school-based management needs to be much more than a change in governance. When done effectively, it constitutes a redesign of the whole school organization such that it becomes a self-improving unit. According to this interpretation, the disappointing results of SBM reflect a failure to build local capacity at the school site for improvement.

We explored these issues in the course of a four-year study of SBM in thirty schools in nine districts in the United States: Bellevue, Washington; Chicago; Denver; Jefferson County, Kentucky; Milwaukee; Prince William County, Virginia; Rochester, New York; San Diego; and Sweetwater (National City), California. We also visited fourteen schools in Edmonton, Alberta, and Victoria, Australia. We focused primarily on urban school districts with student populations of more than sixty thousand. Many of the schools in our sample had a large percentage of students who were eligible for free and reduced lunch. A large number of the schools had a substantial population of English as a second language students and included students of many different ethnic backgrounds. Most of these schools were struggling to meet the needs of their changing populations and had been operating under SBM for at least four years, some of them much longer than that. Finally, the sample districts represented the variety of forms of SBM—principal-based management, community control, and teacher control or administrative decentralization.

The overall intent of our research was to discover what role, if any, SBM played in improving school performance. Thus, we selected sample districts that had devolved real decision-making authority to school sites in the areas of budget, personnel, and curriculum to ensure that the phenomenon we wanted to study—SBM—was in fact in place. It is important to note, however, that across SBM districts reform efforts are sometimes hindered by districts' unwillingness to turn over real power to schools. In the present study, where schools did have real power, we focused on identifying the organizational conditions that helped schools use SBM to bring about changes in teaching and learning. In particular, we examined those factors that enhanced the school's capacity for continuous learning and ongoing improvement. The hypothesis guiding our research was that SBM would lead to improved school performance if the school organization changed (a) in ways that motivated and enabled school people to become involved in making decisions that affected school performance and (b) in ways that promoted the school as a learning community so that school people could collectively learn about new ways of operating and of improving teaching and learning. Our premise was that schools had to develop and try out new approaches to meet the more stringent educational requirements in a changing society and to meet the needs of a changing population of students. To learn how the schools in our sample successfully used SBM to promote educational reform, we conducted site visits over a two-year period and interviewed more than five hundred people, from school board members, superintendents, and associate superintendents in district offices to principals, teachers, parents, and students in schools.[8]

Given the range and diversity of the districts, schools, and forms of school-based management that were included in our analysis, we believe that the lessons learned from this research effort are generalizable to most schools wishing to use SBM to bring about significant improvement in school performance.

Lessons About Successful SBM

The analyses of our data led us to differentiate between schools that were actively using SBM to generate significant restructuring efforts and schools that were struggling in their use of SBM as a governance mechanism and/ or as a means through which to introduce reform in their approaches to

206   teaching and learning. We generated a number of findings regarding the differences between these actively restructuring and struggling schools. We have drawn upon these findings to identify a number of lessons for schools and districts.

LESSON 1

Empower administrators, teachers, parents, and other school constituents by organizing a series of teams or work groups that facilitate widespread involvement.

Finding 1a Schools that were actively restructuring typically dispersed power broadly throughout the school organization and used councils to co-ordinate the efforts of various stakeholders involved in the decision-making process. Struggling schools, on the other hand, tended to concentrate power in the school-site council and got bogged down in power struggles.

    The actively restructuring schools involved a variety of stakeholders in school governance, including individuals from the community. Schools that were most successful were those where staff, parents, and even sometimes students were involved in making decisions. The involvement of all of these school constituents was important for building a school community committed to restructuring, a prevalent finding in other SBM research.[9] In our actively restructuring schools, this widespread involvement was accomplished through the use of subcommittees to the council that were open to membership by interested parents or teachers, and through actively including teacher teams in the consensus-building process for school decisions. Multiple teacher-led decision-making teams were created that cut across the school both horizontally (that is, subschool, grade level) and vertically (math, science, language arts, and discipline) to involve a broad range of school-level constituents in the decision-making process. In addition to being members of grade-level and subject area teams, teachers also were members of council subcommittees and other schoolwide committees addressing a site priority or goal. In these schools, it was common to have teachers working on two or more committees. For example, an elementary teacher might serve on a vertical work team, in which representatives of all grades address a subject area or a school goal, and a horizontal grade-level or subject-area team.

    These decision-making groups, set up to address such topics as curriculum, assessment, and professional development, also helped focus partici- pants' energy on specific tasks rather than on such abstractions as "culture" or "empowerment." In the schools where SBM worked and led to innovations in teaching and learning, the decision-making groups tended to be structured formally, with assigned members and regular meeting times. Because many committees cut across grade level and subject areas, there was wide awareness of the needs of the school as a whole and much more ownership of decisions.

The most effective school councils were those that served largely to coordinate and integrate the activities of the various decision-making groups operating throughout the school, which David also found in her studies of SBM.[10] These councils provided direction for the changes taking place and allocated resources to support them, focusing on the needs of the school as a whole rather than on the needs of individual academic departments or teaching teams. Because whole faculties were involved in the decision-making process, not only the select few on the council, the multiple teams and subcommittees also reduced the workload of council members and broadened the commitment to reform.

Struggling schools, on the other hand, tended to concentrate power in a single school council that often was composed of a small group of committed teachers who were painfully aware they did not have broad representation. These schools claimed that power was dispersed, but subcommittees tended to be stalled and councils got bogged down in establishing power relationships. As a result, struggling schools often were preoccupied with which stakeholder group had control instead of how best to manage, which led to unfocused reform efforts.[11] Turf wars between teacher groups and conflict between teachers and administrators over teacher participation in staff development and school priorities were observed frequently in these schools. One struggling school spent almost a year developing a policy manual that specified who had power and under what conditions. Further, subcommittees and other decision-making groups (if they existed at all) did not have wide participation, so the committed few often felt exhausted and burned out. At the same time, the teachers who were not involved experienced strong feelings of isolation and alienation in the absence of meetings that allowed them to work with other stakeholders on specific projects, such as the development of a schoolwide portfolio assessment system.

208 *Finding 1b* The network of decision-making groups in the actively restructuring schools resulted in a rich connectedness among participants and supported school-level learning activities focused on the school as a whole. These benefits were not found at the struggling schools.

The actively restructuring schools had rich informational linkages and connectedness among participants, including practice-based learning that allowed people to learn from others' experiences and points of view.[12] These linkages have also been found to "encourage teachers to see their schools as friendly and caring places."[13] In our actively restructuring schools, this connectedness among school participants was enabled by the network of decision-making forums, common planning periods, and collaborative teaching teams. In addition, it occurred informally in shared office areas and teachers lounges, and by sharing materials and lesson plans. Struggling schools failed to develop this connectedness among participants. Existing connections broke down and barriers arose because participation mechanisms allowed only a few school constituents to be involved in the decision-making process, and those unable or unwilling to participate therefore mistrusted the process.

Widespread involvement in school learning was promoted through all the participation mechanisms that were thoughtfully designed to facilitate interaction across the traditional boundaries of departments and grade levels. These decision-making groups and the interaction they promoted at the actively restructuring schools helped to minimize balkanization and develop the school as a learning community. Research by David and by the Center on Organization and Restructuring of Schools suggests similar conclusions about the importance of many decision-making groups for building a learning community.[14] In contrast, learning in the struggling schools was found only in small pockets, such as councils or design teams, or among a small group of highly active teachers. These findings reinforce the notion that learning is a collective process and that for an organization to learn to operate differently, the dynamics of learning must be widespread.

Participants in actively restructuring schools also spent time thinking about the whole school organization rather than simply the components of the school. They talked about values and approaches that cut across subjects, grade levels, and classrooms. They talked about the impact that activities in one part of the system had on others. They made decisions based on what would be best for the school overall, rather than making the political trade-offs between various parts of the school that were commonplace in struggling schools. This learning process was particularly hard to accomplish in high schools, where teachers were embedded in departments and even the council members often saw themselves as advocates for a subsystem of the school.

Finding 1c Schools that were actively restructuring used their decision-making authority to make meaningful changes in teaching and learning. Because power was not widely distributed in struggling schools, the decision-making process typically focused on power relationships. In addition to dispersing power, schools where SBM worked used their new power to make decisions that affected teaching and learning and set clear and specific goals to improve school performance.[15] For instance, some actively restructuring schools reallocated their staff time to create resource teacher positions that provided additional assistance to teachers or students. One school had worked hard to get its community to agree to lengthen the school day so that teachers could have a common planning time one morning a week, when school would start late. This is similar to prior findings by Guskey and Peterson that some SBM schools rearrange their schedules so that teachers can have time to work together outside their regular teaching schedule. All of the actively restructuring schools used their staff development money on common thrusts focused around improving teaching and learning and implementing innovations in curriculum and instruction. For example, one actively restructuring elementary school had agreed to use all of its instructional dollars one year to purchase math manipulatives for the entire school. Schools that had the authority to purchase their own services—whether for roof repair or food service—used their savings for instructional needs. None of these kinds of decisions were cosmetic; these decisions confronted the autonomy, isolation, and turf skirmishes so common in schools and facilitated the creation of learning communities centered around teaching and learning.

As a form of governance, SBM in and of itself will not generate improvement in school performance. Instead, it is simply a means through which school-level decision makers can implement various reforms that can improve teaching and learning.[16] In the struggling schools we visited, there was little connection between SBM and curriculum and instructional reform, and councils often got bogged down in issues of power—who could

210   attend meetings, who could vote—not on improving curriculum and instructional practices.

Invest in ongoing and systematic professional development to strengthen
both individual and organizational capacity to achieve reform, especially in
the areas of curriculum, instruction, teamwork, and budgeting.

Finding 2a Knowledge and skills development in actively restructuring
schools was an ongoing process oriented toward building a schoolwide capacity for change, developing a shared knowledge base, and creating a professional learning community. Struggling schools typically restricted professional development activities to one-shot training sessions for a few teachers.

Professional development in schools where SBM worked was a very high
priority. While staff development was present in all schools, in the actively
restructuring schools it was aimed at the development of overall system
capability to achieve collective goals rather than simply personal goals. Interest in developing the knowledge and professional development of teachers and principals was an ongoing process. Staff participated in training
opportunities on a regular basis, rather than sporadically and infrequently
(for example, when SBM was adopted). It was not uncommon for an actively restructuring school to have multiyear commitments to professional
development, which included all teachers. These schools offered follow-up
sessions as well.

In line with the new decision-making responsibilities, actively restructuring schools broadened the subject matter of training and the categories of
staff who were trained. As David and Guskey and Peterson found, broaden-
ing both who was trained and the areas of training was critical in order
for all stakeholders to be active participants in the decision-making process
and for teachers to change their teaching practices and beliefs. In terms
of subject matter, professional development activities at actively restructuring schools were oriented toward building a schoolwide capacity for
change, creating a professional learning community, and developing a
shared knowledge base. In addition to training in teaching, learning, curriculum, and assessment, schools offered instruction in interpersonal skills
(group decision making, consensus building, and conflict resolution), in
management skills (running meetings, budgeting, and interviewing), and

in the process of school improvement. Furthermore, the schools where SBM worked also had greater proportions of the staff take part in professional development. In particular, training in the area of decision-making skills was not limited to members of the school council. As a result, actively restructuring schools had teachers, administrators, office staff, support personnel, parents, and, in some cases at the secondary level, students receiving many different kinds of training. In contrast, struggling schools typically viewed professional development more as an individual activity rather than as a means of creating a schoolwide capacity for improvement. The target group for training was only the comparatively small group of individuals who sat on the formal site council. Furthermore, professional development at these schools tended to be sporadic. In struggling schools, we found more instances of one-time training of the "go, sit, and get" variety rather than ongoing professional development models. Their training tended to be offered only at the start of SBM. One council had been trained on how to make decisions by consensus but not on how to proceed when consensus was not reached. As a result, "meaty" issues at the school were shelved in favor of topics that offered easily reached consensuses.

Finding 2b The actively restructuring schools strategically linked professional development to the school's reform agenda, while struggling schools typically lacked a staff development plan.

Professional development activities at actively restructuring schools were employed more strategically, deliberately tied to the school's reform objectives. These activities were often aligned with the school's mission and goals for introducing innovations in curriculum and instruction and improving student performance, a critical component of effective SBM found by the Center on Organization and Restructuring of Schools. At many of these schools, the council or a separate decision-making group assessed professional development needs and planned and coordinated development activities to meet those needs. Many struggling schools lacked a staff development plan. Usually the principal dispensed funds for training on a case-by-case basis and there was no schoolwide involvement in decisions regarding who or what the training should involve. As a result, the professional development topics at struggling schools were more likely to be narrowly focused and even out of touch with the day-to-day issues faced by teachers. Some teachers were able to opt out of professional development

212 altogether. At one struggling school attempting a schoolwide focus, more than a quarter of the staff were absent on staff development days.

LESSON 3

Get access to a wide variety of information on student, staff, and school performance, and use the information to guide decision making, to provide feedback to school constituents, and to enhance organizational learning.

Finding 3a Considerable information was collected in actively restructuring schools, and this information was used to meet school priorities and to enhance the school's own learning process. Struggling schools often lacked clear priorities and, as a result, did not gather information systematically or comprehensively.

The schools in which SBM was used effectively collected many kinds of data (information on district and site revenues, costs, customer satisfaction, school performance, innovations going on in other schools, and data on the environment) and tried to use it. As David found, schools need sound information about how students are performing and what actions will increase that performance in order to improve teaching and learning. Most of the actively restructuring schools collected daily attendance and tardy data, often disseminating these data to parents on a regular basis. One secondary school regularly printed out the student grade distributions for every class in order to monitor student and teacher performance. Student performance data were maintained in a variety of forms, including portfolios and anecdotal records. Several actively restructuring schools piloted narrative report cards, student profiles in reading and mathematics with grade-level expectations, and student profiles in all subject areas.

These schools also had a strong customer service orientation, which promoted the growth and development of the learning community and helped to determine what information was gathered. They assessed their own progress on an ongoing basis and made decisions based on expected impact on performance outcomes—in other words, they learned from their experiences. Many conducted annual parent and community satisfaction surveys and used the results to help set priorities for the following year. Assessing changes, piloting new approaches, measuring, examining, and seeking causes of trends were other manifestations of self-reinforced learning.

Struggling schools often lacked this emphasis and focus and, as a result, did not gather information systematically or comprehensively. The struggling schools failed to learn from experience because they were not focused on a common understanding of what the school was to become. Instead, strife was a recurring theme as school participants fought to define and defend their authority.

Finding 3b Schools that were actively restructuring had multiple mechanisms for quickly disseminating information to all school constituents, which fostered a sense of trust by ensuring that constituents were aware of the decisions being made. Struggling schools, lacking these broad communication networks, encountered suspicion and resistance to council decisions from an uninformed school community.

The actively restructuring schools used many communication mechanisms to share information. In these schools information not only flowed to the school from the central office but was also disseminated within the school and out to the community. The multiple vertical and horizontal decision-making groups collected and dispensed information within the school and informed parents and the community outside of the school. All of the actively restructuring SBM schools had created networks of teacher teams in which many issues originated and were discussed, and through which a wide variety of information was communicated to all teachers. The net effect was that in these schools there was good communication and reflective dialogue around specific projects. Implementation of curriculum and instruction reforms was consistently described as a collective effort, with constant problem solving and adjustment resulting from continual discussion among teachers about instruction.

Most of the successful SBM schools took systematic and creative approaches to communication with parents and the community, relying as much on face-to-face means as on formal documents. The principals of actively restructuring schools often attended many different types of meetings at which external constituents, such as local businesses, discussed school activities. Many schools held parent-teacher conferences and some offered classes for parents on such topics as computers and student-parent math activities. Several actively restructuring schools installed voice mail for classroom teachers, while another school used grant dollars to hire a

214 part-time ombudsman to serve as a liaison between the school and parent communities.

The actively restructuring schools also recognized the importance of timely and easily understood information. They used the information to improve teaching and learning, and the schools worked to disseminate the information quickly and broadly. Several schools scheduled short grade-level or department meetings immediately after faculty meetings so they could obtain feedback quickly. Two secondary schools used short meetings every morning before school to share information. Grade-level teams met daily or weekly. Content-area teams met at least every two weeks. Committees on school priorities met regularly. Most schools had one and sometimes two afternoons a week that were devoted to rotating committee meetings over a month's time. Among struggling schools, there were few formal mechanisms for sharing information, and the teacher grapevine was often the only means of communication. The information on the grapevine was often incomplete, however, and tended to breed suspicion. In struggling SBM schools we found that teachers often were uninformed about school-wide decisions. As a result, we found several instances of teachers aligning against their peers on the school council because of the mistrust and suspicion that went with the position.

LESSON 4

Design an incentive system that motivates involvement in the reform process and rewards school-level participants for improving their expertise and for producing results, especially student success.

Finding 4a The actively restructuring schools used both monetary and nonmonetary rewards to acknowledge individual and group progress toward school goals more often than struggling schools did. When monetary rewards were used, they were usually given to groups, often schoolwide. Such rewards included differentiated staffing positions with extra compensation for administrative responsibilities, money for professional development, and grants to reimburse teachers for extra time, including, in one district, money for council membership. Differentiated staffing was widely used and accepted as a way of recognizing expertise in Victoria. Some of these differentiated staffing positions had additional pay and modestly reduced teaching loads, some reduced teaching loads only, some just visibility as a leader. All of these positions had to be applied for and were allocated to schools according to enrollment.

At the actively restructuring schools, nonmonetary rewards also were more readily available than at the struggling schools. Many principals at successful SBM schools regularly recognized individuals for work well done; in other schools, principals preferred to recognize group efforts in order to create a sense of community achievement. The principals used various reward strategies, including "pats on the back" and notes of appreciation in school newsletters. At one high school, the principal began every faculty meeting with a list of "thank you's." We also learned about teachers informally recognizing one another's efforts; parents giving thank-you luncheons for teachers; and the scheduling of year-end functions with free dinners, flowers, and parties to celebrate the achievement of school goals. Furthermore, the prestige associated with mentoring or grant writing also served as nonmonetary rewards in our actively restructuring schools, as did reduced teaching loads, which allowed time for these other responsibilities. Guskey and Peterson found that these nonmonetary rewards, mainly in the form of acknowledgments, do much to encourage involvement.

In struggling schools, which operated in a climate of distrust, public recognition was greeted with cynicism. Even monetary rewards were suspect in these schools. Furthermore, the lack of consensus around specific outcomes for schooling was an impediment to establishing a reward structure in struggling schools. School constituents typically did not agree on desired outcomes, and so rewards were, at best, indirect and unfocused.

Finding 4b Teachers in both actively restructuring and struggling schools were beginning to wonder whether they could maintain their level of involvement over the long haul. It has been argued that intrinsic rewards are sufficient to motivate and reinforce teachers. We found that in the actively restructuring schools, many teachers were indeed excited and motivated by the climate of professional collaboration and learning. We also found, however, that some teachers who had been working with SBM for several years were tired and uncertain of their ability to continue working to improve school performance. Our research found that actively restructuring schools placed high demands on all individuals involved. The argument that

216 intrinsic rewards are sufficient to motivate and reinforce teachers for engaging in SBM over the long haul may be too optimistic. As other studies of SBM have also found, dwindling interest and motivation to be involved in the decision-making process is common among both parents and teachers in SBM schools where there are few rewards.[17]

LESSON 5

Create a shared school vision focused on boosting student achievement that guides school-level reform efforts.

Finding 5a Through ongoing dialogue about their purpose and direction, actively restructuring schools developed an active, living vision for the school, while struggling schools were unable to reach consensus on a common direction for teaching and learning. Schools that were most successful in implementing change had a well-defined vision of their mission, values, and goals regarding student outcomes—a vision that guided curriculum and instruction reform as well as conversations in decision-making forums. This "instructional guidance mechanism" served as a constant focus on student learning and was continuously referred to during the decision-making process.[18] In the actively restructuring schools, this vision was frequently generated through ongoing dialogue about the school's purpose, vision, and model of education. This enabled school participants to develop a common understanding of what they wanted their school to become, so they could collectively work to accomplish it. It served to frame discussions about what changes to introduce and what performance outcomes were important.

In general, the vision or instructional guidance mechanism in actively restructuring schools was based on district, state, or national guidelines for curriculum and instruction, such as those produced by the National Council of Teachers of Mathematics. These guidelines provided direction to reform efforts, a critical condition for successful restructuring that David found in her study of SBM, but they were flexible enough to be adapted to the local context. Many of the people we interviewed said the guidelines—in the form of performance standards, curriculum frameworks, and/or assessment systems—specified the "what" of the curriculum but left the "how" up to them. At some actively restructuring schools, for example, teachers themselves wrote a separate curriculum framework for each content area;

other teachers used sections from existing frameworks to come up with their own approaches.

The need for a clear vision and specific goals for meeting that vision has been demonstrated in other studies of SBM as well.[19] In our actively restructuring schools, the instructional guidance mechanism articulated what the school was all about and served as a focus for the reform activities initiated by the school and the SBM council in particular. Successful schools also benefited from a shared understanding and widespread commitment to the instruction and curriculum approaches that had been adopted. Struggling SBM schools, on the other hand, often had power and control issues that interfered with any vision setting. Bogged down in power struggles, they lacked much dialogue about the school's purpose and thus didn't have a common understanding of what the school was to become. Even when they had a vision statement, it was not a living document that was mentioned frequently. Without such a vision, struggling schools were usually less able to achieve real reform.

LESSON 6

Facilitate shared leadership by encouraging teachers to lead work teams and by allowing principals to focus on facilitating change and supporting the emergence of a learning community.

Finding 6a In actively restructuring schools, principals were moving toward the role of manager and facilitator of change and were working hard to foster a strong sense of a school learning community. Principals in struggling schools often operated from their own agendas rather than building a common one, thus alienating school staff and ultimately leading to the rejection of principal leadership. Principals at actively restructuring schools played a key role in several areas: dispersing power, promoting a schoolwide commitment to learning, getting all teachers to participate in the work of the school, collecting information about student learning, and distributing rewards. These successful principals motivated staff, created a team feeling on campus, fostered the school's learning community, and provided a vision for the school. Successful principals also shielded teachers from issues in which they had little interest or expertise so they could concentrate on improving teaching and learning. The principals were often described as facilitators

218   and leaders, as strong supporters of their staffs, and as the people who brought curriculum and instruction innovations to the school and moved reform agendas forward. These same descriptions were found by Murphy and Beck in their study of SBM.[20]

In struggling schools, principals were not routinely respected as legitimate managers. A necessary condition for successful restructuring was a minimum amount of control, specifically focused on factors that affected teaching and learning. But it did not follow that more control led to more, or more positive, changes. SBM was not successful when principals worked from their own agenda rather than helping to develop a common one. This has been found in other studies of SBM as well.[21] Many principals in struggling schools were perceived either as too autocratic by their staffs, who complained that the principals appeared to dominate all decisions, or as insufficiently involved. Principals of struggling schools often loaded up the council with trivial details and typically identified, on their own, a vision for the school presenting it as a fait accompli to the staff. This often led to a power struggle between teachers and the principal, and in some schools, the faculty simply rejected the principal's unilateral agenda for change. Teachers frequently referred to "the principal's vision" in these schools and often were not willing to accept guidance and leadership from the principal because they felt little sense of ownership and accountability to the plan.

Finding 6b Leadership in actively restructuring schools was shared, and often a cadre of teacher leaders emerged to take on the various governance issues surrounding SBM. Less of this shared leadership was found in the struggling schools. Among the governance issues surrounding SBM that teacher leaders assumed in actively restructuring schools were such responsibilities as material selection, budget development, and professional development schedules.[22] In many cases, for example, teachers in actively restructuring schools took the lead in introducing ideas about new instructional practices. Furthermore, these teacher leaders helped to ensure that all stakeholders felt welcome to participate in decisions, particularly those that concerned them directly, and to broaden and sustain the school's commitment to reform. As David found, what emerged from this cadre of teacher leaders in actively restructuring schools was shared leadership and accountability to the schoolwide program among a broad range of individuals. This picture of broad, participatory leadership differed starkly from the struggling schools, where teachers who introduced new practices often did so only in their own classrooms and played no real leadership role in the school.

LESSON 7

Ensure adequate resources by cultivating external funding and by linking the school to community organizations and professional networks.

Finding 7a Schools that were actively restructuring cultivated resources from outside the school, both through involvement in professional networks and through entrepreneurial activity in the local business community. This cultivation of outside resources was not found in struggling schools. Administrators of actively restructuring schools recognized that they needed additional resources to take on the new tasks that SBM demanded. These schools often joined professional networks, such as the Coalition of Essential Schools, for the additional resources that these networks provided, particularly in terms of staff development opportunities. The actively restructuring schools were also very active in their entrepreneurial outreach efforts. For example, some principals served on boards of local business groups or regularly attended their meetings. Other principals diligently fostered press relations with local newspapers. And actively restructuring schools cultivated other outside resources, approaching universities for professional development, area businesses for advice on technology, and private foundations and educational networks for financial support. It was not uncommon for an actively restructuring school to receive additional resources from two or three outside agencies. The Center on Organization and Restructuring of Schools also found that support by outside groups was critical for successfully changing teaching and learning practices and implementing curriculum and instruction innovations.[23] Struggling schools typically did not have these resources, nor were they actively seeking them.

Finding 7b The actively restructuring schools generated connections to their external environment that facilitated the learning and changing process, while such connections were not as apparent in the struggling schools. Schools that were actively restructuring used their connections with the

220   external environment as a source both of technical learning, through research and innovations in other schools, and of learning about such environmental requirements as community changes and preferences. This included ongoing information about how well the school was doing in meeting community requirements and how it compared to other similar schools. The actively restructuring schools shared findings from articles and conferences and both invited external speakers and sent representatives to other schools. Many of these schools were also members of professional networks, such as the National Alliance or the Coalition of Essential Schools, which were sources of new ideas. The actively restructuring schools also surveyed their communities, stayed in contact with families, and learned about what was happening in the organizations that would eventually be the employers of their students. This connection to the external environment was lacking in struggling schools, where participants were focused inward rather than outward.

LESSON 8

Refocus the central office to enable and support school-level reform efforts.

Finding 8a Where SBM worked and schools were using their power to improve teaching and learning, central offices had become more service-oriented and less mandate-minded. Making good use of the power accorded schools also depended on a change in the traditional roles of the superintendent and central offices. As the Center on Organization and Restructuring of Schools and Bryk et al. found, schools need political support from the district office in order to be successful. Superintendents in our study helped by making central offices more service-oriented; as one said, "The schools want helpers, not tellers." In Edmonton, schools had the bulk of money for professional development and maintenance and could purchase those services outside the district. Central office departments offering such services, which had to sell their services to schools in order to stay in existence, became school-oriented. Similarly, district office restructuring and total quality management efforts in San Diego and Prince William County promoted the notion of the schools as the customers of the district departments. Superintendents also provided schools with support by developing a districtwide culture of risk taking. The superintendent in Jefferson County encouraged schools "to go out on a limb" and supported them by offering extra money for professional development to all schools that voted to adopt SBM. In general, schools needed this support from the central office in order to build local commitment for undertaking the massive task of restructuring.

Finding 8b All schools continued to be restricted by district-driven finance systems, which did not provide them with adequate flexibility in employing school funds. SBM requires a new school finance system. Most states have a district-driven finance system. Money is raised by districts and distributed by the state and federal government to local districts. Schools receive resources—teachers, books, transportation, and so on—but they rarely receive money. As Geraci found in his study of Rochester, this lack of local control over the budget is perhaps the biggest obstacle to authentic SBM.[24] The district emphasis on budgetary control needs to change to a school orientation if effective decentralized management is to be implemented.

Decentralizing budget power to the school is the major substantive fiscal route for tying SBM to the school finance system. This shift would entail a state budget providing most dollars in a lump sum directly to schools. This radical approach already is happening in states with charter schools and public school choice programs and elsewhere in the world, including England, New Zealand, and Victoria, Australia. A less dramatic and more practical approach would be for states to require that districts allocate 85–90 percent of all dollars—both general and categorized—to schools in a lump sum. This policy would ensure that the bulk of dollars would be available for use at the school, and it would not disrupt the overall district or school finance structure within any state. Districts taking this approach often continue to pay teachers at the district level and "charge" each school only the average salary for each teacher.

Finding 8c Central offices rarely provided schools with the variety and breadth of professional development activities they needed. As a result, actively restructuring schools sought out training from nontraditional sources.

As David and the Center on Organization and Restructuring of Schools found, districts need to provide schools with the professional development resources necessary to undertake the fundamental changes in teaching and

222   learning that occur with successful SBM. We found a critical need to retrain central office administrators who were more accustomed to being enforcers, regulators, and overseers than to responding to requests from schools for technical assistance. Struggling schools continued to rely on the district for training, and, as a result, the subject matter of professional development activities often was restricted to the topics that were identified by the central office. The actively restructuring schools, on the other hand, often looked outside the district organization to private companies, universities, and research institutes for technical assistance and training in management and group decision making.

Finding 8d Districts often failed to provide schools with the timely information on the management and operation of the school that was needed as key input into the decision-making process.

One key concern of schools was the generally spotty access to up-to-date data related to school management and operations. Traditionally, corporations and district offices have gathered aggregate information most useful for making systemwide decisions, but this is insufficient in SBM, where schools need easy access to the information as well. Victoria's solution was to install an online, interactive computer system in its schools, with data on budgets and personnel, student achievement, electronic invoicing and purchasing, and a master schedule. This computer network was by far the most advanced among the districts we studied, although several other districts, including Edmonton and Jefferson County, have linked school sites electronically with the district office. Most schools, however, were not satisfied with their ability to monitor their own resources or student data accurately and in a timely manner.

Finding 8e Compensation structures were rarely changed in ways that would provide the incentives necessary for sustained involvement in school-based decision making and reform.

Compensation structures have received little attention in SBM. Too many districts mistakenly seemed to assume that no extra energy and commitment is needed to undertake successful SBM. Districts choosing to implement a decentralized, high-involvement approach to management would be wise to take lessons from organizations outside education and restructure compensation in the medium term. The form of changed compensation package can vary, but providing compensation for the vast array of knowledge and skills that teachers must develop to implement innovations in curriculum and instruction is a core element that should probably be included in any revised compensation plan.[25]

School-based management has become a popular reform and is a component of a number of other approaches to reform; however, the promise of SBM has not materialized on a large scale. As authority is devolved to local schools through charter school reforms and other approaches that entail local self-management, policy makers need to recognize the requirements for successful SBM. Our premise is that SBM will not contribute to school improvement if it does not yield new practices and approaches that address the challenges being faced by schools. Thus, successful SBM requires real autonomy at the school site and requires that school-level participants have the capacity to learn how to be more effective at improving performance.

Our research shows that under the right conditions, school-level participants can utilize SBM to introduce innovations and to improve school performance. We found that transferring power from the district office to local schools was a necessary but not a sufficient condition to explain the distinction between schools that used SBM effectively and those that struggled. In addition, schools needed their participants to develop new capabilities and to have access to much more information than in the past. Many successful SBM schools put in place rewards that linked people's efforts to new performance standards. All this happened within an overall school direction that was owned by the school and used as a criterion for decisions and activities. To develop and maintain school reform, the leadership role was key: it helped to support, channel, and energize improvement activity. We also found that shared leadership, particularly between principals and teachers, was essential. Perhaps most importantly, the conditions described above needed to apply to the whole school community. That is, schoolwide reform occurred when involvement was broadened beyond the small group who sat on the school site council.

Successful SBM schools were also characterized by participants who were collectively learning. The learning processes entailed defining a school mission and ongoing dialogue about school purpose, examining educational and management processes, learning from one another and from experience, thinking about the school as a whole rather than concentrating

224   on segments, and actively interacting with and learning from the environment. Further, these activities were not limited to the school site council;
instead, they characterized the whole school and they led to innovations in
teaching and learning in the classroom. Finally, successful SBM schools
were focused on continually improving the education that was delivered
within the school.

Putting the various organizational conditions in place and learning how
to operate effectively in a participatory manner is a challenge entailing
expanded roles, new capabilities, and new norms. Learning how to continuously improve the technical processes in schools in order to more fully
meet today's more demanding educational requirements with the diverse,
complex, and challenging population of students found in our large urban
areas will require extensive learning by local school participants. Finding or
developing leaders who can be effective in high-involvement settings is
essential for the SBM model to operate well.

Many of the successful examples in our research, and other studies
as well, occurred in relatively small schools. The large, segmented high
schools with several thousand students experience great difficulty establishing the conditions for high involvement and learning dynamics. It may
be necessary to break these down into multiple schools of a manageable
size. Even within smaller schools, there may be difficulties in achieving a
shared vision for the school and energizing the large personal investment
that is inherent in fundamental change. These difficulties include divergent
stakeholder preferences for schools and teacher skepticism that they will
truly be able to make meaningful change.

Daunting though it may be, we are left with the challenge that is described throughout this volume. Our large, bureaucratic urban schools have
not met the educational needs of their students, nor have they introduced
the change necessary to keep up with the educational needs of our diverse
society. If we accept the proposition that the environment has changed
in fundamental ways that demand basic changes in the way schools operate, we must ask how schools can best learn appropriate new approaches.
This chapter has demonstrated that if the necessary organizational conditions and learning dynamics are created and maintained, locally managed schools, vested with real power, can transform themselves into high-
performance organizations. Recent findings by researchers at the University
of Wisconsin–Madison are also instructive regarding the link between a

school culture that fosters collaborative group efforts toward learning and student achievement. Based on their study of twenty-four restructured schools, they concluded that the level of professional community in a school contributed to innovative classroom practices and ultimately to higher student achievement.[26]

Thus it seems clear that not all SBM programs are created equal and that future research ought to examine more closely the parameters and dynamics of the SBM process rather than trying to answer a blanket question of whether SBM is an effective way to improve school performance. In our study, we found differences at the district level in terms of the way the SBM plan was defined and its general parameters, and at the school level in terms of the way the SBM plan was implemented. Within the same district, some schools were able to form effective school-level governance mechanisms and focus on school improvement. Other schools were mired in a power struggle, focused on win-lose decisions, concentrated on inconsequential routine decisions, and paid little attention to generating a vision and plan for school improvement. The differences across sites appear to go well beyond the structure of the SBM plan to include other aspects of the school and district organization, such as the training and development support for new ways of operating, the information available to inform SBM decisions, and the development of clear values and purposes.

Effective involvement of people in the improvement of school performance may be made more likely by the existence of school-level decision-making authority, but that is not sufficient. Schools can still fail to become effective decision makers. Furthermore, even if SBM councils become effective at governance, they may not focus their decision-making activities on performance improvement. They may not have the tools and methods to look systematically at the functioning of the school and learn to be more effective in achieving desired outcomes.

9 The Politics of Change

Chester E. Finn, Jr.

An article buried in the November 15, 1995, *New York Times* supplies an apt metaphor for U.S. education: as the dawn of the twenty-first century approaches, more than a quarter of the public schools in the nation's largest city are still heated by coal furnaces.[1]

Portrayed in this startling bit of journalism was coal-stoker Brunel Toussaint, whose job today, as for the past three decades, is shoveling anthracite into the twin boilers—installed in 1924—of Junior High School 99 on Manhattan's East 100th Street. Although he is growing weary and a bit arthritic from the ceaseless heavy lifting, his union—and the school system's skimpy capital budget—preserve both his $35,000 position and the antiquated, costly, and polluting means by which J.H.S. 99's teachers and pupils keep warm in winter.

As the *Times* reporter noted, "It could have been a scene out of early industrial England."

So, one senses, could many scenes upstairs in the classrooms. For it isn't just the heating systems of American education that hew to an obsolete model. And the reasons why the parents and children of New York City cannot realistically expect gas, oil, electricity, solar, or nuclear power to warm (and cool) all their classrooms in the foreseeable future are essentially the same reasons that they cannot realistically expect those classrooms to do a significantly better job of educating the youngsters who sit in them.

Briefly stated, we have entrusted an archaic design to a government monopoly that has scant incentive to alter its accustomed ways, that tailors most of its decisions to the interests of its own employees, that has little need to respond to its clients, that has co-opted (or cowed) those who might otherwise oblige it to change, that has a firm grip on the levers that control its resources, that is not accountable to anyone for its results, and that consequently enjoys near-immunity from incursions by forces outside its own sturdy perimeter.

Are there exceptions to the glum conclusions of the previous paragraph? A few, sure. Other chapters of this book sketch the most promising among them. Indeed, like the rare days when your teenager cleans his room such that you can actually glimpse the floor, the exceptions are what cast the squalid norm into vivid relief.

But those exceptions are also rare, at least where the changes they embody are equivalent to replacing the furnace (and putting Mr. Toussaint out of a job, or perhaps obliging him to learn new skills). Today we have fewer than 500 charter schools in a universe of 85,000 public and 25,000 private schools. Although that number is sure to rise in the next couple of years, charter schools will still be educating less than 1 percent of U.S. youngsters. In a nation with 16,000 local school systems, we find about ten communities experimenting with private contract management of public schools (often just one or two schools among dozens). Their numbers, too, seem certain to rise, but it is unimaginable that they will account for more than a couple of hundred schools by century's end. And yes, two states have withstood a firestorm of political opposition and enacted small voucher programs to serve a handful of inner-city children. If this approach finally passes muster with the courts, it, too, may spread—though the opposition of a single U.S. senator has thus far kept it from spreading to the District of Columbia. So, perhaps, will the number of communities—today just a handful—where the sometimes-inventive school designs of the New American Schools Development Corporation are being tried, often in attenuated form.

All of these are worthy enough efforts based on promising ideas. But every one of them is so difficult to initiate, maintain, and expand as to recall Admiral Rickover's dictum that changing American education is like

228   moving a cemetery. And every one of these initiatives is vulnerable to being
undone after the next school board or gubernatorial election—events in
which the opponents of change can be counted upon to do their considerable utmost to usher into office "friends of public education" committed to
rolling back or at least retarding such unwanted innovations.

It is not really surprising that little has changed. For in spite of all the
ripples on the surface of American education, the deep waters run still. The
inertia is immense, the resistance to innovation awesome. The enterprise is
so vast, so decentralized, and so loosely coupled that it manages to absorb
immense amounts of reform energy without moving more than an inch or
two, rather like a long train that has lots of people shoving the engine yet
producing no visible motion in the caboose. Moreover, the decision-making
system—if such it can even be termed—is constructed so that practically
every faction wields an effective veto over change (at least insofar as it
affects their own community, school, or classroom), while nobody exercises
sufficient power to ensure that lasting change is adopted. Our school system
resembles a giant rubber band; when force is placed upon it, it will bend or
stretch. But its every fiber yearns to resume its previous shape, and, as soon
as the force weakens, it snaps back to where it was. (Baltimore's recent
eviction of Educational Alternatives, Incorporated, from that city's schools
occurred three and a half stormy years after the innovation began, a not
untypical example of how long it takes the enemies of change to restore
business as usual. Of course they were assisted in this instance by EAI's
uninspiring design, sometimes unwarranted claims, and mixed results.)

Antique Practices and Contemporary Fads

Thus we find most of our schools—private as well as public—adhering to a
nineteenth-century design: a calendar shaped for the agrarian age, when air
conditioning hadn't been invented and children were needed in summer to
help on the farm; a school day structured for an era when Mom was waiting
at home at 3 P.M. with milk, cookies, and a ride to Cub Scouts; an organizational plan poised somewhere between the early industrial age and the
"scientific management" schemes of the 1920s; a regulatory regimen re-
sembling a bad dream of Max Weber's; labor-management relations re-
dolent of Detroit in the 1950s; and teaching methods little affected by sound
research into effective instructional techniques.

It has been remarked that if Rip Van Winkle had fallen asleep in the late nineteenth century and awakened today, only two major U.S. institutions would look familiar to him: our churches and our schools. The coal-fired boilers on East 100th Street are only the most visible aspect of an antiquated institutional structure.

At the same time, American education is awash in faddish innovations that sweep through the profession like tropical storms in the Caribbean. Whole-language reading. Constructivist math. Mixed-ability grouping. Multiage grouping. Multiculturalism. Afrocentrism. "Authentic" assessment. Student portfolios. Coalition schools. Comer schools. Levin schools. Boyer schools. Professional development schools. Sex education. Drug abuse education. Environmental education. Conflict resolution education. Outcomes-based education. Cooperative learning. Service learning. Experiential learning. Critical thinking skills. And on and on.

Most of the fads sort themselves into three categories:

- Academic and ideological passions, such as multiculturalism and history-from-the-victim's-standpoint, that migrate from the university campus to the K–12 system. Here is where we should also place the myriad schemes of education school ideologues to create a "more natural" (read "less academic") learning environment.
- Schemes to bring more resources into schools in the name of doing something different, such as the new school designs of Theodore Sizer and James Comer, or adding to the school's mission some duty—sex education, character development—that was previously borne elsewhere in society.
- Efforts to placate noisy factions within the population, either by magnifying and celebrating their differences or—just as often—by denying that those differences have any proper bearing on the schools. Black History Month and bilingual education exemplify the former, while "mainstreaming" youngsters with severe emotional and behavioral problems in regular classrooms illustrates the latter.

Because of this faddishness, American education often appears to be in the throes of ceaseless change. Yet few of these innovations endure. Fewer yield improved results. And nearly all of them are made within the boundaries of the old design, the old ground rules, the old political arrangements, the old government monopoly. Thus waves appear on the surface while fish

230   just a few inches beneath are able to continue swimming in unison with no jostling from the disturbance above.

Some of this deep inertia is cultural—and universal. Every society treats its schools as instruments for socializing and acculturating the young, not for upsetting applecarts. Although there has long been a radical strand within the education profession, most practitioners share the stable middle-class values and attitudes of the taxpayers who pay their salaries and of the parents who supply their students. Unlike some education school radicals, they take for granted that their schools' mission is to prepare young people to enter society, not to overturn it. In that sense, and despite all their faddishness, these are very conservative institutions, not hotbeds of revolution. It is scarcely surprising that they are organized and operated according to static assumptions, timeworn procedures, and familiar ground rules.

This organizational stability and predictability would be welcome if the schools' results were broadly satisfactory. But they are not. Fourteen years after the National Commission on Excellence in Education declared us a "nation at risk," student achievement remains far below the levels needed for sustained prosperity, cultural strength, societal well-being, and civic health. I will not here recapitulate the abounding evidence that undergirds that assertion, save to note that twelfth-grade reading scores were lower in 1994 than in 1992 on the National Assessment of Educational Progress (NAEP)—and 30 percent of high school seniors are not even "basic" readers. That means some 750,000 more youngsters graduate every year without a solid grasp of the most basic academic skill.[2] As for U.S. history, the 1994 NAEP results show just 11 percent of twelfth-graders performing satisfactorily.[3] A recent analysis of the U.S. economy by the Organization for Economic Cooperation and Development (OECD) concluded that our schools "can broadly be characterised as mediocre at best."[4] And in its most recent appraisal of progress toward the education goals set in 1989 by President Bush and the nation's governors, the National Education Goals Panel found improvement on seven indicators, deterioration on another seven, and no change on twelve.[5]

Getting By

The country survives. We cope. We compensate. As has long been the case, a fraction of our population gets a solid education, and among our 110,000

schools are hundreds of fine ones (albeit mostly exemplary versions of the
old model). Our sprawling higher education system also does an immense
amount of remediating—at immense cost—and gives generously subsidized
second and third chances to people coming back to extend their education
at just about any point in their lives. Moreover, we have ample education
options outside the formal schooling system, including employer training
schemes like "Motorola University"; excellent audio and video "self-help"
tapes; a wide array of privately organized after-school and summer programs; and a burgeoning catalogue of information and instruction accessible through one's computer or television set.

Many of the traits that make the United States a generally successful
country also help us compensate for and work around the deficiencies of
our formal schooling system. We are endlessly inventive. We are amazingly
flexible. We are famously entrepreneurial. People from other countries are
amazed at how easy it is to restart one's life here, sometimes pointing it in a
very different direction. And besides exporting tertiary education to an eager world, we readily avail ourselves of talent, energy, and high-quality
training from abroad. That is why U.S. insurance companies send complex
claim-processing files to be worked on in Ireland, and why more than a few
Indian medical schools now hold class reunions in New Jersey.

We cope. But we are not improving the skill and knowledge base—or
work habits and attitudes—of the average high school graduate. Yes, gains
can be seen in school persistence (the dropout rate slowly declines), in
certain measures of minority achievement (although black and Hispanic
Americans remain far behind white and Asian students), and in high school
course-taking patterns. But achievement is not rising, nor are employers
and university professors any better pleased with the preparation of their
entrants than they were a decade ago.

This despite often heroic efforts in recent years to reform our schools and
despite immense increases in the sums we spend on them. Although restive
legislatures, facing reports of high school graduates who could not read,
began enacting minimum competency–style reforms in the 1970s, the contemporary "excellence movement" dates to the mid-1980s. Since that time,
education reform has turned into a substantial industry in its own right,
felling entire forests to print its studies and reports, consuming the energies
of policy makers at every level, spawning a number of new organizations,
absorbing tens of millions of foundation dollars (and billions in local, state,

232 and federal outlays), and transforming the very language of education discourse. We have tried hundreds of reform schemes. Our per pupil expenditure of $6,300 (in public schools) in 1995–1996 is a thousand dollars more (after accounting for inflation) than we were spending a decade earlier and about twice what it was in 1970.[6]

What accounts for the meager results from all this money and effort? The quest for an explanation soon takes us to a fork in the analytic road. One path is taken by those who believe that the reasons are essentially technical: that the main obstacles to improvement arise from our failure thus far to blend the right mix of reform ingredients, or from inadequate resources. In their view, we have not yet found the proper array of standards, course requirements, tests, curricular configurations, federal programs, comprehensive plans for systemic renewal, teacher training schemes, enhanced professional development, reworked time allocations, technology, money, and so on. But if we continue to mix and match, they assure us, one day our alchemy will produce the formula for changing lead to gold.

They might be right. For theirs to be the primary explanation, however, one must assume that our present structural and decision-making arrangements are fundamentally sound, if only we knew how to tweak them properly.

The other path—the one we shall traverse in the remainder of this essay— is taken by people who believe, as I do, that the principal impediments to successful reform are elements of the system itself, structural and political problems that block us from making the kinds of changes we most need and from installing on a large scale the bold reforms with the greatest likelihood of yielding markedly better results.

Ten Structural Barriers to Real Reform

First, the system was designed to furnish ever-increasing services in relatively uniform fashion to an ever-increasing pupil population, but it has none of the elements that are needed to boost quality and productivity. Simply put, we have a quantity-oriented delivery system in an age when what we urgently need is stronger performance and better quality. One is reminded of the period when U.S. automakers were admirably geared to rolling ever more millions of cars off their assembly lines—but far too many of those vehicles were rattling fuel-guzzlers with flashy fins, exploding gas tanks, and ill-fitting doors at a time when American consumers sought efficiency, quality, and smooth, modern lines—features they were more apt to find in Japanese and European vehicles. Detroit eventually responded to these changes in its market, but not until the U.S. manufacturers had incurred heavy losses, and not without fundamentally overhauling their management systems, corporate structures, and leadership.

Today's education system is similarly engineered for quantity at a time when the market seeks performance. As Eric Hanushek and a panel of economists have observed, today's "schools offer virtually no rewards for those who do things more efficiently. . . . Much of the current discussion of school reform involves rather simplistic extensions of existing programs, often just doing more of the same."[7]

The system's primary performance indicators are input-centered. Its chief means of delivery is a bureaucratic management structure that emphasizes compliance with rules, uniformity of treatment, and the precise tracking of resources that segments staff and money into discrete program categories. It is a system that, in its cumbersome way, can always add another program, adjust average third-grade class sizes from 27.2 students to 26.7, and revise the job descriptions of assistant principals. But it has essentially no capacity to ensure that children actually learn, to encourage and reward teacher performance, to weed out incompetent principals, to flatten the management structure, or to substitute one use of resources for another in the interest of boosting efficiency. Insofar as it has any accountability mechanisms, they are programmed around the management of inputs and the delivery of services. The former White House aide James Pinkerton identifies primary and secondary education as one of the strongholds of our "old paradigm" for doing things, which he dubs the "Bureaucratic Operating System."[8]

Second, the education policy-and-governance system is substantially removed from conventional politics and policy leadership. Mayors and governors are chronically frustrated to find themselves with far greater leverage over their welfare, sanitation, and transportation services than over the schools of their state or community. This curious situation resulted from the late nineteenth-century conviction that education should be insulated from common politicians, with their corrupt Tammany-style machines, partisan bickering, and grubby spoils systems, and should instead be entrusted to public-spirited lay boards and expert professionals. The result was an

234 essentially separate education governance system at both state and local levels, consisting of independent policy-setting boards of education that employ licensed educators to run the schools.

Whether this made sense in 1896 is a question we will not linger over. But its effects over time have been perverse—and surely unintended. Public education has developed its own distinctive and insular policy arena that, if not hermetically sealed, is exceedingly hard to break into or influence from outside.

Although the denizens of that arena must usually look beyond its borders for resources, which are generally controlled by the county council or legislature, and must obey often elaborate (and sometimes absurdly prescriptive) state education codes, they have striven with considerable success to shape those outside decisions, too, mostly through electoral activity and heavy lobbying. At least until the last couple of years, they also mostly succeeded in muting partisan differences with respect to education policy. This has turned out to be a mixed blessing. Ostensibly nonpartisan school board elections, for example, which typically do not coincide with the days people go to the polls to pick presidents and governors, tend to draw few voters and to be easily swayed by stakeholder interests. Moreover, school board races, particularly in large communities, no longer enlist platoons of the able, disinterested laymen that the arrangement's architects envisioned. They are far more apt to feature people with singular interests, hang-ups, or grudges of their own (including disgruntled former employees of the school system), slates of candidates assembled by the teachers unions and other groups of current employees, aspiring politicians who view this as a rung on the ladder to power, and individuals seeking money (school board membership often brings a paycheck), media attention, or something with which to fill their days.

The deepening chasm between what the American public deems important in education (safety, discipline, basic skills) and the reform priorities that animate the education establishment (access, inclusion, multiculturalism, and so on) almost certainly can be traced to the insularity of the education policy arena and its removal from the tugs and debates—and incentives and rewards—of conventional politics. Although this is beginning to change as more people run for office in the general-purpose government of their community or state (or nation) on platforms that include specific education policy planks, the capacity of a newly elected mayor or governor (or presi-

dent) to translate his promises into reality still hinges on his ability to manipulate a system over which he usually has no direct control. New York
City Mayor Rudolph Giuliani's efforts to impose his priorities on the city's
schools are one visible recent instance of this, but they are by no means the
only such. Governors John Engler (Michigan), Tommy Thompson (Wisconsin), William Weld (Massachusetts), and Pete Wilson (California) also illustrate the difficulty of bending the education system to the popular will as
interpreted by an elected chief executive.

Third, behind the closed doors of the education policy arena, political
decision making over the past half century has evolved into the brokering of
competing interests among the stakeholders or producers. It's an ant colony
with its own elaborate roles, protocols, and power relationships—all buried
where the sun seldom shines.

Within that colony, factions and stakeholder groups—guidance coun-
selors, school social workers, home economics teachers, baseball coaches,
librarians, curriculum directors, textbook and test publishers, and hundreds
of others—have worked out their own modus vivendi, dividing the resource
pie (and banding together to demand that it be enlarged), accommodating
each other's vital interests, and repelling intruders. Each faction gets its own
"categorical" programs, its own budget lines, its own administrators, its own
defenders at the political level. Frequently lost in this arrangement is the
public interest, not to mention the distinctive needs and varying priorities of
individual clients.

That is why, for example, immigrant parents who want their children to
learn English rapidly have such trouble extricating them from the clutches
of the bilingual education program. The bilingual education crowd gets to
set its own rules, and it sets them so as to expand and solidify its fief.[9] It is
why superintendents and school boards battle against the introduction of
charter schools in their communities. Charters, after all, eat into their enrollments, budgets, and control. It is why the United States employs a higher
percentage of nonteaching personnel in our public schools than any other
OECD country—all those media specialists, drivers, cafeteria workers, security guards, and assistant superintendents have interests that must be
protected, too. And it is why so many youngsters slip through the cracks,
sometimes attending school for years with practically no adult knowing
their names, let alone shouldering responsibility for whether they are actually learning.

The *Washington Post* recently recounted the tale of Demetrius Wilkins, a young man who was given a high school diploma several years ago by the Alexandria, Virginia, public schools even though he could barely read. Soon thereafter, he sought out an adult education teacher who successfully transformed him into a competent reader in six months, something the school system had not managed to do in twelve years, even with the help of the higher-cost special-education class to which he was assigned. Reflecting on this episode, a veteran Alexandria English teacher, Patrick Welsh, had this to say:

> The school system was not totally indifferent to Wilkins's plight. It put him in LD (learning disabled) classes, but little changed. "The LD teachers were nice but it was like they were just there to get me through. We did the same boring sixth-grade stuff year after year," says Wilkins. "It was like just housing me till school was over." . . .
>
> Yet, as Wilkins has since demonstrated, he was fully capable of learning to read. Why couldn't the federally mandated LD program do the job? The trouble, says social worker Thea Hambright, is that "all this energy goes into monitoring whether the social workers and psychologists have their paperwork finished on time. . . . Everything in the school system is fragmented. Different people all know a different piece of a kid, but no one works with or is responsible for the whole kid."[10]

The former National Endowment for the Humanities chairman Lynne V. Cheney borrowed from William James the term "tyrannical machines" to characterize the way dubious practices and assumptions become institutionalized within the education system.[11] The nearly universal requirement that public school teachers be certified by completing an approved program of training in a college of education exemplifies the machines that churn away within this sealed policy arena. Practically nobody outside the education professoriate believes that these programs do much good, even as they consume time and resources that might otherwise be devoted to ensuring that teachers have fair command of the content of their subjects. University programs in school administration are even worse. Yet the requirements remain in force because a skein of institutional interests, jobs, and resource flows has been attached to them, and nobody has the authority to detach it.

Reform efforts are sorely handicapped by the widespread belief—eagerly nurtured by educators—that every stakeholder group must assent to any change before it can be made. This, of course, is a perfect prescription for maintaining the status quo, save for minor innovations on the margin that are lubricated by extra funding. As David N. Plank explains, "The exigencies of bargaining in a pluralist political system have tended to limit reform proposals to those that can win the approval of all interested groups, with the consequence that changes in the structure and operation of state educational systems have not been seriously considered."[12]

Fourth, the same stakeholders have mined the gateways to their policy arena, making it difficult and dangerous for anyone else to disrupt the intricate balance of power worked out among the factions. This has been clear to Washingtonians over the past several years, as they have observed the District of Columbia's education establishment fight every serious proposal to change the city's wretched (but well-financed) school system, using techniques that include ugly charges of racism and colonialism. The District's reform-minded superintendent was unable to prevail with his own school board on a limited contract-management scheme, and the resisters (orchestrated, it appears, by both board members and teachers union) bullied even Newt Gingrich into softening a once potent strategy for transforming the whole system into a far more modest program of marginal change.

Another high-profile episode took place in Jersey City, where, with much fanfare, PepsiCo announced that it would underwrite a new scholarship program to help disadvantaged youngsters attend private and parochial schools—a scheme devised by the city's resourceful mayor, Bret Schundler, to encourage a full-fledged voucher program. That is precisely why defenders of the education status quo in Jersey City threatened boycotts of PepsiCo restaurants and products, broke vending machines, and otherwise did their utmost to intimidate the corporation into backing down. Which, in the event, is what happened—further evidence, if any was needed, that business's zeal to transform American education is commonly circumscribed by considerations of its bottom line. That, of course, is why big business (and the philanthropies it has spawned) has found it convenient to support establishment organizations and their causes rather than any reform schemes that might upset them.

Thus we see local school board elections dominated by candidates recruited (and financed) by teachers unions; state legislatures whose education committees are chaired by union members; and electoral deals worked out—in a kind of high-level Horace's compromise with mayors, governors, even presidents, such that the political success of these officials comes to hinge on their willingness to accommodate the interests of influential education stakeholders. School employees unions are often the biggest contributors to political campaigns and the shrewdest (and most dogged) lobbyists in the anterooms of power. A classic case in point was President Jimmy Carter's creation of a federal education department in return for the National Education Association's political help in 1976.

Many of those interests—for example, teacher certification, tenure, and mandatory collective bargaining—have been codified into laws that are now difficult to change through the political process because of the firm grip that education stakeholders exert upon elected policy makers. For the most part, they do this by courting allies in the Democratic Party. A huge fraction of the delegates to recent state and national Democratic conventions have been teacher unionists. (Neither party nor union will furnish numbers, but it has been estimated by credible analysts that as many as one in seven delegates to recent Democratic national conventions have belonged to the NEA alone.) Union political action committees are also big donors to the campaigns of sympathetic office seekers, and platoons of teachers can be mustered to run phone banks and distribute leaflets (and sometimes drop hints through their pupils about whom parents and grandparents might want to vote for). The occasional electoral upset deals them a setback, as recently happened in Michigan, where the long-mighty unions had grown so accustomed to the Democrats' legislative hegemony that they were entirely unprepared for the GOP takeover (or the shrewd leadership of Governor Engler). But they aren't stupid or rigid; if vouchsafing their interests means manipulating Republicans instead, such a shift is easily made. That is what recently happened in New York City. That is also what happens more and more often in states (such as those in the southwestern and mountain regions) where Republican majorities are the norm. The recent defeat of voucher bills in the Arizona legislature, for example, is attributable primarily to a handful of Republicans whose reelection depends in large part on ensuring that nobody runs too vigorous a campaign against them. Such people are easily whispered to by teachers union leaders and local board members.

More minefields await the intrepid education reformer who tries to circumvent the legislative process and appeal directly to voters. In states where the initiative and referendum are frequently employed to make policy

changes, the education establishment throws immense sums of money and
countless hours of "volunteer" time into campaigns to defeat unwanted
reforms. Recent school voucher initiatives in California, Colorado, and Ore-
gon vividly display this capacity in action, but so do lower-profile fiscal
matters having to do with taxes and education spending.

Circumvention turns out to be nearly impossible, even when election
day appears to bring victory. The stakeholders eventually find ways to stymie unwanted changes. As Plank notes, "In some states . . . education-
minded governors have put forward more radical proposals for reform over
the opposition of important constituencies, including teachers. Even in
states where this strategy was successful and structural reforms were proposed, however, interest groups opposed to reform . . . have for the most
part been successful in forcing compromises . . . or at least in scaling back
major reforms prior to implementation."

Education interest groups are both ubiquitous and tireless. Parents and
business leaders may have scant time to attend policy debates and strategy
meetings, but one can always count on finding participants there from the
teachers union, the superintendents group, and the school board association. They, after all, are paid—by public tax dollars, retrieved through member dues, often extracted involuntarily—to monitor all such gatherings,
whereas consumers must ordinarily support themselves by working at
other jobs. (Often the money flows directly from the taxpayers into the
salaries of union representatives without even passing through members'
dues, as is the case at the federal Education Department, for example, and in
New York City.)

Patience is another asset of the status quo. Education reformers wax and
wane, but established interests endure forever. As George Washington
Plunkitt of Tammany Hall observed decades ago, reformers are "morning
glories," whose interests are ephemeral, while the permanent beneficiaries
of the status quo work at their ownership every day, year in and year out.
An uncommonly zealous governor may succeed in enacting an unusually
bold reform, notwithstanding the objections of unions and school boards.
But in time he will turn his attention to prisons, nursing homes, or economic development. His term will end. A few key legislative allies lose their
elections or retire. His successor arrives in office, perhaps with the help
of voters aggrieved by the inconvenience of the change in its early stages
of implementation. Early evaluations show that the reform did not work

240 perfectly as originally conceived. Proposals are mooted to revise it, perhaps
to save money, perhaps to make it work better, perhaps to foster equity.
Whatever. Establishment interests are always there, doggedly waiting for
the moment to move to weaken, slow down, or repeal key portions of the
change they did not like. They are *always* present. They have elephantine
memories. And they have the fiscal, political, and public relations clout to
reward friends, punish foes, and sway public attitudes. They also have a rare
asset in their capacity (grounded in the American parent's near-automatic
affection for the concept of public education and for his or her own child's
teacher) to paint would-be reformers as "enemies of education" and themselves as "defenders of public schools."

Fifth, although education's producer interests are exquisitely well organized and generously financed to pursue their interests in the political and
policy arenas, the consumers have no effective organization. Often they
cannot rely upon their elected representatives, who are more apt to owe
specific debts to teachers unions than to the nebulous population of families
with children attending public schools. Although education's consumers
are far more numerous than its producers, their numbers are not matched
by any viable means of impressing their priorities on the decision-making
process. They are further handicapped by the difficulty most people have
imagining a school or school system that differs fundamentally from the one
they attended a quarter century earlier. Even people with vivid imagina-
tions are normally less motivated to press hard for something they have
never actually experienced than are the defenders of the status quo to cling
to what they now possess. Consumers, too, are rarely eager to change long-
established routines, at least without compelling reasons. (Thus, for example, the staunch resistance in many communities to a year-round school
calendar, despite evidence that such a change yields both achievement gains
and economic efficiency.) The reasons given them for making the change
are usually less than compelling because the school system, fearful of giving
critics more ammunition, has a greater interest in persuading its public that
all is basically well with the schools as they are.

Sixth, consumers and reformers alike are crippled by the absence of clear
standards, goals, measures, feedback, and real accountability. This is a big
topic that cannot adequately be covered in a few paragraphs.[13] Here is a
summary of the problem:

At almost every level, American education lacks specific objectives that

describe what children should learn and how well they are expected to learn 241
it. The closer one gets to individual schools, teachers, and pupils, the fuzzier
those "standards" get and the more obscure the data about performance.
Without clear standards and reliable indicators of performance in relation to
precise objectives, it is impossible to hold anyone—student, teacher, principal, school system, or state—accountable for success or failure.

Nearly all reports on the performance of the education system are issued
by the same people who run the system. There is no counterpart to what the
corporate world knows as the independent audit. This structural reality,
combined with the strong desire of the establishment to persuade its constituencies that the system is succeeding now, plus the aversion of most educators to tests, comparisons, competition, and "high stakes" accountability,
means that nobody has good, clear, timely, reliable, actionable information
about how anyone is doing in relation to how they ought to be doing.

Yes, there's a lot of testing, and yes, we are barraged by press accounts of
what the latest test scores show. Once in a great while, a poor showing on
some test leads to action (as when California revamped its whole-language
approach to reading instruction after the state's National Assessment scores
plummeted). But such events are as rare as charter schools. And so long as
the system is able to shield its own performance from informed scrutiny,
while engaging in a disinformation campaign to convince people that all is
well, anyone seeking to reform that system will resemble a blindfolded
amateur prizefighter in the ring with a clear-eyed professional. Here is how
former New Jersey governor Tom Kean described his experience in this
arena:

> As part of my blueprint for reform, I proposed a much tougher test [than
> the minimum competency version already in use in New Jersey], this time to
> include writing skills that would be mandatory for high school graduation.
> The test measures basic ninth-grade-level skills. . . . The initial reaction of
> educators to the next test was extremely negative. . . . Educators lobbied me
> strenuously to delay the test, or better, to cancel it. A close look at the argu-
> ment shows an insidious tendency to put the image of schools above the
> welfare of the students.[14]

Seventh, so many cooks stirring the education broth, together with the
nearly infinite capacity of individual schools to resist changes they don't like
and the near-impregnability of a teacher's own classroom, mean that we

have a system that is simultaneously gridlocked and unable to assign responsibility. No one is really in charge, nobody is ultimately responsible, and everybody can blame someone else for whatever isn't working well. The teacher says she is required to use this textbook, is not allowed to discipline that disruptive youngster, and lacks time during the day to provide individual tutoring for the exceptional child. The principal reports that the teacher was foisted on him, that textbook decisions are made downtown or by the state adoption committee, that the school board will not allot extra funds for tutors, and that the courts have tied his hands with respect to discipline. The superintendent explains that the principal has tenure (and his wife's cousin is an alderman). The school board is adamant that disabled and disadvantaged children must receive all the tutorial help even if that leaves none for gifted youngsters. The board chairman says he is following the superintendent's recommendation in this matter and, in any case, is bound by federal and state laws. The governor observes that the schools of this state are locally controlled (and the teachers union and school board association helped elect him). The legislator is terrified that if he presses hard to change the law, he will antagonize either the black caucus or the religious fundamentalists. Besides, the state faces a budget crisis, and the extra money to do anything new must come from Washington. The congressmen sends back a polite form letter indicating that your views will be carefully considered the next time pertinent legislation comes before the House. From the federal Department of Education, there is no reply at all for six months; then you receive a pamphlet entitled "How to Help Your Child Improve in Math."

Eighth, the education establishment cleverly manipulates Americans' strong affection for the concept of public education while imposing a double standard on proposals to reform its reality. We are easily seduced by our innate and uncritical love for anything called public schools. We have grown up thinking of them as good and worthy things, and we give the benefit of the doubt to anyone who claims to support them, just as we cast a jaundiced eye on anything said to weaken them, whether the assertion is true or not. Defenders of the status quo adroitly twist each proposed change into an "effort to destroy our public schools."

In no other institutional domain, save perhaps libraries, does the adjective *public* trigger this warm, supportive feeling. (Consider our response to phrases like "public housing," "public transportation," "public welfare," "public hospitals," "public lavatories," even "public colleges.") It is a feeling

easily exploited by defenders of the old BOS paradigm for education. And   243
they do it shamelessly. When they assert that the such-and-such proposal
"would destroy public education" or "weaken the public schools," what
they ordinarily mean is that it would cause those schools to operate by
different ground rules than they do today.

Recent surveys by Public Agenda indicate that some of the bloom is
fading from this rose as more and more Americans conclude that, when you
get down to specifics, public schools are doing a poor job of providing students with safety, discipline, basic skills, and character development.[15]
These findings have led the perceptive teachers union chief Albert Shanker
to warn his members, "Time is running out on public education. . . . A
majority of Americans believe that the public schools cannot be counted on
to provide the things they consider most important in an education. . . . The
schools have a window of opportunity to regain public support. If that is
ignored we will see the collapse of the system."[16]

Whether regaining support calls for a massive public relations campaign,
as the National Education Association and the American Association of
School Administrators seem to believe, or the more fundamental changes in
the system that Shanker and some of his American Federation of Teachers
colleagues favor, it may be that Americans' blind worship of the theory of
public education is beginning to be replaced by an open-eyed appraisal of its
reality.

But the double standard remains intact and ubiquitous. Simply put, all
proposed changes in the education status quo are subjected to far more
rigorous criteria than is the status quo itself. The latter is able to get away
with widespread malpractice affecting millions of youngsters. Because it is
the way we have always done things, recurrent evidence of its massive
failure triggers no alarms.

Propose a different way of doing things, however, and all the sirens
scream. You are immediately challenged to prove that it will work perfectly, that it has been fully tested and evaluated, that it will have no unexpected or undesirable side effects, that every possible wrinkle has been
ironed out in advance, that every imaginable question about it has an iron-
clad answer—and that it will not deflect any resources from the "regular"
system. Thus we encounter the paradox that nothing can be tried until it has
been proven to work, although it cannot be proven because it has not been
tried because it has not yet been proven. And when a specific innovation

ends unsuccessfully, such as EAI's Baltimore contract, boosters of the status quo promptly assert that all contracting everywhere has been proven to fail and must therefore never be tried again. The reverse argument is never heard: that when a government school fails, it demonstrates that government schooling is a failure.

Ninth, public education has developed a budget and finance system that channels almost all its money into salaries, that treats every change as an additional cost, that has virtually no capacity to substitute one activity or use of funds for another, and yet manages to get an astonishingly small fraction of its dollars into the classroom itself. The percentage of the public school budget devoted to "regular instruction" declined from 61 percent in 1960 to 46 percent in 1990.[17]

A simple calculation makes the point even more vividly. A classroom of twenty-four children accounted for an average total public expenditure of about $150,000 in 1995–1996. Yet the average public school teacher, complete with fringe benefits, costs not quite $50,000. That suggests that some two-thirds of the public funds generated by—and spent on behalf of—those youngsters is not going to their main teacher. Where, then, is it going? Mostly to other people, including all manner of specialists, administrators and nonteaching personnel. That it is nearly all locked up in salaries—and kept there by the force of collective bargaining as well as bureaucratic custom and institutional inertia—means that very little of it is available to replace the coal furnace, fix the leaky roof, extend the school year, or equip the building with networked telecommunications and computer systems.

The education system seems entirely incapable of transferring large sums from one budget function to another. If you propose to do something different, you will be asked where you expect to find the additional money to pay for it, for it is unimaginable that anything else could be cut from the budget. When money is tight, class sizes may grow. But perish the thought that an unnecessary administrator, superfluous sheet metal instructor, unwanted bilingual program, or inept library aide would be let go or replaced by a bit of modern technology, much less that the special education program (with its immense costs, entrenched interests, and redundant procedures) might be reined in.

Even when a radical structural change is introduced, the budget—and its many dependents—fight back. The main source of EAI's trouble with the Hartford school system, which it had contracted to manage, was the com-

pany's proposal to dismiss a number of unneeded employees (pupil enrollments having markedly shrunk in recent years, with no contraction of the
personnel rolls) and transfer the money into a major technology upgrade.
This was unacceptable to the unions (and local politicians) and led in short
order to a major downscaling of EAI's duties in Hartford.

Tenth, the education profession does not attract risk takers and change
agents. Although any enterprise with five million employees is bound to
have people of every sort, security, predictability, and congenial human
relations rank higher on the priorities of most educators than do rigor,
experimentation, and entrepreneurship. Moreover, their "progressive"
philosophical makeup—carefully nurtured in the colleges of education—is
apt to assign greater value to self-esteem, respect for differences, emotional
well-being, and nonjudgmentalism than to intellectual distinction, compet-
itiveness, and accountability.

One can argue that educators' pay isn't enough to justify taking many
risks or upsetting applecarts—or to elicit more work than the typical 180-
day school year and six-hour day. If we want the high-wire, high-intensity,
round-the-clock dedication of securities traders, perhaps we should expect
to fork over Wall Street–level salaries. But pay isn't the whole story. The
education china shop today contains so much clutter and so many delicate
pieces that anyone entering it is well advised to move with care. One can
easily run afoul of one's principal, one's school board, a student's parents,
a litigation-crazed public-interest law firm, even one's own peers. Thus
teachers who have received prizes and awards for classroom excellence, or
who have gone to the considerable bother and expense of getting themselves board certified, often find themselves scorned or ridiculed as rate
busters by their teaching colleagues. Thus the founders of a Massachusetts
charter school faced intimidation and harassment by public school employees that was intense enough to cause several of them to leave town.[18] On
balance, prudence and good sense would seem to argue for leaving things as
they are, shutting the classroom or office door and quietly minding one's
own business, not making noise or disrupting the comfortable assumptions
of others.

Indeed, the surest way to get in trouble in American education is to try to
change things. Going with the flow, one avoids controversy and keeps one's
job. Paddling against the tide, one is sure to be buffeted and quite likely to
capsize. And the higher one's rank, the greater the risks of risk taking—and

the less security one enjoys. (Public school teachers typically gain permanent tenure after three years; urban superintendents are lucky to last that long.) Consider the fate of John Murphy, one of the nation's most respected school executives, who recently surrendered the helm of North Carolina's largest school system after less than four years.

Murphy is a veteran practitioner of education change who believes deeply in standards and accountability, who handpicks every principal, who surrounds them—and himself—with factual evidence of the performance of each school in the system as gauged on numerous measures, who envisions schools that depart boldly from the familiar model, who doesn't hesitate to dismiss or transfer nonperformers, and who is firm with everyone—local tycoons and newspaper editors as well as school employees—about what he expects from them.

He can also be a proud, headstrong, and difficult person, but he does not shrink from battles. A book he wrote quotes Machiavelli on the dangers that lurk in the "creation of a new system" and advises education change agents to "have your bags packed and be ready to move."

That's what Murphy himself has had to do, even though the schools of Charlotte-Mecklenburg improved greatly under his stewardship. As the *New York Times* education writer Peter Applebome reports, "There is widespread agreement that his tenure has been overwhelmingly positive for children in the district. . . . Test scores—including those of minorities—are up. Thirty-six of 38 performance indicators show improvement, much of it substantial. And . . . almost everyone agrees that Dr. Murphy has put in place a sophisticated system to monitor and reward excellence."[19]

So what went wrong? As Applebome recounts, "The problem with getting a hard-charging C.E.O.-type to run a school system can be getting someone who is a hard-charging C.E.O." Even in a state with relatively weak teachers unions, Murphy ran "afoul of some educators when his changes meant reassigning or demoting people he thought were not performing." Some of this took on a racial tinge, leading to criticism from the left. Meanwhile, religious fundamentalists who won some school board seats objected to Murphy's relentless emphasis on educational outcomes, giving him critics on the right. Nor were Charlotte's powerful business community and local politicians universally charmed by his outspoken support for a school bond issue (which failed) and his bitter criticism of those who opposed it.

The erosion of Murphy's base of support was gradual and cannot be traced to a single cause, like New York Mayor Rudolph Giuliani's vendetta against former school chancellor Ramon Cortines or the Milwaukee teachers union's alarm over former superintendent Howard Fuller's flirtation with private contracting and school choice—alarm so keen that the union ran its own candidates in the next school board election and produced a majority that prompted Fuller's resignation. But now, like Cortines, Fuller, and dozens of others, Murphy must go. So, typically, must other educators who break a little china, change the system's ground rules, unsettle established interests, and challenge the community's comfortable assumptions about its schools. Is it any wonder that they are few and far between?

Cracks in the Glacier

As is now clear, most of the forces in American education work to keep it from changing, and the more radical the change the harder those forces go about their work. Yet not everything is gloomy from the reformer's standpoint. Several contemporary developments, while still modest in scale, now gleam through the cloud layer. These include:

- A few states and communities have begun to blunt the claws of their teachers unions. While the headline of a recent article in *School Board News*, "Dark Days For Teacher Unions," is surely premature, Michigan, Illinois, and Indiana exemplify historically strong union states that have moved to limit the scope of collective bargaining, to break the union monopoly on insurance for teachers, or to boost the penalties for striking. Tenure laws are under assault in a half dozen jurisdictions. Nobody is counting the unions out—and the continuing AFT-NEA merger negotiations could yield a political powerhouse—but they're on the defensive more often than in the past. And the simultaneous onslaught of multiple changes that they abhor (for example, voucher bills, charter school bills, private contracting schemes, efforts to ease tenure laws, and reallocation of funds) leaves even their deep pockets, resourceful strategists, and indefatigable lobbyists hard-pressed to defend every bastion.
- A "new paradigm" of public education is making some headway in intellectual, policy-making, and political circles. Instead of the Bureaucratic Operating System depicted by Pinkerton, it anticipates a performance-

based system, a decentralized universe of diverse models, multiple providers, and consumer choices, usually stitched together by standards and
accountability for results. This amounts to nothing less than redefining
public education in terms of serving the public rather than being the
servant of a government monopoly. Most of the bold reforms discussed
elsewhere in this book illustrate this new paradigm in action. If it continues to spread, it must ultimately prove fatal to the monopoly.

- An important part of education's new paradigm, and of "reinventing government" more broadly (whether one prefers the Clinton-Gore version
or the Gingrich approach), is the serious entry of private enterprise into
the vast K–12 education market. Of course, it has long been there, selling
computers, textbooks, chalk, milk, and chicken nuggets, leasing school
buses and contracting for janitorial services. In recent years, private organizations have also supplied specialized instruction in foreign languages,
science, and remedial reading to school districts. But the operation of
entire schools or school systems, and the delivery by private providers of
complete packages of curriculum and instruction, are new to public education. They are growing. They directly threaten the monopoly. So do
other imaginative private-sector strategies, such as the creation in more
than a dozen cities of privately funded scholarship schemes designed in
part to bring pressure for school choice to bear on public education policy
makers. Although the jury is still out as to whether these various inter-
ventions yield higher pupil achievement, there is no doubt that they are
forcing changes in the old ground rules and hoary operating assumptions.

- Accompanying the new paradigm, and a corollary of private sector involvement, is widening acceptance within education policy deliberations
of what may be termed a productivity agenda, centering on standards,
performance, efficiency, and accountability. Described in detail in Hanushek's *Making Schools Work* and in a recent report by the Consortium on
Productivity in the Schools, it is also what business leaders are propound-
ing when they press for standards-based school reform and what elected
officials are after when they demand more return on the education dollar.
Although the backlash against outcomes-based education has intimi-
dated some, the quest for stronger performance may yet embolden more
lay reformers to gain control of the standards, measures, and criteria by
which progress will henceforth be gauged.

- A few politicians are beginning to be rewarded at the polls for taking on

the education status quo and challenging the field's established interests.
It is hard to interpret Engler's smashing 1994 reelection, for example, as anything but a public mandate to continue making bold changes in the schools of Michigan. Candidates offering radical change swept into state superintendent posts in Arizona, Florida, and Georgia that year. And although no large changes in policy and structure have yet occurred at the federal level, the new congressional majority has placed some fresh ideas on the Washington table.

- Some of the newcomers are chipping cracks in the once-solid facade of the education establishment. More than a dozen state-level education policy makers have formed a new organization—the Education Leaders Council—to advance the "new paradigm" agenda, and some are defecting from such old-line groups as the Council of Chief State School Officers, the National Association of State Boards of Education, and the Education Commission of the States. If these cracks widen, the old organizations will be less able to claim that they represent their entire constituencies, and policy makers may be less apt to heed their views. (Another rift has developed between American Federation of Teachers chief Albert Shanker and a group called the Council of the Great City Schools. This, too, stems from sharp disagreement over important policy issues.)
- Having tried for at least a decade to push their way into the education policy arena, more and more purposeful noneducators are finally gaining entry. In addition to the governors and business leaders who arrived first, recent entrants include a number of mayors (such as Schundler in Jersey City, Daley in Chicago, Norquist in Milwaukee, Goldsmith in Indianapolis, Schmoke in Baltimore, and Menino in Boston), some tough-minded lawyers (such as Clark Durant, who chairs the Michigan state board), a handful of energetic, persistent, and well-informed critics (William Bennett and Lynne Cheney, for example) and philanthropists (Peter Flanigan, Michael Joyce, Robert Schwartz), and even the occasional ex-military officer (General John Stanford is now Seattle's superintendent).

How deep into the glacier do these cracks extend, and what are the odds that it will begin to break up rather than continue grinding down everything in its path? There is no way to know for sure whether we're living in the early days of a big thaw or in the shadow of an ice age. Either could happen. Recent history favors the established interests and predicts the recuperation of the status quo. Yet if, as some analysts think, the United States is on the threshold of a profound political and ideological shift, including the repudiation of century-old assumptions about the proper ordering of our domestic social policies, the repeal of key elements of the New Deal, and the reining-in of major elements of the Great Society, the implications for education reform could be huge.

If we move from an overhaul of the welfare system to an equally thoroughgoing reconstruction of our educational arrangements, the glacier could well shatter. Unlike welfare policy, however, large changes in K–12 schooling are far more likely to be made at the state or local level than in Washington. Although it is inconceivable (and probably undesirable) that all these jurisdictions would move together, they are known for copying one another. If a dozen governors, mayors, or legislative leaders are able to display stronger educational performance, improved school efficiency, or enhanced parent satisfaction in the aftermath of such bold reforms as those now being tried, others are certain to follow their lead. If, on the other hand, established interests are able to suppress these reforms before they can prove themselves, we'll gradually revert to the familiar status quo. Deep waters continue to run still. The fish swim undisturbed, and the surface waves prove deceptive.

10 Somebody's Children: Educational Opportunity for *All* American Children

Diane Ravitch

Certain values are paramount in any discussion of education in the United States: equality, excellence, and pluralism. As a nation we support the principle of equality of educational opportunity. We support the principle of educational excellence. Our pursuit of equality and excellence must be joined, because educational opportunity—if equal—should be equal in excellence, not equal in mediocrity. And finally, we support the liberal democratic ideas of diversity and pluralism, for we recognize that in a free society, healthy differences of opinion and practice not only promote progress but are required for it.

In the United States today, we have an education system from kindergarten through twelfth grade that embraces these ideals in theory but fails to achieve them in reality. Whether we look at the results of international

252 assessments, standardized tests, or performance-based assessments, our students do not achieve high levels of excellence; and, in spite of considerable progress over the past generation, there continue to be large gaps in achievement between children from different social classes and different racial or ethnic groups.[1] For many children, especially children who are poor and belong to racial minorities, both equality and excellence in education remain out of reach. In addition, although our public schools honor diversity and pluralism by bringing together students from many different backgrounds, they simultaneously dishonor those values by requiring conformity to state-imposed policies on controversial issues about which reasonable people differ and by prohibiting the use of public funds in schools that differ from the majoritarian consensus (for example, single-sex schools and schools for those with strong religious convictions).

On February 15, 1994, Secretary of Education Richard Riley delivered a speech at Georgetown University on the state of American education, in which he noted, "Some schools are excellent, some are improving, some have the remarkable capacity to change for the better, and some should never be called schools at all."[2]

I was struck by the reference to schools that "should never be called schools at all." Who attends them? Chances are these students are African-American and Hispanic; chances are they are from very poor families, in which a single parent is struggling to make ends meet. These are the children who are compelled to attend schools that most teachers shun, if they can, in neighborhoods that people of means avoid, if possible.

The secretary closed his speech with a famous quotation from John Dewey: "What the best and wisest parent wants for his [and, may I say, her] child, that must be what the community wants for all of its children. Any other ideal for our schools is narrow and unlovely; it destroys our democracy."

The question must arise, "Who are the best and wisest parents, and what would they do if their children were assigned to one of those places that are not fit to be called schools?"

Somebody's children are compelled—one might say condemned—to attend schools that should never be called schools at all. Somebody's children go to those schools. Not mine. Not yours. Not the secretary's. Not the president's or the vice president's. Surely not the mayor's or the superintendent's or even the teacher's. What would the best and wisest parents do if their children were zoned into schools that are physically unsafe and educationally bankrupt? They would move to a different neighborhood or put their children into private schools. That's what the president and the vice president did. That is what well-to-do and middle-class parents do.

But somebody's children are required to go to those schools. Some parents who do not have the money to move to a better neighborhood or to put their child into a private school have been told that their child must stay there no matter how bad the school is. If they are parents with motivation and energy, they are told by school officials and policy makers that they must stay right where they are, because they are the kind of parents who might someday help to improve that dreadful school. The people who tell them this would not keep their own child in that school for even a day.

What should we do about those children and those schools? Many people say, "We must reform those schools." Of course, they are right. For policy makers and academics, this is the appropriate response to clearly inadequate schools. But for parents, this is an outrageous proposition, for our own children live this day, in the here and now, and they cannot wait around to see whether the school will get better in five or ten years. I suggest that we project our passion for our own children's welfare—as Dewey suggested—onto those parents who lack our money, power, and education; they love their children as much as we love ours. Their desperation about their children's future is greater than ours because they know that the odds are stacked against them. They should not be expected to wait patiently for the transformation of the failing institutions where their children are required to go each day, the places that the secretary of education says do not deserve to be called schools at all. We surely would not be willing to make the same sacrifice of our own children. Why should they?

Dewey was right: what the best and wisest parents want for their children is what the community should want for all its children. Not the promise of good education someday, maybe, but the reality of good education today.

So the problem I now address is: how can we quickly improve the educational opportunities available to those children who are now attending schools that should not be called schools?

I suggest that states, cities, or the federal government should provide means-tested scholarships to needy families, who may use them to send

254   their children to the school of their choice, be it public, independent, or
religious. In higher education, needy students are eligible for Pell grants,
which can be used to attend any accredited institution, regardless of its
sponsorship. In effect, I am suggesting Pell grants for elementary and secondary education. The number and size of such scholarships can be strictly
controlled by public authorities, in order to gauge the cost and consequences (although care should be taken to assure that public authorities do
not make the number and size so small as to render the program meaningless). The size of the scholarship should vary in relation to family income;
the needier the child, the larger the grant. Children with disabilities should
receive the full amount of financial aid to which they would be entitled
under state and federal law because their education is expensive, no matter
who provides it. Because funds will necessarily be limited, highest priority
for such scholarships should go to children who are currently enrolled in
schools that have been identified by public authorities (for example, the
state commissioner of education or the city superintendent) as the lowest-
performing in the district.

Usually, these schools are well-known to officials, parents, and the press.
In New York State, for example, the state commissioner of education has
identified certain "schools under registration review" because of extremely
poor pupil performance and high dropout rates. It would not be difficult to
select objective criteria to identify such schools, including attendance rates
for students and teachers, dropout rates, and various measures of pupil
performance. Parent education and family income obviously contribute to
pupil performance, but we must take care not to build into public policy a
sense of resignation that children's socioeconomic status determines their
destiny. Public policy must relentlessly seek to replicate schools that demonstrate the ability to educate children from impoverished backgrounds instead of perpetuating (and rewarding) those that use the pupil's circumstances as a rationale for failure.

When allowed full choice among public schools, parents help identify the
least effective by voting with their feet. If allowed the opportunity to receive
scholarships to attend the school of their choice, whether public or nonpublic, parents of poor children would become empowered consumers
rather than hapless clients ignored by an unresponsive bureaucracy. In addition to providing immediate assistance to the neediest students, this strat-

egy would help to transform or even close those schools that have been unchanged by all previous reform efforts.

Of course there is the danger of perverse incentives. So that dropping out is not encouraged or rewarded, dropouts should not be eligible for such scholarships. It is possible that parents might send their children to a school with a terrible reputation in hopes of winning a scholarship, but that seems unlikely.

There are many different ways to structure a scholarship program for needy students and many different policy considerations involving criteria for eligibility, size of individual scholarships, cost, transportation, support services for parents, evaluation, and so on. As cities and states seek to implement school choice, many different approaches will be tried. I do not offer a single solution to any one of these questions, because experience to date is too limited to provide definitive answers. The issue at hand is not the specific details that should be adopted in a given program but the general principles that should guide the development of such programs in the future.

Of one thing I am convinced: the big, anonymous comprehensive high school that was the hallmark of American education for most of this century is incapable of meeting the needs of endangered youngsters in the cities. The "shopping mall high school," as it was appropriately called by Arthur Powell, Eleanor Farrar, and David Cohen, offers something for everyone, cafeteria-style, but it cannot provide the individual support and nurturance that most of these young people need. The typical comprehensive high school is large and impersonal, with a studied air of neutrality towards all students. But that is exactly what these children do not need. They need schools that work closely with each student and his or her family; they need schools that are designed to be intensely engaged with each child as a unique person. Children need to be in schools where there are many adults who know their names and care about them, know when they are absent, know when they have a problem, think about their futures, and expect to talk frequently to their parents or guardians.

I am persuaded that the most successful urban schools are those that have a sense of purpose, a mission, an identity of their own. Some of these schools are public, some are not. Paul Hill and his colleagues describe them as "high schools with character." Theodore R. Sizer writes, "Good schools are thoughtful places. The people in them are known. The units are small

256   enough to be coherent communities of friends." Anthony Bryk, Valerie Lee,
       and Peter Holland analyze the way that Catholic schools create a strong sense
       of community, with a coherent philosophy, shared values, and common
       purpose.[3] Hill and his colleagues call such places "focus schools," which

> resemble one another, and differ from zoned comprehensive public schools,
> in two basic ways. First, focus schools have clear uncomplicated missions
> centered on the experiences the school intends to provide its students and on
> the ways it intends to influence its students' performance, attitudes, and
> behavior. Second, focus schools are strong organizations with a capacity to
> initiate action in pursuit of their missions, to sustain themselves over time, to
> solve their own problems, and to manage their external relationships.[4]

Most children need to be in focus schools, schools with a high degree of
autonomy and self-direction, schools with a clear sense of purpose, schools
where they are known, schools that are small enough to create a sense of
community, schools where no one is anonymous or overlooked. Students
in the inner city have the greatest need to attend schools where adults know
them, watch over them, watch out for them, and care for them. In today's
society, with most parents working, children need schools that function in
loco parentis, with the knowledge and assent of parents who welcome a
partnership with the school.[5]

There are two complementary strategies to expand the numbers of focus
schools: One is to provide means-tested scholarships to poor children, allowing them to attend any school that accepts public accountability for education standards and civil rights laws. The other is to promote the spread of
charter schools and special-purpose public schools managed under contract
by public or private organizations. The virtue of charter schools is that they
encourage innovation with accountability; they are public schools, regardless of who manages them, operating with public funds, open to all who
apply.

The charter/contracting strategy is politically practical and avoids the
inevitable constitutional problems that will accompany any choice plan that
includes private and religious schools. These two paths will create a more
diverse, pluralistic system of good schools from which parents and students
may choose. One creates demand for special-purpose schools by supplying
scholarships, the other creates a new supply by encouraging the creation of
additional special-purpose schools.

Both strategies should be pursued at the same time. Both are necessary if there is to be any prospect of large-scale change, because otherwise supporters of the status quo will severely restrict the number of charters granted and will seek to marginalize charter schools as appropriate only for a tiny minority of students with special interests. Taken together, both strategies would expand educational opportunities for poor children. Wherever specialized magnet schools or choice programs have been made available, parents have responded enthusiastically, largely because of their perception that their child may be neglected in the anonymity of the typical large comprehensive school, as well as the implicit (and usually explicit) promise that the new, small schools offer an individualized education, in which no child is overlooked.

Although it is tempting to support public choice only, because it is less controversial, I argue the case for full choice involving both state and non-state schools because, first, opening choice to all schools will rapidly expand the supply of places available, and second, including private and religious schools, so long as they are willing to comply with state education standards, is a matter of justice. I do not advocate full choice solely on grounds that competition is good, although I do think that competition is good. I have difficulty thinking of any monopoly that effectively serves the public and simultaneously meets individual needs. Nor do I argue for full choice on grounds that private schools are by their nature better than public schools; I do not believe that. On the contrary, I know that there are many excellent public schools, as there are many mediocre private schools.

No, what I argue is that it is unjust to compel poor children to attend bad schools. It is unjust to prohibit poor families from sending their children to the school of their choice, even if that school has a religious affiliation. It is unjust to deny free schooling to poor families with strong religious convictions, equally unjust as it would be to prohibit the use of federal scholarships to attend Notre Dame, Yeshiva, or Princeton. It is unjust that there is no realistic way to force the closure of schools that students and their parents would abandon if they could.

For the following reasons, the policy of means-tested scholarships would benefit low-income children and their families, while encouraging pluralism:

A means-tested choice program would strengthen the role of parents and families in children's lives. Public policy should aim to enhance the role of parents in

258   their children's lives. There is clear evidence that parent participation is much greater in Catholic schools than in public schools, and it is probably greater in "focus" public schools than in ordinary public schools.[6]

A means-tested choice program would allow low-income students to move to a better school—public, private, or religious. As the charter school movement spreads across the country, there are increasing opportunities for students to move to small, purposeful schools. A model school created by Wayne State University in Detroit was heavily oversubscribed. Rice University was inundated with applications for a new school near its campus in Houston. Catholic schools have a strong track record, especially with disadvantaged urban students, who have a lower dropout rate and higher test scores than their peers in public schools.[7] One reason for the difference is the fact that students in Catholic schools are much likelier to be placed in college preparatory programs, regardless of their race or social class. So, for example, in 1990, 66 percent of high school sophomores in Catholic schools were on a college track, compared with 39 percent of public school sophomores.[8]

A means-tested choice program would enable students to attend schools where teachers and parents agree on a code of conduct. Participating in a close, consensual community would help to protect and nurture youngsters and to buttress them against the dangers of the street. Under a program of choice, eligible students will be able to attend a school where there is focus, mission, and identity. It is only in such a setting that students who are now alienated will begin to see themselves as responsible participants, surrounded by adults and other students who are affected by their decisions and actions. Under the current system, there is no incentive to establish new focus schools. In a choice program, there will be encouragement to create many such schools.

A means-tested choice program would minimize conflict within school systems by giving options to people with conflicting values. Some parents prefer a school that requires uniforms; others do not. Some may want progressive pedagogy; others may not. Although some individual schools of choice may be homogeneous in their basic values, the system as a whole would foster greater pluralism and diversity.

A means-tested choice program would help school districts use every educational resource in the community to meet a surge in enrollments. The United States is once again in the midst of a large increase in school enrollments. The National Center for Education Statistics projects that enrollment in grades K–8 will increase from 35.2 million in 1992 to 39.7 million by the year 2004, an increase of 13 percent, and that enrollment in grades 9–12 will grow from 12.9 million in 1992 to 16.0 million in 2004, an increase of 24 percent.[9] Increases of this magnitude will force public officials either to invest billions of dollars in constructing new schools or to use all existing facilities fully.

The best response to these enrollment increases is to take advantage of all schools through a choice system that is well organized, well supervised, and coordinated with existing public schools.

A means-tested choice program would encourage individual decision making, a fundamental value in a democratic society. It is hard to think of any other part of American life in which choice is portrayed as an evil. Having the ability to choose among competing products and services allows us to exercise some control over our lives; the absence of choice means that someone else has made a vital decision for us, as though we were incompetent to manage our own lives. It is possible to argue that life is unfair and that poor people have no right to demand the kind of mobility available to people of means. But the example of higher education suggests a workable model for providing scholarships for poor students in elementary and secondary schools.

My proposal is not new; many others have made similar suggestions.[10] It is, however, new for me. I have reconsidered my views on the relation between public and nonpublic schools. I do so not because of any animus towards public education. I attended public schools in Houston, Texas, for thirteen years. I am a supporter of public education. From July 1991 until January 1993, I was an assistant secretary of education in the administration of President George Bush. That administration strongly endorsed the principle of school choice, and it might have been reasonable to suppose that I did too. In truth, I was unresolved about the issue. Indeed, in 1983 I argued in *The New Republic* that tuition tax credits were a bad idea because they might undermine the independence of nonpublic schools. During my time in the federal government I devoted my energy to advocating the creation of voluntary national standards and seldom spoke about choice. Frankly, I avoided the topic because I knew that I could make the argument for both sides. I was impressed by the research about Catholic schools by James Coleman, Andrew Greeley, and others, but I had not made up my mind and did not intend to be pushed, for political reasons, to say something that I was not sure about.

A number of events and ideas have helped clarify my thinking about choice. Many years have passed in which the problems of the most desperate inner-city schools have remained fundamentally unchanged, despite wave after wave of reforms and programs. Trying harder has helped some schools, but the worst are untouched. Certain personal experiences also changed my perspective. I recall, in particular, a visit to Britain in the fall of 1992, when I went to learn about that nation's efforts to create a national curriculum and national assessments. I was also curious to learn about "grant-maintained" schools, and I asked to visit a typical one. These are the schools where parents have voted to leave the jurisdiction of the local board of education and to receive public funding directly from the national government.

To my surprise, I was sent to a Roman Catholic girls' school in London, where most of the students were members of racial minorities. The nun who showed me around was in street dress, as were the teachers. The money that previously was consumed by the local school board (about 15 percent of the school's budget) was now contributed directly to the school. The school used a capital grant from the government and its additional funds to build a new science laboratory, make long-deferred repairs, and hire additional teachers. For the first time, the staff was allowed to select the school's food supplier, and competitive bids were solicited. The local school board (which previously held a monopoly) was unable to submit a bid, because it did not know how much its food services cost. The school selected a caterer after comparing price and quality among bidders. In other words, instead of acting as the last link in a bureaucratic chain, the staff in the school became free to act as adults, making responsible decisions. As I went from classroom to classroom, I saw teenage girls preparing for the national examinations in an atmosphere that was orderly, cheerful, and well main-tained. What I most vividly recall is the comment of my guide, who said, "You can always tell a grant-maintained school by the smell of fresh paint."

Not only do the British provide public funds for religious schools, they insist that religious and moral education is a regular part of the national curriculum, whatever the student's beliefs. So do many other nations. This is obviously not the practice in the United States. Opposition to funding nonpublic schools, especially religious ones, is powerful here, and admitting any demonstration of religious faith into the public school is anathema. We have been told for many years that the use of any public funds in a religious school violates the constitutional principle of separation of church and state and that it amounts to an illegal establishment of religion.

Yet when we look at other developed democracies that share our ideals, we find that our so-called "wall of separation" is anomalous. Every other Western nation provides state aid to religious and other private schools. Denmark, for example, provides direct government funding for nongovernmental schools so that parents can exercise religious and political freedom. These state-funded nonpublic schools attract only about 5–6 percent of the total enrollment, a testament both to popular support for state schools and to Denmark's commitment to religious and political pluralism. Like Denmark, other nations act on the principle that it would be a denial of religious freedom to distribute public funds only to state schools. After the fall of communism, many parents and teachers in Eastern Europe demanded alternatives to state schools, which had proved themselves to be instruments by which to impose ideological and political conformity.[11]

The more I learned about schooling in other democracies, the more I wondered about the roots of our own practices. Why do we insist that public funds go only to state schools when other Western nations do not? Why do we adamantly refuse any public funding for those who attend religious schools, but only at the primary and secondary levels? Why is Mary Jones— a young woman from an impoverished family—ineligible for public funds when she is an eighteen-year-old senior at St. Mary's Academy yet eligible for a federal Pell grant when she is an eighteen-year-old freshman at St. Mary's College? Is it fair to deny free education to needy citizens whose sincere religious convictions make it impossible for them to send their children to secular state schools? Why is public funding available only to schools that exclude religious values? Why is there free speech in public schools for all controversial views except religious ones? Why would it be an "establishment of religion" if students with public grants attended schools sponsored by scores of different religious groups? Does the Constitution require hostility to religion or only neutrality toward all religions?

Public schools are defined as "only those schools owned and operated by the government," yet places of public accommodation (hotels, restaurants, buses, theaters, and so on) are defined as public not on the basis of who owns and operates them but by whom they serve.[12] Thus the paradox: a school in an exclusive suburb that educates affluent students at a cost of $15,000 per student per year is "public," while an inner-city parochial school that educates impoverished minority students at a cost of $2,000 per year is not "public."

I am a historian of education, and my first book—*The Great School Wars: New York City, 1805–1973, a History of the Public Schools as Battlefield of Social Change*—dealt at length with the issues of public and nonpublic schools. I thought that I had adequately examined the evolution of the secular public school. But the more I questioned my own views, the more I began to doubt what I once knew. I looked again at familiar literature with a fresh eye and found answers that I had not seen or had not wanted to see before.

The rise of the American common school during the nineteenth century cannot be understood without reference to the dominant influence of evangelical Protestantism in their formation and, more specifically, to the relentless efforts by evangelical Protestants to deny public funds to Catholic schools. The historian David Tyack has documented the extensive role of evangelical Protestant clergymen as leaders of the common school movement and as state superintendents who "spread the gospel of the common school in their united battle against Romanism, barbarism, and skepticism."[13] The historian Lloyd Jorgenson has described "the Protestant Common School Movement" and its close ties to nativism and the Know-Nothing Party. The object of the common school movement was not to establish nonreligious, secular schools, but to establish schools that were state-controlled, nonsectarian, and Christian.[14]

The goal of the common school movement was not to create secular schools but to assure that all public funds were devoted solely to nondenominational Protestant schools and that no public funds could be used for "sectarian" schools. Catholic schools were, of course, sectarian schools, as were denominational Protestant schools. The common school reformers achieved their purpose: throughout the nineteenth century and well into the twentieth, students in nonsectarian public schools read the Protestant Bible, sang Protestant hymns, recited Protestant prayers, and learned a Protestant version of European history.[15]

As Jorgenson notes, political leaders did not claim that it was unconstitutional to spend public funds in Catholic schools; instead, they passed laws in the states to prevent it and even attempted to pass a constitutional amendment to make sure that no public money could be allotted to the schools of the "papists." The leaders of the common school movement did not justify this policy by invoking the principle of separation of church and state; their argument was "simple and blunt: the growth of Catholicism was a menace to republican institutions and must be curbed." Over the years, rioters,

clergymen, voters, and politicians have tried to suppress Catholic schools as
an affront to "American" values. Jorgenson finds it "ironic that policies born
of religious intolerance should today be regarded with reverence."[16]

Over the years, we have developed a theory of public education that is
unnecessarily constricted. Public education, in current theory, occurs only
in schools operated and controlled by the government. Yet it is the education of the public—all the public—that should concern us. When public
officials use the phrase "all our children," they often do not literally mean
all our children; they mean "all our children who attend state schools." This
seems fundamentally unfair and undemocratic. If there were an epidemic of
polio, would public officials vaccinate all children, or only those who attend
state schools? If public funds are made available to educate children with
severe disabilities, should they be used for all children with severe disabilities or only those who attend state schools? If ignorance is to be vanquished, should it be vanquished among all our children or only among
those children in state schools?

The questions that must be seen as central to the reform of education are
these: How can we expand educational opportunity for poor children in
urban areas, where academic achievement is lowest and where social conditions are worst? How can we provide them with access to schools that
have a strong sense of community, shared moral values, and a commitment
to their success? How can we do this now rather than someday? My answer
is that those children who are most at risk of failure should receive scholarships, to be used in the schools of their choice. If the scholarships are generous enough, and if enough students receive them, many schools will
welcome scholarship students, and new schools will open to supply the
demand for good education.

Interestingly, Theodore Sizer and Phillip Whitten offered a similar program, which they called "A Proposal for a Poor Children's Bill of Rights," in
1968. They suggested that poor children should receive a coupon equivalent to about three times the average national expenditure, to be used in
the school of their choice, and that the value of the coupon would be so
attractive that schools would compete to enroll poor children. Among the
benefits that they saw were the empowerment of parents of poor children
and the elimination of inferior schools; the largest benefit, they predicted,
would be the eventual savings on the cost of police, welfare, and prisons, as
well as other public expenditures associated with poverty. In response to the

264   fear that poor parents were unequipped to choose the right school for their children, the authors wrote: "We feel, unhappily, that giving parents more power can only be seen as the least of evils. We trust them little, but still more than we trust the present monopoly of lay boards and professional schoolmen."[17]

Since Sizer and Whitten offered their proposal, social conditions in which poor and minority children live have worsened in many respects. Fundamental changes in the family over the past generation have added new disadvantages to those who are neediest. From 1960 to 1991, the proportion of poor children living in female-headed households grew from 23.7 percent to 59 percent. Among poor black children, the proportion living in a female-headed household during that period increased from 29.4 percent to 83.1 percent.[18] At the same time that female-headed households became the predominant family structure in poor black communities, other social indicators went from bad to worse: the suicide rate for youngsters of all races ages fifteen to nineteen nearly tripled, and the homicide rate for this group more than tripled. During the same three decades, the arrest rate for youngsters fourteen to seventeen nearly tripled.[19] When we add to these dire statistics the other conditions of social distress—teen pregnancy, drug and alcohol abuse, AIDS, and homelessness—we must recognize that many young people, particularly those who are poor and members of racial minorities, are living in cruel, desperate, and frightening circumstances.

What can schools do to support and protect young people from the pressures that threaten them? There are many things that schools can do, and there are many things that they cannot do. They cannot by themselves end poverty, though children who do not get a good education are likely to be condemned to a lifetime of poverty. They cannot by themselves create jobs or improve housing conditions or stop the violence on the streets. There are other public and private agencies with these purposes, and the schools must collaborate with them. But schools in big cities can and must make changes that enable them to nurture and guide the young people who are growing up in a milieu fraught with peril.

There are strong objections to full school choice. I will review the main objections in order to suggest why I think that a system based on choice is preferable to a system built on compulsion.

"A choice program—even if means tested—would destroy the public school sys-

tem." Some people oppose even public school choice, on the ground that those running the system know best what is in everyone's interest. Opposition is even stronger to choice programs that allow families to use public funds to send their children to nonpublic schools. Critics fear that if nonpublic choice were available, huge numbers of families and children would flee from their local public schools or leave public education altogether. Yet there is no evidence for such fears. According to a poll commissioned by the Carnegie Foundation for the Advancement of Teaching, only 19 percent of public school parents would like to send their children to a private school.[20] Furthermore, the same poll shows that most parents—87 percent—are satisfied with their children's public schools. The Carnegie Foundation interpreted these figures as evidence that few people are interested in choice; I interpret them to mean that between 13 and 19 percent of families would leave the public schools if they could afford to. Assuming that many of these families would not qualify for means-tested scholarships, I conclude that in a system that permitted means-tested choice of all schools, the public schools would continue to enroll 80 percent or more of all students, instead of today's 90 percent. There is no reason to fear a wholesale exodus from a fundamentally sound institution. Not only would the public school system not be destroyed, it would be strengthened by the ability to shut down bad schools.

"There is no precedent for allowing students to use government funds for education in private or religious institutions." For many years, the federal government has provided scholarships (Pell grants) to college students to attend the college or university or proprietary school of their choice. Students may use their Pell grants to attend Princeton or Georgetown or the local state university. The federal government does not care whether students attend public, private, or religious institutions, so long as the institution is approved by an accrediting agency. Eighty percent of students enroll in public institutions, no doubt because public universities cost less than private ones. The same dynamic would hold in primary and secondary education, and the overwhelming majority—80 percent or more—would continue to attend state schools. Public higher education has not been destroyed by a system that allows students to use federal scholarships at nonpublic institutions; on the contrary, most people believe that the United States has the best and the most pluralistic system of higher education in the world.

266   In addition, private and sectarian organizations receive public funds to manage Head Start centers, special education programs, hospitals, nursing homes, social service agencies, and a variety of other public activities.

In 1993, a unanimous U.S. Supreme Court made clear (in *Florence County School District Four v. Carter*) that a school district must reimburse parents who educated their learning-disabled child in a private school, after the parents rejected the school district's "individual education plan" as inadequate. The Court held that the usual state requirements "do not apply to private parental placements." The school district set as a goal for Shannon Carter that she would progress four months in reading and mathematics for every year of schooling; in her private placement, she progressed three grade levels in three years. The state complained that the private school selected by Shannon's parents did not have the approval of the state education agency; in response, the Supreme Court quoted a lower court approvingly: "It hardly seems consistent with the Act's goals to forbid parents from educating their child at a school that provides an appropriate education simply because that school lacks the stamp of approval of the same public school system that failed to meet the child's needs in the first place." In short, the Supreme Court has no problem with paying public funds to a nonpublic school when it is freely chosen by parents and when—as in the case of Shannon Carter—it meets needs that are not met in the public schools.

"An education finance system that includes religious schools would be unconstitutional." There is no question that under current law, it would be unconstitutional for a public authority to provide funds directly to religious schools. However, financial assistance that goes directly to parents, to spend at the school of their choice, would not violate the principle of separation of church and state. The U.S. Supreme Court in 1983 (in *Mueller v. Allen*) upheld a Minnesota state law that allowed all parents of school-age children to deduct expenses for tuition, textbooks, and transportation from their state taxes, regardless of where their children attended school, even though most of the benefits were likely to flow to parents of children in sectarian schools. In 1986 a unanimous Supreme Court (in *Witters v. Washington Department of Services for the Blind*) upheld the grant of state aid to a blind student who was attending a Bible college, preparing to be a minister. Justice Thurgood Marshall wrote the opinion, stressing the importance of individual choice: "[A] State may issue a paycheck to one of its employees, who

may then donate all or part of that paycheck to a religious institution, all without constitutional barrier; and the State may do so even knowing that the employee so intends to dispose of his salary. . . . In this case, the fact that aid goes to individuals means that the decision to support religious education is made by the individual, not the State." In 1993 the Supreme Court (in *Zobrest v. Catalina Foothills School District*) found no conflict with the establishment clause when a public school district was asked to provide a sign language interpreter for a deaf student in a Roman Catholic high school. Again, the Court relied on the fact that the decision was made by the parents: "By according parents freedom to select a school of their choice, the statute ensures that a government-paid interpreter will be present in a sectarian school only as a result of the private decision of individual parents."

In his textbook, the legal scholar Laurence H. Tribe writes that recent Supreme Court decisions "suggest that the Court would uphold an educational voucher scheme that would permit parents to decide which schools, public or private, their children should attend. The establishment clause probably would not stand as an obstacle to a purely neutral program, at least one with a broad enough class of beneficiary schools and one that channeled aid through parents and children rather than directly to schools."[21]

"A choice system would put an intolerable burden on already strained state and local budgets." Apparently many people voted against the school choice proposal in California's 1993 referendum because they feared that it would cripple the state budget. That proposal, however, was not means tested. A scholarship that was available only for poor children would have measurable, predictable, and limited impact on the budget. It would be available to a limited number of students and could be expanded only as feasible. Such a program would cost the public no more—and, if bureaucracy is substantially reduced, possibly less—than the state currently spends for those children now in public schools.[22] The state would be responsible for monitoring the quality of services provided instead of acting as the sole provider of services itself.

To be sure, the availability of public transportation would serve as a constraint on choice. Public authorities cannot be expected to create a massive network of minivans. They should, however, supply free bus passes for schoolchildren, which is usually sufficient in big cities to permit many choices. Choice would not be unlimited, but it never is. Students could not "choose" to attend a school ninety miles away, nor could they choose a school that is already full. On the other hand, I see no reason to prohibit out-of-district choice, so long as the receiving school has space available and has the programming to meet the needs of the student.

"A choice program will 'skim off' the best students, leaving public schools only with the poorest and most difficult ones." A means-tested scholarship makes "skimming off" highly improbable, for only the neediest students—those who are very poor and those who are now in low-performing schools—will be eligible for these scholarships.

Good schools in big cities will not be adversely affected by a means-tested choice program, although they are likely to get many more applicants. Their students do not want to leave; their parents know that they are getting a good education and have no interest in removing them. In New York City a small number of excellent, mixed-ability schools—called education option schools—regularly receive eight or ten applications for every opening; many of their applicants currently attend private and parochial schools. This demonstrates that there is a vigorous, unfilled market for good public schools in the big cities.

As cities introduce varieties of public school choice, including charter schools and magnet schools, they expand the number of focus schools that are available to students. The growing number of these new-style public schools reduces still further the number of students who would leave the public school system if offered a means-tested scholarship. Indeed, the spread of full choice is likely to induce cities to increase the number of focus schools in order to meet the demand from students and parents.

"A choice program would worsen segregation in big-city districts." It is hard to see how segregation could become worse if means-tested scholarships were provided to poor students who are currently enrolled in inner-city schools with almost exclusively African-American and Hispanic populations. If anything, allowing choice to these students may well reduce inner-city segregation.

"No evidence shows that choice would raise the academic achievement of poor, inner-city students." Since there have been no large-scale demonstrations that permit full choice to all students, with means-tested scholarships for poor children, it is impossible to say whether poor children would achieve higher test scores or higher graduation rates under such a plan. Choice is not a panacea, and there is no reason to expect that it would produce miraculous results overnight. But it is at least possible that permitting students to enroll

in schools of choice will reduce student alienation and increase parental participation, both of which may contribute to higher attendance rates, improved academic performance, and increased graduation rates.

On the other hand, the existing system of hierarchical, bureaucratic controls must be judged by the same exacting standard; it has been in existence for well over a century. Surely it is fair to ask, "Is the existing system capable of raising the achievement of poor, inner-city students? Does anyone expect dramatic improvement in big-city school systems as they are now organized?" If the answers are yes, then choice should be rejected; if no, then choice should be explored in meaningful, large-scale, long-term demonstration projects.

"Some parents would not take advantage of a choice program." If a district announced that it intended to provide scholarships for the neediest children in the lowest performing schools, there would probably be parents who do not respond to invitations to choose a new school. But because the overwhelming majority of needy children have parents or guardians who care about their education, the number of nonparticipants would be small. In the few cases where no family member stepped forward to choose a school for a scholarship student, the decision could be made by a panel of community-based child advocates, such as representatives of local community organizations, parent associations, and churches. In any event, it would be the responsibility of the school system to assure that every parent and guardian received good information about the choices available and that each student enrolled in a school with appropriate programs and a commitment to his or her education.

"Public funds might support schools that teach bizarre religious ideas, antiscientific ideas, or racist ideas." During the California voucher controversy, there was concern that public funds might support schools run by religious cults, creationists, or racists. It should not be difficult to avert this problem. First, no school should be eligible to receive public scholarships if it excludes students on grounds of race or religion. Second, all schools that accept public-scholarship students should be required to prepare their students to pass state subject-matter assessments. The state should require that students are able to pass the city or state's examinations in mathematics, science, history, civics, English, and foreign languages at rates no worse than comparable public schools. Third, schools that teach racial or religious hatred should be barred from participation in the choice program. Nonpublic

270 schools that do not meet these requirements should be excluded from the
choice program.

"Nonpublic schools might shun students with handicapping conditions." Students with special needs should be eligible for a scholarship to go where
their needs can best be met; if the size of the scholarship is large enough,
new schools will be created to cater to the needs of these children. As the
Supreme Court has already ruled, the parents of disabled students have the
right to obtain a free, publicly financed education in the private sector if the
state cannot provide it. Some states already pay private school tuition for
students with special needs that can't be met in the public schools.

"Some public schools would lose most of their students." If a district provides
scholarships on the basis of need, as well as to those enrolled in the worst
schools, then some schools may have a sharp drop in enrollment. Allowing
parents to remove their children is an important signaling device to public
school officials; they would restructure or close schools that no one wanted
to attend instead of forcing poor children to remain in them. Very bad
schools should be closed and replaced by new schools, with a new principal, new faculty, and new mission. The means-tested scholarship would
strengthen the public schools by providing a mechanism that identifies and
eliminates the worst schools.

*"Public authorities could not hold nonpublic schools accountable if they were not
directly controlled and regulated by the state."* On the contrary, public authorities would find it easier to ensure accountability of nonpublic schools than it
is now to ensure accountability of public schools. At present there are usually few, if any, consequences for failing public schools. What happens to
public schools where the leadership is poor, teaching is ineffective, and
children are not learning? The state can't punish the school by taking away
money because that only makes matters worse; if it gives the school more
money, then it seems to be rewarding failure, which discourages effective
schools that win no rewards for success. The state can take over bad schools
or send in monitors, but these strategies have not thus far proved effective.

With nonpublic schools and public charter schools, the state could act
decisively and impose real accountability. If such schools failed to meet their
contractual obligations or demonstrated educational inadequacy, the state
could cancel their charter or withdraw their eligibility to receive public
scholarships. In fact, public authorities would have more power over nonpublic and charter schools than they currently have over public schools,

with the ultimate power to exclude them from the choice program. Those nonpublic schools that did not wish to accept public accountability would not participate in the program.

"Schools with different values are socially divisive." Actually, our most divisive school-related conflicts occur because we impose a single set of state-defined values on everyone in public schools. Scarcely a week goes by without the eruption of a bitter controversy in a public school somewhere over social, political, and religious differences. The state board of education and the local board of education are often combat zones where warring groups fight about condom distribution, textbooks, outcome-based education, prayer in the schools, political messages on T-shirts, and other contentious issues. As pluralism in the school and society grows, the conflicts will become more intense. Inevitably, some parents win and some lose. Some families are forced to live with decisions by the school board that are deeply offensive to them. Those of us who are liberal and secular feel comforted when our side wins and frightened when the other side wins. Yet why should people who are not liberal and secular be compelled to submit their children to values that they find deeply obnoxious? Why should those who are liberal and secular be compelled to submit their children to values that they find oppressive and narrow-minded? Perhaps they are both right, and each should be in a school in which there is no state-imposed uniformity of opinion. Under a means-tested choice program, schools should differ from each other in a variety of ways, so long as they respect the Constitution and the laws of the state and comply with the state's education standards.

If we cease trying to impose state-defined values and instead permit diversity of values, there may well be more harmony and less divisiveness. In a review of school choice in other nations, Charles Glenn reports that "choice reduces the level of conflict over the purpose and control of schooling, and thus encourages broad societal support."[23] In schooling, one size does not fit all.

"Newcomers to the United States would not be assimilated to the mainstream if they attended ethnic or religious schools." Most people, including new immigrants, would continue to patronize traditional public schools, because they are free, convenient, and satisfactory to the overwhelming majority of parents. Those parents who do not choose to patronize public schools do not threaten the stability of the nation. There is no evidence that people who attended religious schools or other private schools are less patriotic, less

272   civic-minded, less likely to vote in elections, or less willing to serve their country than those who attended public schools. Nor is there any evidence that those who attended religious or other private schools are less tolerant than those who attended public schools.

The public schools may not be the primary instrument of civic assimilation in our society. American society itself—its laws, its cultural pluralism, its openness, its tolerance for diversity, its encouragement of freedom of expression and enterprise—may be the most effective instrument of social assimilation. Although a few groups like the Amish or Hasidic Jews choose to live apart from society, most Americans—regardless of the kind of school they attended—have no trouble assimilating into American society. And even separatist groups like the Amish or Hasidic Jews, it seems to me, should be allowed to use means-tested scholarships, if they wish, to attend the schools of their choice. As a mature democracy, we should be long past the time when we feared that any deviation from the mainstream threatened the stability of our society. Our commitment to pluralism and diversity should be strong enough to tolerate the very small number of devout separatists who do not wish to assimilate.

In 1859, John Stuart Mill considered some of the same questions in his famous essay "On Liberty." In that magnificent defense of freedom of opinion Mill asserted, "If all mankind minus one, were of one opinion, and only one person were of the contrary opinion, mankind would be no more justified in silencing that one person, than he, if he had the power, would be justified in silencing mankind." When he turned his thoughts to education, Mill argued:

> If the government would make up its mind to *require* for every child a good education, it might save itself the trouble of *providing* one. It might leave to parents to obtain the education where and how they pleased, and content itself with helping to pay the school fees of the poorer classes of children, and defraying the entire school expenses of those who have no one else to pay for them. . . . An education established and controlled by the State, should only exist, if it exist at all, as one among many competing experiments, carried on for the purpose of example and stimulus, to keep the others up to a certain standard of excellence.[24]

Mill believed that students should be required to take annual examinations to ascertain whether they had acquired "a certain minimum of general knowledge," but he maintained that examinations on disputed topics—like religion or politics—"should not turn on the truth or falsehood of opinions, but on the matter of fact that such and such an opinion is held, on such grounds, by such authors, or schools, or churches." He saw no danger in students' learning the religion of their parents, but he warned that "all attempts by the State to bias the conclusions of its citizens on disputed subjects, are evil."

Like Mill, I worry about the power of the state to mold opinion and to establish official knowledge. With the current move to establish clear academic standards, such a worry is more than theoretical. Yet standards offer a realistic means of public accountability for schools of choice, be they public or private. The public has a right to know that its money is well-spent, that the state does not support institutions that violate civil rights laws, and that children are educated to high standards. Those schools that accept students with public scholarships should expect to be reviewed periodically by public authorities, who remain responsible for safety, health, and overall educational quality.

I began this essay with a statement of commitment to the coequal goals of pluralism, equality, and excellence. This proposal promotes pluralism because it would create incentives for a diverse, pluralistic system of schools with many different kinds of sponsors, all dedicated to educating the public. It supports excellence, because public officials would be responsible for setting standards for quality and reviewing the performance of all educational institutions that receive public funds, with the power to withdraw approval from those schools that failed to meet their stated performance goals. It serves equality, because it would endow poor children with sufficient resources to escape from failing schools and to gain entry to the public or nonpublic school of their choice. The intention is to empower public officials to act as guardians, auditors, and evaluators, while empowering those children and families who are now ill-served by current institutions.

Nobody's children should be compelled to attend a bad public school. A good school system must offer equal educational opportunity to everybody's children.

Notes

Introduction

1. Seymour Mandelbaum, *Boss Tweed's New York* (New York: John Wiley, 1965); Jerome Mushkat, *Tammany: The Evolution of a Political Machine* (Syracuse: Syracuse University Press, 1971).

2. Martin J. Schiesl, *The Politics of Efficiency: Municipal Administration and Reform in America, 1880–1920* (Berkeley: University of California Press, 1979); Joseph P. Viteritti, *Bureaucracy and Social Justice* (Port Washington, N.Y.: Kennikat, 1979).

3. David Tyack and Elizabeth Hansot, *Managers of Virtue, Public School Leadership, 1820–1980* (New York: Basic, 1982), pp. 129–166.

4. Raymond Callahan, *Education and the Cult of Efficiency* (Chicago: University of Chicago Press, 1962); David Tyack, *The One Best System* (Cambridge: Harvard University Press, 1974).

5. See generally Susan H. Fuhrman and Richard F. Elmore, "Ruling Out Rules: The Evolution of Deregulation in State Education Policy," *Teachers College Record,* vol. 97 (Winter 1995).

6. Lonnie Harp, "Code Revisions Spur Change in Texas Climate," *Education Week,* January 17, 1996.

7. Lonnie Harp, "Michigan Education Code Overhaul Shifts Power," *Education Week,* January 10, 1996.

8. Jeanne Ponessa, "Ill. Districts Jump at Chance for Waivers to Rules," *Education Week,* September 20, 1995.

276

9. Marilyn Tallerico, "Governing Urban Schools," in Patrick B. Forsythe and Marilyn Tallerico, eds., *City Schools* (Newberry Park, Calif.: Corwin, 1993).

10. Jeffrey Mirel, "School Reform, Chicago Style: Educational Innovation in a Changing Urban Context, 1976–1991," *Urban Education*, vol. 28 (July 1993).

11. Committee on Economic Development, *Putting Learning First* (New York: CED, 1994), p. 15.

12. Bruce Bimber, *The Decentralization Mirage* (Santa Monica, Calif.: RAND, 1994); Bruce Bimber, *School Decentralization: Lessons from the Study of Bureaucracy* (Santa Monica, Calif.: RAND, 1993); Daniel Brown, "The Decentralization of School Districts," *Educational Policy*, vol. 6 (1992).

13. Education Commission of the States and Center for School Change, *Charter Schools: What Are They Up To?* (1995); Keith A. Halpern and Eliza R. Culberson, *Charter Schools: Blueprint for Change* (Washington, D.C.: Democratic Leadership Council, n.d.).

14. Denis P. Doyle, "The Role of Private Sector Management in Public Education," *Phi Delta Kappan* 76 (October 1994).

15. Mark Walsh, "Baltimore Vote Ends City's Contract with EAI," *Education Week*, December 6, 1995; George Judson, "Baltimore Ends City Experiment," *New York Times*, November 23, 1995; George Judson, "Education Company Banned from Hartford Schools," *New York Times*, February 1, 1996.

16. Peter Applebome, "Lure of Education Market Remains Strong for Business," *New York Times*, January 31, 1996; Mark Walsh, "Sylvan Makes Quiet Inroads into Public Schools," *Education Week*, November 29, 1995.

17. Milton Friedman, "The Role of Government in Education," in R. A. Solo, ed., *Economics and the Public Interest* (New Brunswick, N.J.: Rutgers University Press, 1955).

18. Milton Friedman, *Capitalism and Freedom* (Chicago: University of Chicago Press, 1962).

19. John E. Chubb and Terry M. Moe, *Politics, Markets, and America's Schools* (Washington, D.C.: Brookings Institution, 1990).

20. Jeffrey R. Henrig, *Rethinking School Choice: Limits of the Market Metaphor* (Princeton: Princeton University Press, 1994).

21. *Brown v. Board of Education*, 347 U.S. 484 (1954); Amy Stuart Wells, *Time to Choose: America at the Crossroads of School Choice Policy* (New York: Hill and Wang, 1993), pp. 63–74; *Griffen v. County School Board of Prince Edward County*, 377 U.S. 218 (1964).

22. David Armor, *Forced Justice: School Desegregation and the Law* (New York: Oxford University Press, 1995), pp. 13–16, 180–194, 211–234; Christine Rossell, *The Carrot or the Stick for Desegregation Policy* (Philadelphia: Temple University Press, 1990).

23. Henrig, *Rethinking School Choice*, p. 108.

24. Peter W. Cookson, *School Choice: The Struggle for the Soul of American Education* (New Haven: Yale University Press, 1994), pp. 58–64. 277

25. Allyson Tucker and William F. Lauber, *School Choice Programs: What's Happening in the States* (Washington, D.C.: Heritage Foundation, 1995).

26. Joe Nathan and Wayne Jennings, *Access to Opportunity: The Experience of Minnesota Students in Four Statewide School Choice Programs* (Minneapolis: Center for School Change, University of Minnesota, 1990). See also Joe Nathan and James Ysseldyke, "What Minnesota Has Learned About School Choice," *Phi Delta Kappan*, May 1994.

27. Carnegie Foundation for the Advancement of Teaching, *School Choice* (Princeton: Carnegie Foundation, 1992).

28. Edith Rasell and Richard Rothstein, eds., *School Choice: Examining the Evidence* (Washington, D.C.: Economic Policy Institute, 1993).

29. Valerie J. Martinez, R. Kenneth Godwin, Frank R. Kemerer, and Laura Perna, "The Consequences of School Choice: Who Leaves and Who Stays in the Inner City," *Social Science Quarterly*, vol. 76 (September 1995).

30. Abigail Thernstrom, *School Choice in Massachusetts* (Boston: Pioneer Institute, 1991).

31. Anthony Bryk, Valerie E. Lee, and Peter Holland, *Catholic Schools and the Common Good* (Cambridge: Harvard University Press, 1992); James S. Coleman, Thomas Hoffer, and Sally Kilgore, *High School Achievement: Public, Catholic, and Parochial Schools* (Chicago: University of Chicago Press, 1992).

32. See Joseph P. Viteritti, "Stacking the Deck for the Poor: The New Politics of School Choice," *The Brookings Review*, vol. 14 (Summer 1996).

33. Bruce Fuller, Richard Elmore, and Gary Orfield, eds., *Who Chooses? Who Loses? Culture, Institutions, and the Unequal Effects of School Choice* (New York: Teachers College Press, 1996); Terry M. Moe, ed., *Private Vouchers* (Stanford: Hoover Institution Press, 1995).

34. See Joseph P. Viteritti, "Choosing Equality: Religious Freedom and Educational Opportunity Under Constitutional Federalism," *Yale Law and Policy Review*, vol. 15 (1996).

35. *The Blum Center's Educational Freedom Report* (Milwaukee: Marquette University, 1995).

36. John E. Chubb and Terry M. Moe, *A Lesson in School Reform from Great Britain* (Washington, D.C.: Brookings Institution, 1992); Kathryn Stearns, *School Reform: Lessons from England* (Princeton: Carnegie Foundation, 1996).

37. Education Commission of the States, *Charter Schools: Initial Findings* (Denver: ECS, 1996).

38. Roger Barker and Paul Gump, *Big School, Small School* (Palo Alto: Stanford University Press, 1964); John Goodlad, *A Place Called School: Prospects for the Future* (New York: McGraw-Hill, 1984); Thomas J. Sergiovanni, "Small Schools, Great Expectations," *Educational Leadership* 53 (November 1995).

278   1. New York

1. For a history of the New York City school system, see Diane Ravitch, *The Great School Wars: New York City, 1805–1973* (New York: Basic, 1974).

2. For an analysis of the political and institutional environment of educational policy making in New York, see Joseph P. Viteritti, *Across the River: Politics and Education in the City* (New York: Holmes and Meier, 1983).

3. Seymour Fliegel and James MacQuire, *Miracle in East Harlem: The Fight for Choice in Public Education* (New York: Times Books, 1993); Kay S. Hymowitz, "Up the Up Staircase: A Place to Unlearn the Lessons of the Street," *City Journal*, vol. 4 (Spring 1994).

4. For the 1993–1994 school year, 1,034,235 students were enrolled in 1,071 schools. Board of Education of the City of New York, *Annual Report, 1994–95*, p. 2.

5. See David Rogers, *110 Livingston Street: Politics and Bureaucracy in the New York City School System* (New York: Random House, 1968).

6. Number of employees as of November 1994. Board of Education of the City of New York, "Vital Statistics," n.d. The budget for the 1995–96 fiscal year was $8,352,749,859. Board of Education of the City of New York, Budget Operations and Review Circular no. 3, 1995–1996, January 5, 1996.

7. Rudolph F. Crew, "Proposal for the Reorganization of the Central Division/Offices of the Board of Education of the City of New York," March 1996, p. 24. Quotations from p. 1.

8. New York City Board of Education, School board budget reports, 1995–1996 (1996), p. 3.

9. "Education at a Glance: OECD Indicators on Education" (Paris: Organization of Economic and Cultural Development, 1992).

10. See, for example, Seymour Melman, "The Rise of Administrative Overhead in the Manufacturing Industries of the United States," *Oxford Economic Papers*, vol. 3 (February 1951); Gerry E. Hendershot and Thomas F. James, "Size and Growth as Determinants of Administrative-Production Ratios in Organizations," *American Sociological Review*, vol. 37 (April 1972); John Kasarda, "The Structural Implications of Social System Size," *American Sociological Review*, vol. 39 (February 1974).

11. See, for example, "Rethinking School Safety: The Report of the Chancellor's Advisory Panel on School Safety," February 1993.

12. The Special Commissioner of Investigation for the New York City School District, "An Investigation into Recruiting, Screening, and Hiring Practices at the Board of Education's Division of School Safety," November 1995.

13. Special Commissioner of Investigation for the New York City School District, "Papers, Pencils, and Planes to the Caribbean: Corruption in the Purchasing of School and Office Supplies," October 1994.

14. The Special Commissioner of Investigation for the New York City School

District, "An Investigation into the Management and Delivery of Food Services by the Board of Education of the City of New York," June 1995.

15. The Special Commissioner of Investigation for the New York City School District, "A System Like No Other: Fraud and Misconduct by New York City School Custodians," November 1992.

16. The City of New York, Office of the Comptroller, Bureau of Audit, "Audit Report on The New York City Board of Education Controls over Custodial Employees Work Hours," March 14, 1996.

17. Alan Finder, "Panel Says Crumbling Schools Pose Hazards to Students," *New York Times*, June 22, 1995.

18. Sarah Kershaw, "School Board Overcharged, Will Examine All of Its Leases," *New York Times*, April 17, 1996.

19. New York State Senate, Committee on Investigations, Taxation and Government Operations, "School Construction: A Continuing Problem," April 23, 1996. This report confirmed the findings of an earlier inquiry conducted by the same senate committee, "Failing Grades for the School Construction Authority," September 1994.

20. Board of Education of the City of New York, "Educational Progress of Students in Bilingual and ESL Programs: A Longitudinal Study, 1990–1994," October 1994.

21. *Aspira v. Board of Education*, 72 Civ. 4002 (S.D. N.Y. 1974).

22. *Bushwick Parents Association v. Richard P. Mills*, Index no. 5181-95.

23. Joseph P. Viteritti and Robert F. Pecorella, "Community Government and the Decentralization of Service Delivery," Report to the New York City Charter Revision Commission, November 1987.

24. Ravitch, *The Great School Wars*, pp. 292–379. See also David John Ayers, *The Effects of Ethnicity, Class, and Occupational Affiliation upon Political Style: A Theoretical and Historical Analysis of the Sociological Influences Shaping Competing Positions in the Controversy over the Movement for Community Control of Public Schools in New York City, 1966–1969*, Ph.D. diss., New York University, 1996.

25. The Special Commissioner of Investigation for the New York City School District, "From Chaos to Corruption: An Investigation into the 1993 Community School Board Election," December 1993.

26. William J. Cook, "Corruption and Racketeering in the New York City School Boards," in Robert J. Kelly, Ko-Lin Chin, and Rufus Schatzberg, eds., *Handbook of Organized Crime in the United States* (Westport, Conn.: Greenwood, 1994).

27. Patricia Mangan, "No Apple for School Boards," *Daily News*, May 31, 1995.

28. Raphael Sugarman, "New York City's District Board Members Flunking Out," *Daily News*, March 30, 1995.

29. New York State Department of Education, *School Report Cards* (1997). See Raymond Hernandez, "Rating of Schools Shows Skills Lag in New York City," *New York Times*, January 3, 1997.

280   30. Board of Education of the City of New York, "The Class of 1994: Longitudinal Report," n.d.

31. Id.

32. The State Education Department, The University of the State of New York, "State Education Commissioner Orders 'Corrective Action' in 16 New York City Schools," press release, October 19, 1995.

33. The State Education Department, The University of the State of New York, "Roman Catholic Schools in New York State: A Comprehensive Report," May 1993, pp. 39, pp. 42–43.

34. Id., p. 28. The public school figure includes $529 per pupil for support services that are not reflected in the Catholic school data, such as transportation, health services, and textbook aid.

35. The Student Sponsor Partnership, "Internal Program Evaluation, 1996," n.d. See also Paul T. Hill, "Private Vouchers in New York City: The Student Sponsor Partnership Program," in Terry M. Moe, ed., *Private Vouchers* (Stanford: Hoover Institution Press, 1995).

36. Quoted in Sol Stern, "The School Reform that Dares Not Speak Its Name," *City Journal*, vol. 6, (Winter 1996), p. 29.

37. Id., p. 28.

38. Clifford J. Levy, "As Albany Cuts Funds, Lobbies Spend More," *New York Times*, March 14, 1996.

39. The meeting was convened jointly by the finance and education committees on April 25, 1996. These remarks are based on personal observations.

40. This finding is based on data provided by the Public Education Association.

41. Michael Friedman Rice, *Authority and Influence in New York City School-Based Management*, Ph.D. diss., New York University, 1993.

42. New York Network for School Renewal, "An Innovative Model for Systemic School Change," n.d.

2. The Charter School Movement

1. Louann Bierlein and Lori Mulholland, "The Promise of Charter Schools," *Educational Leadership*, September 1994, 34–40.

2. Lori Mulholland and Louann Bierlein, *Understanding Charter Schools*, Fastback 383 (Bloomington, Ind.: Phi Delta Kappa Educational Foundation, April 1995), pp. 9–11.

3. Joe Nathan, "Charter Public Schools: A Brief History and Preliminary Lessons" (Minneapolis: University of Minnesota, Center for School Change, Hubert H. Humphrey Institute of Public Affairs, October 1995), pp. 1–2. See also Mulholland and Bierlein, *Understanding Charter Schools*.

4. Ray Budde, "Education by Charter," *Phi Delta Kappan* 70 (March 1989); Albert Shanker, "Restructuring Our Schools," *Peabody Journal of Education* 65 (1988).

5. Arizona, Kansas, and Hawaii joined the list in 1994, and Michigan also   281
   enacted the second version of their law after the first had been declared
   unconstitutional. Wyoming, Texas, Arkansas, Alaska, Delaware, New
   Hampshire, Rhode Island, and Louisiana were added in 1995, followed by
   New Jersey, Illinois, Florida, North Carolina, South Carolina, Connecticut,
   and the District of Columbia in 1996.

6. Some contend that a number of charterlike schools are being developed in
   states that do not have formal charter school laws. Indeed, the small schools
   in New York City and the "schools-within-schools" in Philadelphia, as well as
   many site-based managed schools across the country, have many characteristics of charter schools. But there are a number of significant differences
   between these schools and those being created under the charter concept: (1)
   they do not have automatic freedom from state laws or policies and receive
   freedom from local policies only as allowed by the district and / or the union;
   (2) they do not have control over personnel, in that they can neither set
   teacher salaries nor hire or dismiss at will (they are allowed to bypass many of
   the district/union seniority rules for hiring, but still must follow the district
   salary schedule and policies); (3) they do not have control over their budgets
   (for example, they cannot set salaries or decide to contract out for private
   custodial or other services); (4) they cannot easily be started by outside
   groups (for example, the YMCA cannot offer a proposal to open and run one
   of these schools from scratch); and (5) these schools are not on a contract or
   charter (they indeed must continue to attract students to stay alive, but they
   do not have defined outcomes which they must meet or go out of business).

7. Drew Lindsay, "Policy End Run: Taking a Case for Change to the People's
   Court" *Education Week* 15 (December 12, 1995), 1, 16–17.

8. Mark Buechler, "Charter Schools: Legislation and Results After Four Years"
   (Bloomington: Indiana University, Indiana Education Policy Center, January 1996).

9. See Louann Bierlein and Mark Bateman, "Opposition Forces and Education
   Reform: Will Charter Schools Succeed?" in Todd DeMitchell and Richard
   Fossey, eds., *Vain Hopes and False Promises: The Failure of Law-Based School
   Reform* (Lancaster, Pa.: Technomic, 1996), for a more detailed analysis of
   these seven critical charter school law components.

10. Susan Fuhrman and Richard Elmore, "Ruling Out Rules: The Evolution of
    Deregulation in State Education Policy" (New Brunswick: Rutgers, State
    University of New Jersey, Consortium for Policy Research in Education,
    March 1995), pp. 12–13.

11. Ted Kolderie, "The Charter Idea in the 1995 Legislative Sessions" (St. Paul,
    Minn.: Center for Policy Studies, 1995).

12. See Louann Bierlein, "Charter Schools: Initial Findings" (Denver: Educa-
    tion Commission of the States, February 1996), for detailed charter school
    demographic information.

282   13. Cynthia Grutzik, Dolores Bernal, Diane Hirshberg, and Amy Stuart Wells, "Resources and Access in California Charter Schools: A Preliminary Overview," paper presented at the annual meeting of the American Educational Research Association, San Francisco, April 1995. This preliminary research has been met with significant criticism; see Eric Premack, "Who Benefits from California's Charter Schools Legislation?" (Berkeley, Calif.: Institute for Policy Analysis and Research, 1996).

14. Ronald Corwin and John Flaherty, eds., "Freedom and Innovation in California's Charter Schools" (Los Alamitos, Calif.: Southwest Regional Laboratory, November 1995).

15. Marcie Dianda and Ronald Corwin, "Vision and Reality: A First-Year Look at California's Charter Schools" (Los Alamitos, Calif.: Southwest Regional Laboratory, 1994).

16. Thomas Vitullo-Martin, "Diversity in the Characteristics of Students Enrolled in Charter Schools" (East Lansing: Michigan Center for Charter Schools, November 1994), p. 4.

17. Alex Medlar and Joe Nathan, "Charter Schools . . . What Are They Up To? A 1995 Survey" (Denver: Education Commission of the States, 1995), p. 13.

18. Chester Finn, Louann Bierlein, and Bruno Manno, "Charter Schools in Action: A First Look" (Washington, D.C.: Hudson Institute, January 1996).

19. Minnesota Department of Education, Federal Charter School Grant Application (St. Paul: Minnesota Department of Education, June 1995), p. 8; K. L. Billingsley and Pamela Riley, "The Empire Strikes Back: How California's Educational Establishment Is Hindering the Growth of Charter Schools" (San Francisco: Pacific Research Institute for Public Policy, 1995), p. 3.; Yvonne Chan, principal of Vaughn Next Century Learning Center, personal communication, April 10, 1995.

20. Susan Urahn and Dan Stewart, "Minnesota Charter Schools: A Research Report" (St. Paul: Minnesota House of Representatives, Research Department, 1994), pp. 42–45.

21. Henry Becker, Kathryn Nakagawa, and Ronald Corwin, "Parental Involvement Contracts in California's Charter Schools: Strategy for Educational Improvement or Method of Exclusion?" (Los Alamitos, Calif.: Southwest Regional Laboratory, April 1995).

22. Jose Afonso, Massachusetts Secretary of Education's office, personal communication, October 21, 1995.

23. See Finn, Bierlein, and Manno, "Charter Schools in Action," p. 4.

24. Finn, Bierlein, and Manno, "Charter Schools in Action," p. 3.

25. See Louann Bierlein, "Charter Schools: A New Approach to Public Education," *NASSP Bulletin* 79 (September 1995), 12–20, for additional information on other impacts.

26. Joy Fitzgerald, "Charter Schools in Colorado" (Denver: Colorado Children's Campaign, March 1995).

27. Mary Anne Raywid, "The Struggles and Joys of Trailblazing: A Tale of Two Charter Schools," *Phi Delta Kappan* 76 (March 1995), 555–560; quotation from page 560.
28. Billingsley and Riley, "The Empire Strikes Back," p. 2.
29. A number of reports describe the barriers and struggles facing charter school implementers; see Buechler, "Charter Schools," pp. 35–40; Fitzgerald, "Charter Schools in Colorado," pp. 11–15; Urahn and Stewart, "Minnesota Charter Schools," pp. 46–50; and Medlar and Nathan, "Charter Schools," p. 28. Bierlein and Bateman, in *Vain Hopes*, offer a detailed analysis of the many forces opposing charter schools.
30. Edutrain had its charter revoked within a few months of opening for alleged financial mismanagement: a larger number of students were being reported than were actually in attendance, an expensive staff retreat was held, and the principal was leasing a sports car with school funds. See Sarah Lubman, "Charter Is Revoked for Local School of Los Angeles," *The Wall Street Journal*, December 7, 1994, p. A4. Citizen 2000 filed for bankruptcy after the revelation that the company made claims for state school aid for one hundred more students than it actually taught. See Lyn Schnaiberg, "For First Time, 'Hands-Off' Ariz. Revokes Charter for School," *Education Week*, November 27, 1996.
31. Although a great deal of behind-the-scenes opposition continues, the National Education Association recently launched a national "charter schools initiative" to provide technical assistance to charter school developers across a number of states. Some speculate that this is a means to ensure that district collective bargaining provisions are adopted by these charter schools; others believe that NEA may have really changed its position on charter schools. In 1996 the American Federation of Teachers released a report endorsing charter schools but advocating local control, teacher certification, and compliance with local labor agreements. See *Charter School Laws: Do They Measure Up?* (Washington, D.C.: American Federation of Teachers, 1996).
32. Milo Cutter, teacher and leader of City Academy, personal communication, July 13, 1995.
33. Billingsley and Riley, "The Empire Strikes Back," pp. 8–10. This report also offers numerous examples of activities undertaken by the state department of education and various school districts to stymie charter school development.
34. See Urahn and Stewart, "Minnesota Charter Schools," p. 2; and Buechler, "Charter Schools," p. 33.
35. Jeanne Allen, *Monthly Newsletter* (Washington, D.C.: The Center for Education Reform, June 1995).

3. Contracting in Public Education

1. Thomas Toch, "Do Firms Run Schools Well?" *U.S. News and World Report*, January 8, 1996, pp. 46–49.

284   2. Dean Millot, *What Are Charter Schools?* Seattle, University of Washington Program on Re-Inventing Public Education, 1995.

3. Toch, "Do Firms Run Schools Well?"

4. Because EAI used a different instructional sequence from other Baltimore city schools, and because the other schools spent the entire year preparing for the citywide achievement tests, use of the school system's tests put EAI at a major disadvantage. This will become a familiar problem as charter schools and schools with distinctive designs like those associated with the New American Schools Development Corporation (NASDC) are evaluated. See, for example, Karen J. Mitchell, *Reforming and Conforming: NASDC Principals Talk About the Impact of Accountability Systems on School Reform* (Santa Monica, Calif.: RAND, 1992).

5. See Ted Kolderie, "The States Would Have to Withdraw the Exclusive," Minneapolis, Center for Policy Studies, University of Minnesota, 1992; Joe Nathan, *Public Schools by Choice: Expanding Opportunities for Parents, Students and Teachers* (Bloomington, Ind.: Meyer Share, 1989).

6. Howard Davies, *Fighting Leviathan: Building Social Markets that Work* (London: The Social Market Foundation, 1993).

7. Ted Kolderie, "The States Would Have to Withdraw."

8. See Mary Beth Celio, *Building and Maintaining Systems of Schools: Lessons from Religious Order School Networks.* Working Papers of the University of Washington Graduate School of Public Affairs, 1995.

9. Id.

10. See, for example, Joan Lipsitz, *Successful Schools for Young Adolescents* (New Brunswick, N.J.: Transaction, 1983); and Paul T. Hill, Gail E. Foster, and Tamar Gendler, *High Schools with Character* (Santa Monica, Calif.: RAND, 1990).

11. See Booz-Allen and Hamilton, *Financial Outlook for the Chicago Public Schools,* prepared for the Civic Committee of the Commercial Club of Chicago, 1992; and Bruce S. Cooper, *School-Site Cost Allocations,* paper presented at the General Meeting of the American Educational Finance Association, 1993.

12. Paul T. Hill and Josephine Boran, *Decentralization and Accountability in Public Education* (Santa Monica, Calif.: RAND, 1991).

13. David B. Tyack, *The One Best System: A History of American Urban Education* (Cambridge: Harvard University Press, 1974).

4. Lessons in School Reform from the Edison Project

1. Patrick M. Reilly, *Wall Street Journal,* August 2, 1993; *Business Week,* August 2, 1993; *New York Times,* October 30, 1994; *The New Yorker,* October 31, 1994.

2. Tom Toch, "Whittling Away the Edison Project," *U.S. News and World Report,* August 16, 1993.

3. E. D. Hirsch, Jr., *Cultural Literacy: What Every American Needs to Know* (Boston: 285
Houghton Mifflin, 1987).

4. For an overview of the standards wars that is both practical and scholarly,
see Diane Ravitch, *National Standards in American Education: A Citizen's Guide*
(Washington, D.C.: Brookings Institution, 1995).

5. For a discussion of the experiences of several states, see Judith McQuaide
and Ann-Maureen Pliska, "The Challenge of Pennsylvania's Education Reform," *Educational Leadership* 51 (December 1993–January 1994); and Lynn
Olson, "Who's Afraid of O.B.E.?" *Education Week* 12 (December 15, 1993).

6. Connecticut's battle illustrates this problem, as reported in George Judson,
"Bid to Revise Education Is Fought in Connecticut," *New York Times*, January 9, 1994.

7. Edison Project, *Partnership School Design* (New York: Edison Project, 1994).

8. Edison Project, *Student Standards for the Readiness Academy; Student Standards
for the Primary Academy; Student Standards for the Elementary Academy;* and
Student Standards for the Junior Academy (New York: Edison Project, 1994).

9. Ravitch, *National Standards*, especially chapter 5 on the politics of standards.

10. See, for example, Stanley M. Elam, Lowell C. Rose, and Alec M. Galleys,
"The 23rd Annual Gallup Poll of the Public's Attitude Toward the Public
Schools," *Phi Delta Kappan* 73 (September 1991).

11. Carnegie Foundation for the Advancement of Teaching, *School Choice: Special
Report* (Princeton: Carnegie Foundation, 1992).

12. A response to the Carnegie report, with special attention to New York City, is
offered in Seymour Fliegel with James MacGuire, *Miracle in East Harlem: The
Fight for Choice in Public Education* (New York: Times Books, 1993).

13. Jean Johnson and John Immerwahr, *First Things First: What Americans Expect
from the Public Schools* (New York: Public Agenda, 1994).

14. See especially Toch, "Whittling Away."

15. Because the surveys needed to gauge very accurately the willingness of
parents to pay tuition, the sample was limited to households earning above
$30,000 annually in 1993, the lower boundary of what we believed might
be full-tuition families. The surveys therefore do not reflect the views of
low-income parents. Edison's other market research, however, included a
full page of communities and family income levels.

16. David B. Tyack, *The One Best System: A History of American Urban Education*
(Cambridge: Harvard University Press, 1974).

17. The best recent treatment of the evolution of the federal system is Paul E.
Peterson, *The Price of Federalism* (Washington, D.C.: Brookings Institution,
1994).

18. Department of Education, National Center for Education Statistics, *Digest of
Education Statistics, 1993* (Washington, D.C.: U.S. Department of Education,
National Center for Education Statistics 1994), tables 41, 88.

286   19. Tyack, *The One Best System.*

20. John E. Chubb: "Federalism and the Bias for Centralization," in John E. Chubb and Paul E. Peterson, eds., *The New Direction in American Politics* (Washington, D.C.: Brookings Institution, 1985).

21. Peterson, *The Price of Federalism,* offers a comprehensive analysis of state resurgence.

22. On state reform efforts see Denis P. Doyle, Bruce S. Cooper, and Roberta Trachtman, *Taking Charge: State Action in School Reform in the 1980s* (Indianapolis: Hudson Institute, 1991).

23. Ravitch, *National Standards,* pp. 160–168.

24. *Philadelphia Inquirer,* June 1, 1992.

25. Vance H. Trimble, *An Empire Undone: The Wild Rise and Hard Fall of Chris Whittle* (New York: Birch Lane, 1995), ch. 22.

26. Larry R. Vaughn, "Why I Turned to the Edison Project," *School Administrator,* August 1995.

27. John E. Chubb and Terry M. Moe, *Politics, Markets, and America's Schools* (Washington, D.C.: Brookings Institution, 1990), ch. 4.

28. John T. Bruer, *Schools for Thought* (Cambridge: MIT Press, 1993).

5. School Choice in Milwaukee

1. The research reported in this chapter is based on the examination of documentary sources as well as interviews with principals, administrators, government officials and community leaders in Milwaukee and Madison in November and December 1994. Respondents were promised anonymity. Quotations for which no citation is given are from these interviews. We thank the Annie Casey and John Olin Foundations for their support for this research. The findings and views reported in this chapter are the authors' and should not be attributed to either foundation.

2. Wisconsin State Senator Gary George, quoted in Steve Schultze and Priscilla Ahlgren, "School Choice Empowers Poor, Lawmaker Says," *Milwaukee Journal,* March 23, 1990.

3. Stephen Marshall, legislative aide to Wisconsin Representative Polly Williams, quoted in Paul Taylor, "Milwaukee's Controversial Private School Choice Plan Off to Shaky Start," *Washington Post,* May 25, 1991.

4. Carnegie Foundation for the Advancement of Teaching, *School Choice* (Princeton: Carnegie Foundation for the Advancement of Teaching, 1992), p. 73.

5. Albert Shanker, "Where We Stand: All Smiles," advertisement in *New York Times,* January 30, 1994. Also see similar assessment by a spokesperson for the American Federation of Teachers quoted in Daniel McGroarty, "School Choice Slandered," *The Public Interest* no. 117 (Fall 1995), 96.

6. Texas State Teachers Association/National Education Association, "Our

Public Schools . . . the Best Choice for Texas, Issue: Public vs. Private"   287
(Austin: Texas State Teachers Association, 1995).

7. Curtis Lawrence, "Choice Programs Showing Little Success, Study Says,"
   Milwaukee Journal Sentinel, July 15, 1995.

8. Laura Miller, "Wis. Vouchers for Religious School Urged," *Education Week,*
   January 25, 1995, p. 11.

9. McGroarty, "School Choice Slandered," 111. See John F. Witte, Christopher
   A. Thorn, Kim M. Pritchard, and Michele Claibourn, "Fourth Year Report:
   Milwaukee Parental Choice Program," Department of Political Science and
   the Robert M. La Follette Institute of Public Affairs, University of Wisconsin-
   Madison, December 1994. One of the authors of this chapter has also crit-
   ically assessed the methodological underpinnings for the conclusions Witte
   reaches in his evaluation. See Paul E. Peterson, "A Critique of the Witte
   Evaluation of Milwaukee's School Choice Program," Center for American
   Political Studies, Harvard University, Occasional Paper 95-2, February 1995.

10. "New Learning Curves," *Wall Street Journal,* January 30, 1995.

11. John Pisciotta, *The Milwaukee School Choice Program: Lessons for Texas* (San
    Antonio: Texas Public Policy Foundation, 1995), p. 26.

12. George A. Mitchell, *The Milwaukee Parental Choice Plan* (Milwaukee: Wiscon-
    sin Policy Research Institute, 1992), p. 1.

13. A privately funded school-choice program in Milwaukee, Partners Advanc-
    ing Values in Education (PAVE), suffers from fewer limitations than does the
    state-funded program. More than a hundred private and secular schools
    participate. Early reports suggest that the program is considerably more
    successful than the state-funded program. See Janet R. Beales and Maureen
    Wahl, "Given the Choice: A Study of the PAVE Program and School Choice
    in Milwaukee," Los Angeles: Reason Foundation, Policy Study No. 183,
    January 1995.

14. Nicholas Masters, Robert Salisbury, and Thomas Eliot, *State Politics and the
    Public Schools* (New York: Knopf, 1964); Paul E. Peterson, "The Politics of
    American Education," in Fred N. Kerlinger and John B. Carroll, eds., *Review
    of Research in Education* (Itasca, Ill.: F. E. Peacock, 1974), pp. 350–66.

15. Peter Brimelow and Leslie Spencer, "Comeuppance," *Forbes,* February 13,
    1995, p. 122.

16. Id.

17. Department of Education, Office of Educational Research and Improve-
    ment, National Center for Education Statistics, *Digest of Education Statistics,
    1991* (Washington, D.C.: Government Printing Office, 1991), tables 34, 116.

18. James G. Cibulka, "Restructuring Wisconsin's Educational System: How
    Effective Is the Department of Public Instruction?" (Milwaukee: Wisconsin
    Policy Research Institute, 1991), vol. 4, no. 4.

19. Susan Mitchell, *Why MPS Doesn't Work* (Milwaukee: Wisconsin Policy Re-
    search Institute, 1994), pp. 1, 34–36.

288   20. E. P., "Wisconsin Governor Again Seeks Choice, Both for Milwaukee and Across the State," *Education Week*, February 1, 1989, p. 10.

21. "Thompson 'Choice' Plan Too Flawed," *Milwaukee Journal*, January 22, 1989.

22. Priscilla Ahlgren, "Union Key in Defeating Choice Plan," *Milwaukee Journal*, July 6, 1989.

23. Kimberly McLarin, "In Test of School-Voucher Idea, the Sky's Not Falling But Neither Is Manna," *New York Times*, April 19, 1995.

24. Taylor, "Milwaukee's Controversial Private School Choice Plan."

25. Lacking this exclusion, the voucher proposition on the ballot in California became an immediate big-ticket budget item, a fact successfully used by voucher opponents to generate opposition to the proposition. See Myron Lieberman, "The School Choice Fiasco," *The Public Interest* 114 (Winter 1994), 17–34.

26. In the 1991–1992 school year, the estimated per pupil payments to choice schools came to $2,729, about 41 percent of the per pupil cost of educating a student in the Milwaukee public schools, as reported in Wisconsin Department of Public Instruction, *Basic Facts About Wisconsin's Elementary School Districts, 1991–92*, cited in Mitchell, *The Milwaukee Parental Choice Plan*, p. 12.

    The amount was also about half the national average cost of educating a public school student, which in 1991 was estimated to be $5,748. See U.S. Department of Education, Office of Educational Research and Improvement, National Center for Education Statistics *Digest of Education Statistics, 1991*, table 158.

27. "[Thomas] Fonfara (Thompson's adviser on education issues) said he expected private schools either to waive the difference or to make some sort of payment arrangements with the parents"; Richard P. Jones, "The ABC's Haven't Been Written for Thompson's Education Plan," *Milwaukee Journal*, January 15, 1989.

28. Mitchell, *The Milwaukee Parental Choice Plan*, p. 12.

29. Milwaukee Parents for School Choice, press release, August 1, 1995, p. 1.

30. Pisciotta, *The Milwaukee School Choice Program*, p. 5.

31. John F. Witte, "Choice and Control: An Analytical Overview," in William H. Clune and John Witte, eds., *Choice and Control in American Education*, vol. 1 (London: Falmer, 1990), p. 43.

32. John F. Witte, "Understanding High School Achievement: After a Decade of Research, Do We Have Any Confident Policy Recommendations?" Paper prepared for the Annual Meeting of the American Political Science Association, San Francisco, August 30–September 2, 1990. Findings from the paper are reported in "Paper Launches Academic Attack on Chubb-Moe Book on Education," *Education Week*, November 14, 1990, p. 1. Witte's work is discussed by Albert Shanker, the president of the American Federation of Teachers, in an advertisement in the *New York Times*, November 18, 1990.

33. John Witte, quoted in George Mitchell, Open Letter to John Witte, February 28, 1995, in Mitchell, *The Milwaukee Parental Choice Plan*.

34. Cibulka, "Restructuring Wisconsin's Educational System," p. 42.

35. Id., pp. 15, 17, 19, 43.

36. *Milwaukee Journal*, July 23, 1990.

37. *Milwaukee Sentinel*, August 8, 1990, quoted in Mitchell, *The Milwaukee Parental Choice Plan*, p. 6.

38. Quoted in Mitchell, *The Milwaukee Parental Choice Plan*, p. 6.

39. Mark J. Rochester, "State Mailed Letters Too Late, Parents Say," *Milwaukee Journal*, July 2, 1991.

40. Quotation from *Wisconsin Statutes* S. 119.23(2)(b).

41. Amy Stuart Wells, "Milwaukee Parents Get More Choice on Schools," *New York Times*, March 28, 1990.

42. Barbara Miner, " 'Choice' School in Turmoil Because of Staff Cuts, Changes," *Milwaukee Journal*, November 23, 1990.

43. Witte's report characterized four of the original choice schools as being in "serious financial difficulty" and, in addition to Juanita Virgil, found two more to be "on the verge of closing in the Spring of 1990"; John F. Witte, Andrea B. Bailey, and Christopher A. Thorn, "Third Year Report: Milwaukee Parental Choice Program," Department of Political Science and the Robert M. La Follette Institute of Public Affairs, University of Wisconsin-Madison, December 1993, p. 10.

44. Special supplement to the *Milwaukee Community Journal*, May 4, 1994, prepared by and about the Harambee Community School on the occasion of the celebration of the twenty-fifth anniversary of its founding.

45. Taylor, "Milwaukee's Controversial Private School Choice Plan."

46. Witte, "Choice and Control," p. 12.

47. Id., p. 13.

48. Special supplement to the *Milwaukee Community Journal*, May 4, 1994.

49. Administrator views are supported by data reported in the Witte evaluation, which indicates that choice students, when in public school, had "higher than average behavioral problems"; John F. Witte, "First Year Report: Milwaukee Parental Choice Program," Department of Political Science and the Robert M. La Follette Institute of Public Affairs, University of Wisconsin-Madison, November 1991, p. ii.

50. Paul E. Peterson, Barry Rabe, and Kenneth Wong, *When Federalism Works* (Washington, D.C.: Brookings Institution, 1985).

51. John T. Benson also had close ties to WEAC, which spent $175,000 on his reelection campaign. Benson criticized the choice program for failing to provide "the dramatic academic improvements in student achievement that would label it a success." But neither Benson's language nor his administrative decisions were as hostile to the choice plan as Grover's had been. See David Prosser, "Who Is Fighting Education Reform?" A Special Report from

290   Wisconsin's State Assembly Speaker, May 19, 1995; John T. Benson, Letter to Donald Schneider, Chief Clerk, Wisconsin State Senate, January 6, 1994.

52. In early 1995 Howard Fuller resigned as Milwaukee's school superintendent, after a slate of candidates backed by the teachers union was elected to the school board. Whether or not the choice schools continue to have good relations with Fuller's successor will provide a further indicator of the extent to which the choice program has become institutionalized.

53. Witte, Bailey, and Thorn, "Third Year Report," p. 10.

54. Karen Herzog, "Once-Retired Principal Takes New Approach," *Milwaukee Sentinel,* October 17, 1994.

55. State of Wisconsin, Legislative Audit Bureau, "An Evaluation of Milwaukee Parental Choice Program," Report 95–3, February 1995, table 5, p. 26.

56. David Ruenzel, "A Choice in the Matter," *Education Week,* September 27, 1995, p. 28.

57. Carnegie Foundation, *School Choice,* p. 69.

58. Data on the mobility rates among students in low-income elementary schools in grades 2 through 5 are provided in John F. Witte, Andrea B. Bailey, and Christopher A. Thorn, "Second Year Report: Milwaukee Parental Choice Program," Department of Political Science and the Robert M. La Follette Institute of Public Affairs, University of Wisconsin-Madison, December 1992, pp. 19–20.

59. Peterson, "A Critique of the Witte Evaluation," pp. 29–36. See also Paul E. Peterson, "The Milwaukee School Choice Plan: Ten Comments on the Witte Reply," Harvard University, Center for American Political Studies, Occasional Paper 95–3, March 1995.

60. Ruenzel, "A Choice in the Matter," p. 28.

61. The Witte evaluation is reported in the following documents: Witte, "First Year Report"; Witte, Bailey, and Thorn, "Second Year Report"; Witte, Bailey, and Thorn, "Third Year Report"; Witte et al., "Fourth Year Report: Milwaukee Parental Choice Program," Department of Political Science and the Robert M. La Follette Institute of Public Affairs, University of Wisconsin-Madison, December 1994. The quotations are from Witte et al., "Fourth Year Report," p. v.

62. Jay P. Greene, Paul E. Peterson, and Jiangtao Du, with Leesa Boeger and Curtis L. Frazier, "The Effectiveness of School Choice in Milwaukee: A Secondary Analysis of Data from the Program's Evaluation." Harvard University Program in Education Policy and Governance, Occasional Paper 96–3, August 1996.

6. Catholic Lessons for Public Schools

1. The ideas put forth in the chapter are drawn from a long collaborative relationship with Anthony S. Bryk, including the 1993 publication of our

book. See Anthony S. Bryk, Valerie E. Lee, and Paul B. Holland, *Catholic Schools and the Common Good* (Cambridge: Harvard University Press, 1993). Because we worked together so closely on the research and ideas that are represented in the book, it is not possible to separate which ideas, which writing, and which conclusions have sprung from which person.

2. The third Baltimore Council of Bishops, in 1884, commanded Catholic parents to send their children to parochial schools. Individual parishes were strictly enjoined to erect a school near each church within two years if one did not already exist. Although these decrees were never fully realized, they stood as Church doctrine for almost a century.

3. From a high of 5.5 million students in 1965, the Catholic school enrollment dropped to 2.5 million in 1990. From enrolling 12 percent of the school-age population in 1965, in 1990 the schools enrolled only 5.4 percent. The numbers of schools declined accordingly, from thirteen thousand in 1965 to around nine thousand in 1990 (National Catholic Educational Association, 1990).

4. This second wave of findings, and comments on them, are summarized in an entire issue of the journal *Sociology of Education* (58[2] [1985]). The general conclusions about the findings from HS&B were summarized by Christopher Jencks in an article in that issue. Jencks wrote that the accumulated evidence indicates that average achievement is somewhat higher in Catholic high schools than in public high schools, and it also suggests that Catholic high schools may be especially helpful for disadvantaged students.

5. According to the National Center for Education Statistics (1995), U.S. Catholic high schools enrolled about 680,000 students in 1990–1991, a decline of 7 percent from three years before. Private high schools enrolled about 880,000 students in 1990–1991, compared with the 13.7 million students in public high schools. Catholic elementary schools enroll about 7 percent of the total U.S. elementary school population. Enrollment in Catholic schools is still declining, and Catholic schools are still closing, but at much less precipitous rates than in the late 1960s and 1970s.

6. The actual figure, from HS&B data for 1982 graduates, is $5,745. Bryk, Lee, and Holland, *Catholic Schools,* p. 70.

7. The nature of remediation is also quite different in public and Catholic high schools. Typically, a Catholic ninth-grader without adequate skills to succeed in Algebra 1, for example, would be placed in an Algebra 1 class but would also be required to take another math class each day until his or her computational skills reached the class level. In a public high school, on the other hand, such a student would be probably be enrolled in a general math class *instead* of Algebra 1. That student would be unlikely ever to learn algebra.

8. In addition to *Catholic Schools,* these ideas are spelled out in detail by Anthony S. Bryk and Mary E. Driscoll, *The School as Community: Theoretical*

Foundation, Contextual Influence, and Consequences for Students and Teachers (Madison: National Center for Effective Secondary Schools, University of Wisconsin, 1988); and Valerie E. Lee, Anthony S. Bryk, and J. B. Smith, "The Effect of High School Organization on Teachers and Students," in L. Darling-Hammond, ed., *Review of Research in Education* 19 (1993): 171–268.

9. Recent evidence suggests that teachers who take responsibility for their students' learning, as a group, have profound influence on learning and its equitable distribution—in Catholic and public schools alike. See Valerie E. Lee and J. B. Smith, "Collective Responsibility for Learning and Its Effects on Gains in Achievement for Early Secondary School Students," *American Journal of Education* 104(2) (1996): 103–147.

10. Chubb and Moe consider the two components of bureaucratic influence—administrative constraint and personnel constraint—to be the antithesis of decentralized governance. Their analyses show the most constraints of either type in low-achieving schools and the fewest in high-achieving schools (table 5–8, p. 162). See John E. Chubb and Terry M. Moe, *Politics, Markets, and America's Schools* (Washington, D.C.: Brookings Institution, 1990). By far the most important element in predicting the degree of both administrative and personnel constraint is school sector (table 5–11, p. 178). In the book's final analysis, school sector is shown to be the major explanatory factor for effective school organization (table 5–13, p. 182). Autonomy, according to Chubb and Moe, is crucial for effective school organization, and private control of schools is the key to autonomy.

11. Gerald Grant, *The World We Created at Hamilton High* (Cambridge: Harvard University Press, 1988), pp. 55, 59.

7. Chicago School Reform

1. The title of the *Chicago Tribune* series, "Chicago Schools: 'Worst in America,'" drew directly on the statement made by Bennett during a brief visit to Chicago. The *Tribune* described the school system as "a disgrace" (*Chicago Tribune*, May 1988).

    This chapter is drawn from a book in preparation by A. S. Bryk, J. Q. Easton, D. Kerbow, S. G. Rollow, and P. Sebring, *Democratic Participation and Organizational Change: The Chicago School Experience*, to be published by Westview. The theory of democratic localism appears in chapter 2 of that book, for which Sharon Rollow was the primary author. David Kerbow was the primary author of chapter 5, where the path analysis results are reported.

2. While decrying the overall dysfunction in the system, the *Tribune* also chronicled stories of many individual teachers, parents, and school system officials who strove valiantly to do good work. They literally saved some students' lives, but ultimately they proved powerless to change their schools

and the larger system. For a more general discussion of this problem in urban school reform, see Seymour B. Sarason, *The Predictable Failure of Educational Reform: Can We Change Course Before It's Too Late?* (San Francisco: Jossey-Bass, 1990).

3. In this regard, advocates for expanded democratic participation actually share a common ground with other reformers who advance very different solutions, such as educational markets (John E. Chubb and Terry M. Moe, *Politics, Markets, and America's Schools* [Washington, D.C.: Brookings Institution, 1990]) and systemic reforms (Marshall Smith and Jennifer O'Day, "Systemic School Reform," *Politics of Education Yearbook* [Washington, D.C.: Falmer, 1990]). All see the current institutional structure of public schooling as a major impediment to significant change. These analyses typically begin with the observation that how a school works (or fails to work) is shaped, in both obvious and subtle ways, by its external environment. In this regard, schools are viewed as "open systems," where the nature of core practices and their overall effectiveness largely reflect how these external influences operate. When we confront school failure on a massive scale, as in Chicago, it seems highly plausible that the root cause of this failure is not inside each individual school but rather in the external environments that they share. From this perspective, pervasive bad school practices are symptoms of some larger external causes—in particular, how schools are governed.

4. G. Alfred Hess, Jr., and Diana Lauber, *Dropouts from the Chicago Public Schools* (Chicago: Chicago Panel on Public School Policy and Finance, 1985).

5. Designs for Change, *The Bottom Line: Chicago's Failing Schools and How to Save Them* (Designs for Change Research Report No. 1: January 1985).

6. For a detailed discussion of the role of the Chicago business community in school reform see Dorothy Shipps, "Big Business and School Reform: The Case of Chicago, 1988" (Ph.D. diss., Stanford University, 1995), which chronicles the activities of the Civic Committee and its satellite organizations, Chicago United and Leadership for Quality Education, in mobilizing for reform. Shipps draws out the historical links between this current activity and a larger, centurylong effort by this elite organization of business leaders to shape public education in the city.

7. *Chicago Schools: "Worst in America"* (Chicago: Chicago Tribune, 1988).

8. Kenneth Wong and Sharon G. Rollow, "A Case Study of the Recent Chicago School Reform," *Administrator's Notebook* 34 (Chicago: Midwest Administration Center, University of Chicago, 1990), 5–6.

9. David Cohen, quoted in Donald R. Moore, "Voice and Choice in Chicago," in William H. Clune and John F. Witte, eds., *Choice and Control in American Education*, vol. 1 (London: Falmer, 1990).

10. Alex Pointsett, "School Reform, Black Leaders: Their Impact on Each Other," *Catalyst* 1(4) (1991), 7–11.

11. When PA 85–1418 was first passed, many Chicago teachers viewed it nega-

tively. See John Q. Easton, Anthony S. Bryk, Mary E. Driscoll, John G. Kotsakis, Penny A. Sebring, and Arie J. van der Ploeg, *Charting Reform: The Teacher's Turn* (Chicago: Consortium on Chicago School Research, 1991). On the national scene, Chicago's reform was cited as being at odds with major efforts to promote school improvement through teacher professionalism (Ann Lieberman, "Restructuring Schools: What Matters and What Works," *Phi Delta Kappan,* June 1990, 759–764), strengthening the instructional leadership skills of principals (Kenneth Leithwood and Deborah Montgomery, *Improving Principal Effectiveness: The Principal Profile* [Toronto: Ontario Institute for Studies in Education, 1986]), and bolstering the technical core of instruction in urban schools (Robert Slavin and Nancy E. Madden, "What Works for Students at Risk: A Research Synthesis," *Educational Leadership* 46 [February 1989], 4–13).

12. John E. Chubb and Terry M. Moe, "Politics, Markets, and the Organization of Schools," *American Political Science Review* 88 (December 1988).

13. Moore, "Voice and Choice."

14. For a detailed historical treatment of democratic localism and educational governance, see Michael B. Katz, *Restructuring American Education* (Cambridge: Harvard University Press, 1987).

15. The impetus for community control in New York was somewhat different from the push for reform in Chicago. In Chicago, parents argued that the schools were failing their children academically. While these same concerns were raised in New York, parents there were primarily concerned about the socialization of their children and the role of school personnel in that development. They did not want "outsiders"—white, Jewish education professionals—to have undue influence. See Mario Fantini, Marilyn Gittell, and Richard Magat, *Community Control and the Urban School* (New York: Praeger, 1970); and Mario Fantini and Marilyn Gittell, *Decentralization: Achieving Reform* (New York: Praeger, 1973).

16. For a specific account with regard to Chicago school reform, see Michael B. Katz, "Chicago School Reform as History," *Teachers College Record* 94 (Fall 1992), 56–72. For more general treatments of this idea, see Harry C. Boyte, *The Backyard Revolution: Understanding the New Citizen Movement* (Philadelphia: Temple University Press, 1980); and Sara M. Evans and Harry C. Boyte, *Free Spaces: The Sources of Democratic Change in America* (Chicago: University of Chicago Press, 1986).

17. The description provided in this section is based on the original Chicago School Reform Act of 1988, PA 85–1418. Although there were some minor adjustments along the way, these provisions remained basically unchanged until the spring of 1995, when the Illinois legislature passed a second major Chicago school reform bill.

18. When the legislation was first passed, school staff elected two teacher representatives. This procedure has since been changed; now the staff "nomi-

nates" its representatives, who are appointed by the board of education. In high schools, students elect a representative, who can vote on everything but personnel issues.

19. Even in settings that appear genuinely committed to this aim, it has not generally occurred. For example, in the 1970s, Salt Lake City instituted local governing boards on which parents and professionals were equally represented. Parental influence, however, remained limited even here, regardless of the formal balance of power on these boards. See Betty Malen and Rodney T. Ogawa, "Professional-Patron Influence on Site-Based Governance Councils: A Confounding Case Study," *Educational Evaluation and Policy Analysis* 10 (Winter 1988), 251–270. We note that Chicago's reform is also quite different from parental involvement provisions that exist in federally funded programs like Head Start and Title VII Bilingual. Although parents who participate in these programs may gain new leadership and parenting skills, their influence with regard to policy and decision making, as well as their ability to challenge professional control, has remained minimal. See Josie Yanguas and Sharon G. Rollow, "The Rise and Fall of Adversarial Politics in the Context of Chicago School Reform: Parent Participation in a Latino School Community" (Center for School Improvement, University of Chicago, 1994), photocopy.

20. Material distributed by the Citywide Coalition for Chicago School Reform, of which both Designs for Change and the Chicago Panel on Public School Policy were members, made frequent reference to this literature. See, for example, Charles L. Kyle and Edward R. Kantowicz, *Kids First—Primero Los Niños: Chicago School Reform in the 1980s* (Springfield: Sangamon State University, Illinois Issues, 1992).

21. Albert L. Bennett, Anthony S. Bryk, John Q. Easton, David Kerbow, Stuart Luppescu, and Penny A. Sebring, *Charting Reform: The Principals' Perspective* (Chicago: Consortium on Chicago School Research, 1992); and Anthony S. Bryk, John Q. Easton, David Kerbow, Sharon G. Rollow, and Penny A. Sebring, *A View from the Elementary Schools: The State of Reform in Chicago* (Chicago: Consortium on Chicago School Research, 1993), reported that most principals still found this procedure time-consuming and cumbersome and, consequently, continued to rely on less formal means to persuade a teacher that she or he would be happier elsewhere.

22. Michael Madigan, speaker of the Illinois House of Representatives, told the reform caucuses in a directive sent during the legislative write-up process that he would not support a bill that included any provisions objectionable to the CTU. Given his virtual complete control over House activities, this directive was tantamount to a mandate.

23. This provision remains controversial. Principals in Chicago must annually evaluate their faculties, which are almost entirely tenured. Since it is very difficult to remove incompetent teachers, a negative evaluation often does

little more than exacerbate an existing personnel problem. Because two members of the faculty have an opportunity every four years to influence whether the principal's contract will be renewed, relations have become even more sensitive. Many principals object to this aspect of the reform legislation.

24. Many of these provisions required initiative on the part of the central office, which was slow to embrace reform. Although a set of citywide objectives was established, they were not directly connected to the school improvement planning process and were used little by schools. Provisions concerning intervention in nonimproving schools were largely ignored. In general, the "systemic agenda" contained in PA 85–1418 received little attention during the first five years of reform. In the past year, however, renewed interest has focused on all of these areas.

25. See G. Alfred Hess, Jr., "Buying Aids or Teachers? The Reallocation of Funds Under Chicago School Reform" (Atlanta: Annual Meeting of the American Educational Research Association, 1993), for a further discussion of the reallocation of funds under Chicago school reform.

26. Shipps, "Big Business."

27. In fact, Chicago has always benefited from activist CBOs and citywide organizations whose primary focus was educational improvement. Controversial in this history has been a split over leadership, representation, and motives between the neighborhood-based community organizations influenced by Alinsky and the more affluent citywide reform groups. For more discussion of this history, see Saul Alinsky, *Rules for Radicals* (New York: Vintage, 1971); Michael Herrick, *The Chicago Schools: A Social and Political History* (Beverly Hills, Calif.: Sage, 1971); D. J. Hogan, *Class and Reform: School and Society in Chicago, 1880–1930* (Philadelphia: University of Pennsylvania Press, 1985); and Julia Wrigley, *Class Politics and Public Schools: Chicago, 1900–1950* (New Brunswick, N.J.: Rutgers University Press, 1982). See Pointsett, "School Reform," for a viewpoint on this controversy in Chicago's current reform.

28. William S. McKersie, "Philanthropy's Paradox: Chicago School Reform," *Educational Evaluation and Policy Analysis* 15(2) (Summer 1993), 109–128.

29. See, for example, James P. Comer, *School Power: Implications of an Intervention Project* (New York: Free Press, 1980).

30. In fact, an emphasis on short-term trends in student achievement could actually be detrimental. As schools seriously engage change, uncertainty rises, and controversy is likely as established routines are discarded but new, tested practices have yet to become routinized. See, for example, Michael B. Fullan, *The New Meaning of Educational Change* (New York: Teachers College Press, 1991), Ann Lieberman, "Restructuring Schools: What Matters and What Works," *Phi Delta Kappan,* June 1990, 759–764; and Karen S. Louis and Matthew B. Miles, *Improving the Urban High School* (New York: Teachers

College Press, 1990). In this transitional period, a school may even look worse by old standards. If staff are not adequately prepared for the confusion and conflict associated with organizational change, the restructuring may be abandoned in return for the security of the old ways.

31. It is important to remember that even five years after the Illinois legislature first passed a school reform bill, the development of the reform was still at a fairly early stage. Although the legislation was originally passed in 1988, implementation was deferred until the fall of 1989. Organizing the first local school council elections, training councils, and writing bylaws dominated most of the first year. Thus, the 1989–1990 school year was taken up almost entirely with initiating the structures and processes of local school governance. See John Q. Easton and Sandra L. Storey, *Local School Council Meetings During the First Year of the Chicago School Reform* (Chicago: Chicago Panel on Public School Policy and Finance, 1990) for a description of the first-year activity of LSCs. Also during that year, half of the schools were required to evaluate their principal and to make a decision either to retain or to hire a new one. The other half of the schools made that decision in the spring of 1991. The schools that reviewed their principal in spring 1990 were ready to begin their school improvement efforts the following fall; schools that had to wait until spring 1991 to make a change in principal leadership, however, might not really have begun improvement activities until fall 1991. In practical terms then, by 1993 about half of the schools had three years to initiate improvements while others had only two years. Thus, in many school communities the change process was still fairly new, and any fair evaluation of the progress during this initial period must take this into account.

32. Anthony S. Bryk and Penny A. Sebring, *Achieving School Reform: What We Need to Know* (Chicago: Consortium on Chicago School Research, 1991).

33. This indeed is proving to be the case. The first consortium study to examine the progress of reform in high schools was recently released as Penny B. Sebring, Anthony S. Bryk, John Q. Easton, Stuart Luppescu, Yeow Meng Thum, Winifred A. Lopez, and BetsAnn Smith, *Charting Reform: Chicago Teachers Take Stock* (Chicago: Consortium on Chicago School Research, 1995). The picture here appears considerably more negative—that of more deeply troubled institutions with far fewer reform success stories.

34. Formally, this was defined as schools with a composite average on the Illinois Goals Assessment Program (IGAP) in reading and mathematics at grades 3, 6, and 8 (or whatever subset of these were present in the school) of less than 235 in the year prior to school reform. When the IGAP program was established, "national norms" were equated to a score of 250 with a test standard deviation of 100. For any typical Chicago elementary school with approximately one hundred students per grade, a composite score of 235 or less, averaged across multiple grades in reading and math, is several standard errors below norms.

298   35. G. Alfred Hess, Jr., *Restructuring Urban Schools: A Chicago Perspective* (New York: Teachers College Press, 1995); and Sharon G. Rollow and Anthony S. Bryk, "Catalyzing Professional Community in a School Reform Left Behind" Atlanta: Paper presented at the annual meeting of the American Educational Research Association, 1993.

36. The combination of longitudinal case studies and a large systemwide database was essential here. The case studies provided a mechanism for both identifying key concepts (the governance and school improvement types) and validating the indicators of these concepts. That is, as we assembled survey and administrative data to measure the key concepts, we could cross-validate the measures against actual field reports from more than forty schools. For more details see Anthony S. Bryk, John Q. Easton, David Kerbow, Sharon Rollow, and Penny A. Sebring, *Democratic Localism as a Lever for Institutional Renewal* (Boulder, Colo.: Westview Press, forthcoming).

37. Much of the past research on school-level politics has focused on the relationships between the principal and faculty. See, for example, Steven J. Ball, *The Micro-Politics of the School: Towards a Theory of School Organization* (London: Methuen, 1987); Joseph J. Blase, "The Micro-Politics of the School: The Everyday Political Orientation of Teachers Toward Open School Principals," *Educational Administration Quarterly* 25 (November 1989), 377–407; and Joseph J. Blase, ed., *The Politics of Life in Schools: Power, Conflict and Cooperation* (Newberry Park, Calif.: Sage, 1991). These studies document that there is little public political activity in many schools. Rather, teachers and the principal seem to tacitly accept and understand their respective domains of practice and responsibility, having long ago negotiated treaties about how they will behave toward each other and the organization of their work. There is little need for public discussion, so faculty and other school meetings become perfunctory. Most of the political activity that does occur takes place in private, as individuals meet with their principal to negotiate their personal needs. Through these negotiations the principal seeks to satisfy as many as possible and to keep the lid on nascent dissent and potential demands for more substantive change.

    In general, these pluralist negotiations can effect incremental reforms, but rarely do they address the basic structure of political systems—the power relations, the representation of interests within them, and how things get done. It is for these reasons that they are often described as maintenance politics.

38. For a further elaboration of these ideas, see Fred M. Newmann and Gary G. Wehlage, *Successful School Restructuring: A Report to the Public and Educators by the Center on Organization and Restructuring of Schools* (Madison: Board of Regents of the University of Wisconsin System, 1995).

39. For full details of the analysis see Bryk et al., *Democratic Localism.*

40. Terrence E. Deal and Kenneth D. Peterson, *The Leadership Paradox: Balancing*

Logic and Artistry in Schools (San Francisco: Jossey-Bass, 1994), argue that
entrepreneurship has both an instrumental and symbolic dimension. Such
behavior involves both gathering resources and expertise for the school
(instrumental) and articulating the values and ideas that can anchor and
motivate a common agenda for change (symbolic).

41. For a further discussion of Chicago school reform as a social movement, see
Michael B. Katz, "Chicago School Reform as History," *Teachers College Record*
41 (Fall 1992), 56–72.

42. In *A View from the Elementary Schools,* Bryk et al. present direct commentary
from adult and student participants in six actively restructuring schools.
They generally shared the sentiment that much more needed to be accomplished.

43. The principles in this firm, James Champy and Mike Hammer, popularized
this term as applied to organizations in their best-selling book *Reengineering
the Corporation* (New York: HarperCollins, 1993) and in the subsequent volume by Champy, *Reengineering Management* (New York: HarperCollins,
1995). They were selected over several other major corporate consultant
firms, including Arthur Andersen.

44. This is a profound historical development. A major tenet of the progressive
movement since early in this century has been the need to buffer the governance of school affairs from the patronage politics that characterizes city
affairs. See Lawrence A. Cremin, *American Education: The Metropolitan Experience, 1876–1980* (New York: Harper and Row, 1988). With one stroke of the
pen, enormous contract and personnel authority was in essence shifted to
the mayor's office.

45. It is a great political irony that a Republican legislature gave back to the son,
Mayor Richard M. Daley, what an earlier legislature had taken away from
Chicago largely because of the actions of his father, Richard J. Daley. The
creation of the School Finance Authority and the restrictive budgeting requirements under which the CPS had been forced to operate for over a
decade resulted from fiscal abuses during the elder Daley's tenure as mayor,
which in turn precipitated the school system financial crisis of 1979: James
D. Squires, preface to *Chicago Schools: Worst in America* (Chicago: R. R. Don-
nelley and Sons, 1988).

46. Careline Hendrie, "109 Chicago Schools Put on Academic Probation," *Education Week,* October 9, 1996.

47. Because science and social studies tests have been added recently, they are
not useful for pre- and postreform trend analyses. Similarly, the state high
school testing program shifted from grade 11 to grade 10 in 1993, so these
data are also unusable for trend analyses under reform.

48. For example, the Nobel laureate in physics Leon Letterman helped organize
the Teachers' Academy of Math and Science, which has engaged in extensive professional development work with Chicago elementary schools. Sim-

300   ilarly, both the Illinois Writing Project and the Chicago Area Writing Project
         have teacher networks organized around writing instruction.

49. A student who is "on grade level" is expected to gain 1.0 grade equivalents
    per year. Against this yardstick, a 0.5 grade equivalent improvement over
    five years implies a 50 percent increase in school productivity.

50. The report by the Chicago Public Schools with the Chicago Urban League
    and the Latino Institute, *Chicago's Public School Children and Their Environ-
    ment* (Chicago: Chicago Public Schools, 1995), documents this. Also see Ball
    Foundation, *Using What We Have to Get the Schools We Need: A Productivity
    Focus for American Education* (Glen Ellyn, Ill.: Ball Foundation, 1995), which
    advances this argument about increasing school productivity in the context
    of declining school inputs.

51. David Kerbow, "Pervasive Student Mobility: A Moving Target for School
    Improvement" (Chicago: Chicago Panel on Public School Policy and the
    Center for School Improvement, 1995).

52. Robert H. Meyer, "Value-Added Indicators of School Performance," in Eric
    Hanushek, ed., *Improving the Performance of America's Schools* (Washington,
    D.C.: National Academy Press, forthcoming) presents important empirical
    work that documents the confounding effects of mobility on drawing in-
    ferences about school impact from school-average test score trends. Consis-
    tent with the arguments made here, he too argues for the use of "value
    added" indicators.

53. Anthony S. Bryk, Paul E. Deabster, John Q. Easton, Stuart Luppescu, and
    Yeow Meng Thum, "Measuring Achievement Gains in the Chicago Public
    Schools," in G. Alfred Hess, ed., *Education and Urban Society* 26 (May 1994).

54. In a letter to the editor, Simon, Katz, and Fein, who have been observers of
    Chicago's reform, suggest that in Chicago reform is "more than educational
    change. . . . In Chicago school reform is a social movement that embraces
    and reflects the city's diversity." It is "one of the great adult education move-
    ments in American history," which has "rekindled optimism, unleashed
    energy and activated coalitions across race, class, gender and politics" (*Chi-
    cago Tribune*, March 7, 1991).

55. On the schools' seeming intractability, see Larry Cuban, "Reforming Again,
    Again, and Again," *Educational Researcher* 19 (January–February 1990), 3–
    13; and Sarason, *Predictable Failure*.

8. Successful School-Based Management

This chapter draws from research conducted by the University of Southern
California's Center on Educational Governance under grants from the U.S. Department of Education, Office of Educational Research and Improvement; the
Carnegie Corporation of New York; and the Finance Center of the Consortium
for Policy Research in Education. The opinions expressed are those of the au-

thors and do not necessarily reflect the views of the sponsors or the University of Southern California. We would also like to gratefully acknowledge the assistance of Amy Van Kirk in the preparation of this chapter.

1. Betty T. Malen, Rodney T. Ogawa, and Jennifer Kranz, "What Do We Know About School-Based Management? A Case Study of the Literature, A Call For Research," in William H. Clune and John F. Witte, eds., *Choice and Control in American Education,* vol. 2 (London: Falmer, 1990).

2. Council of Great City Schools, *National Urban Education Goals, 1992–93 Indicators Report* (Washington, D.C.: Council of Great City Schools, 1994).

3. Priscilla Wohlstetter and Roxane Smyer, "Models of High-Performance Schools," in Susan A. Mohrman, Priscilla Wohlstetter, and associates, *School-Based Management: Organizing for High Performance* (San Francisco: Jossey-Bass, 1994).

4. Rodney T. Ogawa and Paula A. White, "School-Based Management: An Overview," in Mohrman, Wohlstetter, and associates, *School-Based Management.*

5. Malen et al., "What Do We Know?"; Anita A. Summers and Amy W. Johnson, "Doubts About Decentralized Decisions," *School Administrator* 52 (March 1995), 350–367.

6. Susan Moore Johnson and Katherine C. Boles, "The Role of Teachers in School Reform," in Mohrman, Wohlstetter, and associates, *School-Based Management.*

7. Mohrman, Wohlstetter, and associates, *School-based Management.*

8. Priscilla Wohlstetter, Roxane Smyer, and Susan A. Mohrman, "New Boundaries for School-Based Management: The High-Involvement Model," *Educational Evaluation and Policy Analysis* 16 (Fall 1994), 268–286; Peter J. Robertson, Priscilla Wohlstetter, and Susan A. Mohrman, "Generating Curriculum and Instructional Innovations Through School-Based Management," *Educational Administration Quarterly* 31 (Fall 1994), 375–404; Center on Educational Governance, *Successful School-Based Management: Putting the Pieces Together* (Los Angeles: University of Southern California, Center on Educational Governance, 1995).

9. Thomas R. Guskey and Kent D. Peterson, "The Road to Classroom Change," *Educational Leadership* 53 (December–January 1996), 10–14; Joseph Murphy and Lynn Beck, *School-Based Management as School Reform: Taking Stock* (Thousand Oaks, Calif.: Corwin, 1995).

10. Jane L. David, "School-Based Decision-Making: Linking Decisions to Learning," third-year report to the Prichard Committee (Palo Alto, Calif.: Bay Area Research Group, 1994).

11. Anthony S. Bryk, John Q. Easton, David Kerbow, Sharon G. Rollow, and Penny A. Sebring, "The State of Chicago School Reform," *Phi Delta Kappan,* September 1994, pp. 74–78.

12. John Seeley Brown and Paul Duguid, "Organizational Learning and Com-

302   munities-of-Practice: Toward a Unified View of Working, Learning, and Innovation," *Organization Science* 2(1), 40–57.

13. Anthony S. Bryk, Valerie E. Lee, and Peter B. Holland, *Catholic Schools and the Common Good* (Cambridge: Harvard University Press, 1993), p. 278.

14. Fred M. Newmann and Gary G. Wehlage, "Successful School Restructuring: A Report to the Public and Educators" (Madison: University of Wisconsin-Madison, Center on Organization and Restructuring of Schools, 1995).

15. David, "School-Based Decision-Making"; Newmann and Wehlage, "Successful School Restructuring."

16. Helen Marks and K. Seashore Louis, "Does Teacher Empowerment Affect the Classroom? The Implications of Teacher Empowerment for Teachers, Instructional Practice, and Student Academic Performance," (Madison: University of Wisconsin, Center on Organization and Restructuring of Schools, 1995).

17. David, "School-Based Decision-Making"; Guskey and Peterson, "The Road to Classroom Change."

18. David, "School-Based Decision-Making"; S. C. Gleason, N. Donohue, and G. C. Leader, "Boston Revisits School-based Management," *Educational Leadership* 53(4) (Dec.–Jan. 1996), 24–27; Guskey and Peterson, "The Road to Classroom Change"; Newmann and Wehlage, "Successful School Restructuring."

19. Terrence Deal and Kent D. Peterson, *The Leadership Paradox: Balancing Logic and Artistry In Schools* (San Francisco: Jossey-Bass, 1994); Guskey and Peterson, "The Road to Classroom Change."

20. Murphy and Beck, *School-Based Management.*

21. Jane Clark Lindle, "Lessons from Kentucky About School-Based Decision-Making," *Educational Leadership* 53(4) (Dec.–Jan. 1996), 20–23.

22. Gleason et al., "Boston Revisits."

23. Newmann and Wehlage, "Successful School Restructuring."

24. Bill Geraci, "Local Decision-Making: A Report from the Trenches," *Educational Leadership* 53 (December–January 1996), 50–52.

25. Edward E. Lawler, *High-Involvement Management* (San Francisco: Jossey-Bass, 1986).

26. Newmann and Wehlage, "Successful School Restructuring."

9. The Politics of Change

1. Jacques Steinberg, "Time Stands Still in Some School Boiler Rooms," *New York Times,* November 15, 1995.

2. Department of Education, National Center for Education Statistics, *1994 NAEP Reading: A First Look, Findings from the National Assessment of Educational Progress* (Washington, D.C.: Department of Education, Office of Educational Research and Improvement, 1994).

3. Department of Education, National Center for Education Statistics, *NAEP*   303
1994 U.S. History: A First Look, Findings from the National Assessment of Educational Progress (Washington, D.C.: Department of Education Office of Educational Research and Improvement, 1994), v.
4. Organization for Economic Cooperation and Development, *OECD Economic Surveys, 1993–94* (Paris: OECD, 1994).
5. National Education Goals Panel, *The National Education Goals Report: Building a Nation of Learners, 1995* (Washington, D.C.: Government Printing Office, 1995).
6. Department of Education, *1995 Back to School Forecast: Enrollments, Graduations, and Degrees Up*, press release, August 31, 1995, 8 (table 4). See also National Center for Education Statistics, *Digest of Education Statistics, 1994* (Washington, D.C.: Department of Education, Office of Educational Research and Improvement), 165 (table 166).
7. Eric A. Hanushek et al., *Making Schools Work: Improving Performance and Controlling Costs* (Washington, D.C.: Brookings Institution, 1994).
8. James P. Pinkerton, *What Comes Next: The End of Big Government—And the New Paradigm Ahead* (New York: Hyperion, 1995), 55.
9. Jacques Steinberg, "Lawsuit Is Filed Accusing State of Overuse of Bilingual Classes," *New York Times*, September 19, 1995.
10. Patrick Welsh, "Why a 12th-Grader Can't Read," *Washington Post*, November 26, 1995.
11. Lynne V. Cheney, *Tyrannical Machines: A Report on Educational Practices Gone Wrong and Our Best Hopes for Setting Them Right* (Washington, D.C.: National Endowment for the Humanities, 1990).
12. David N. Plank, "Why School Reform Doesn't Change Schools: Political and Organizational Perspectives," in William Lowe Boyd and Charles Taylor Kerchner, eds., *The Politics of Excellence and Choice in Education* (New York: Falmer, 1988).
13. The interested reader may consult Diane Ravitch, *National Standards in American Education: A Citizen's Guide* (Washington, D.C.: Brookings Institution, 1995), especially chapters 1 and 2; and Chester E. Finn, Jr., *We Must Take Charge: Our Schools and Our Future* (New York: Free Press, 1991), particularly chapters 8, 9, and 10.
14. Thomas H. Kean, *The Politics of Inclusion* (New York: Free Press, 1988).
15. Jean Johnson et al., *Assignment Incomplete: The Unfinished Business of Education Reform* (Washington, D.C.: Public Agenda, 1995).
16. Albert Shanker, "Where We Stand: Down the Tubes?" *The New Republic*, November 6, 1995, 23 (advertisement).
17. Hanushek et al., *Making Schools Work*, 38.
18. Jordana Hart, "Marblehead School Backers Say They're Harassed," *Boston Globe*, August 23, 1995.
19. Peter Applebome, "Class Notes," *New York Times*, November 22, 1995.

10. Somebody's Children

A slightly different version of this essay appears in Irwin Garfinkel, Jennifer L. Hochschild, and Sara S. McLanahan, eds., *Social Policies for Children* (Washington, D.C.: Brookings Institution, 1996). Used by permission.

1. For a summary of data about test scores, dropout rates, and graduation rates, see Department of Education, National Center for Education Statistics, *The Condition of Education, 1992* (Washington, D.C.: Department of Education, National Center for Education Statistics, 1992), pp. 39–60. For information about performance assessments, see John A. Dossey et al., *Can Students Do Mathematical Problem-Solving? Results from Constructed-Response Questions in NAEP's 1992 Mathematics Assessment* (Washington, D.C.: Department of Education, Office of Educational Research and Improvement, 1993).

2. Department of Education, Public Affairs, "State of American Education," remarks prepared for Richard W. Riley, secretary of education, speech delivered at Georgetown University, February 15, 1994, pp. 2, 13.

3. Paul T. Hill, Gail E. Foster, and Tamar Gendler, *High Schools with Character* (Santa Monica, Calif.: RAND, 1990); Theodore R. Sizer, *Horace's School: Redesigning the American High School* (Boston: Houghton Mifflin, 1992), p. 128; Anthony S. Bryk, Valerie E. Lee, and Peter B. Holland, *Catholic Schools and the Common Good* (Cambridge: Harvard University Press, 1993).

4. Hill, Foster, and Gendler, *High Schools with Character*, p. vii.

5. There is a large body of research supporting the proposition that students fare better in a small school with a clear mission than in a large, anonymous school where there is minimal engagement between adults and children. In addition to the works cited here by Sizer, *Horace's School;* Hill, Foster, and Gendler, *High Schools with Character;* and Bryk, Lee, and Holland, *Catholic Schools;* see Linda Darling-Hammond, *Standards of Practice for Learner-Centered Schools* (New York: NCREST, Teachers College, 1992), p. 20: "Studies of school organizations, including two massive studies of secondary schools conducted by the National Institute of Education, have found that student achievement, positive feelings towards self and school, and positive behavior (including attendance, retention, and low levels of violence) are higher in smaller settings and those where students have close, sustained relationships with smaller numbers of teachers over their school career."

Fred M. Newmann, "Reducing Student Alienation in High Schools: Implications of Theory," *Harvard Educational Review* 51 (1981), 550, writes, "Organizational theory and the literature on the social psychology of organizations suggest six general issues relevant to reducing student alienation: the basis of membership, the nature of organizational goals, organizational size, decision-making structure, members' roles, and the nature of work. My review of the literature on these six issues leads me to propose the following guidelines: voluntary choice, clear and consistent goals, small size, participation, extended and cooperative roles [for teachers], and integrated work."

According to William J. Fowler and Herbert J. Walberg, "School Size, Characteristics, and Outcomes," *Educational Evaluation and Policy Analysis* 13 (2) (Summer, 1991), 200, "Increased school size has negative effects upon student participation, satisfaction, and attendance and adversely affects the school climate and a student's ability to identify with the school and its activities. Students who are dissatisfied, who do not participate in school activities, who are chronically absent, and who do not identify with the school will achieve less, whether on achievement tests or on postschooling outcomes."

6. Unpublished data from the National Education Longitudinal Survey:88 Base Year Data, Department of Education, 1992.

7. Id.; unpublished data from the almanac of the National Assessment of Educational Progress, Department of Education, for reading and mathematics, 1992. On the National Assessment of Educational Progress tests of reading and mathematics in 1992, disadvantaged urban students in the eighth grade in Catholic schools scored significantly higher than their public school peers in reading (but not in mathematics); in twelfth grade, disadvantaged urban students in Catholic schools scored significantly higher in both reading and mathematics. See also Anthony S. Bryk, Valerie Lee, and Julia Smith, "High School Organization and Its Effect on Teachers and Students: An Interpretive Summary of the Research," in William H. Clune and John F. Witte, eds., *Choice and Control in American Education: The Theory of Choice and Control in American Education* (London: Falmer, 1990); James S. Coleman, Thomas Hoffer, and Sally Kilgore, *High School Achievement: Public, Catholic, and Private Schools Compared* (New York: Basic, 1982); and James S. Coleman and Thomas Hoffer, *Public and Private High Schools: The Impact of Communities* (New York: Basic, 1987).

8. Department of Education, *America's High School Sophomores: A Ten Year Comparison, 1980–1990* (Washington, D.C.: Department of Education, 1992), p. 17.

9. Department of Education, National Center for Education Statistics, *Projections of Education Statistics to 2004* (Washington, D.C.: Department of Education, National Center for Education Statistics, 1993), p. xi.

10. Senators Daniel Patrick Moynihan and Robert Packwood made a similar proposal in the late 1970s. See also John E. Coons and Stephen D. Sugarman, *Family Choice in Education: A Model State System for Vouchers* (Washington, D.C.: Institute of Governmental Studies, 1971); John E. Coons and Stephen D. Sugarman, *Education by Choice: The Case for Family Control* (Berkeley: University of California Press, 1978); John E. Chubb and Terry M. Moe, *Politics, Markets and America's Schools* (Washington, D.C.: Brookings Institution, 1990).

306 11. Denis P. Doyle, "Family Choice in Education: The Case of Denmark, Holland, and Australia," commissioned by the National Institute of Education, March 22, 1984. See also Charles L. Glenn, *Choice of Schools in Six Nations: France, Netherlands, Belgium, Britain, Canada, West Germany* (Washington, D.C.: Department of Education, 1989).

12. Doyle, "Family Choice," pp. 4, 26.

13. David Tyack, "The Kingdom of God and the Common School: Protestant Ministers and the Educational Awakening in the West," *Harvard Educational Review* 36 (Fall 1966), 450.

14. Lloyd P. Jorgenson, *The State and the Non-Public School, 1825–1925* (Columbia: University of Missouri Press, 1987), p. 69.

15. This was the case at the public high school that I graduated from in Houston in 1956.

16. Jorgenson, *The State*, pp. 138–140, 216, 221; see also pp. 138–140.

17. Theodore Sizer and Phillip Whitten, "A Proposal for a Poor Children's Bill of Rights," *Psychology Today,* August 1968, 59–63.

18. Department of Education, *Youth Indicators, 1993* (Washington, D.C.: Department of Education, 1993), pp. 48.

19. Id., pp. 116–117. The rates for suicide, homicide, and arrests are national, not localized to disadvantaged urban communities. They are not likely to be better in those communities and are probably worse.

20. Carnegie Foundation for the Advancement of Teaching, *School Choice* (Princeton, N.J.: Carnegie Foundation for the Advancement of Teaching, 1992), p. 104.

21. Laurence H. Tribe, *American Constitutional Law* (Mineola, N.Y.: Foundation, 1988), p. 1223.

22. There are large cost differences between public and nonpublic schools, especially Catholic schools. Some observers attribute the difference solely to labor costs and predict that the cost of Catholic schools would equal those of public schools if they were to pay their teachers the same as public teachers. However, part of the differential is attributable to the overadministered bureaucratic structure of public education. A report by the Organization for Economic Cooperation and Development found that the United States has a higher proportion of nonteaching personnel than any other OECD nation. See Center for Educational Research and Innovation, *Education at a Glance* (Paris: OECD, 1993).

23. Glenn, *Choice of Schools in Six Nations,* p. 218.

24. John Stuart Mill, *The Six Great Humanistic Essays of John Stuart Mill* (New York: Washington Square Press, 1963), pp. 230–233.

Contributors

DIANE RAVITCH is a senior research scholar at New York University and holds the Brown Chair in Education Policy at the Brookings Institution. She served as assistant secretary in the U.S. Department of Education (1991–1993). She is the author of six books and more than three hundred articles and reviews, including *National Standards in American Education, The Schools We Deserve, The Troubled Crusade,* and *The Great School Wars: New York City, 1805–1973.*

JOSEPH P. VITERITTI is a research professor of public administration and adjunct professor of law at New York University. He is the author of several books and more than seventy-five articles, book chapters, and papers, including *Across the River: Politics and Education in the City* and *Bureaucracy and Social Justice.* He has served as special assistant to the chancellor of the New York City School System (1978–1981) and as a senior adviser to the superintendents of schools in Boston (1981) and San Francisco (1992).

LOUANN A. BIERLEIN is education adviser to the governor of Louisiana and former director of the Louisiana Education Policy Research Center at Louisiana State University. She is the author of numerous studies and essays on charter schools and a book, *Critical Issues in Educational Policy.*

308   ANTHONY S. BRYK is professor of education at the University of Chicago and founding director of the Consortium on Chicago School Research. He is the coauthor of *Catholic Schools and the Common Good* and *Democratic Participation and Organizational Change: The Chicago School Experience* with Kerbow, Rollow, and others (forthcoming). DAVID KERBOW and SHARON ROLLOW are research associate and director of research, respectively, at the Center for School Improvement at the University of Chicago.

JOHN E. CHUBB is a founding partner with the Edison Project in New York and a nonresident senior fellow in the Governmental Studies Program at the Brookings Institution. He has been an education adviser to the White House and to several state governments and local school districts. He is the coauthor of *Politics, Markets, and American Schools* and *A Lesson in School Reform from Great Britain*.

CHESTER E. FINN, JR., is the John M. Olin Fellow at the Hudson Institute, where he cochairs the Educational Excellence Network. He served as assistant secretary in the U.S. Department of Education (1985–1988). He is the author of *We Must Take Charge: Our Schools and Our Future; What Do Our 17-Year-Olds Know?* (with Diane Ravitch); and *Scholars, Dollars, and Bureaucrats*.

PAUL T. HILL is a research professor in the School of Public Affairs and director of the Center on Re-Inventing Public Education at the University of Washington, and a senior social scientist with the RAND Corporation. He is the coauthor of *Private Providers and Public Purposes: Contract Schools in American Education* and *High Schools with Character*.

VALERIE E. LEE is an associate professor of education at the University of Michigan and a principal investigator with the Center on the Organization and Restructuring of Schools at the University of Wisconsin. She is the coauthor of *Catholic Schools and the Common Good*, which won the Willard Waller Award from the American Sociological Association.

PAUL E. PETERSON is the Henry Lee Schattuck Professor of Government and director of the Program on Education Policy and Governance at Harvard University. He is the author of *The Price of Federalism; City Limits; The Politics of School Reform, 1870–1940; School Politics Chicago Style;* and *Race and Authority in American Politics* (coauthor). CHAD NOYES is a graduate student in the Department of Government at Harvard University.

PRISCILLA WOHLSTETTER is an associate professor of education and director of the Center for Educational Governance at the University of Southern California. She is coauthor with SUSAN ALBERS MOHRMAN of *School Based Management: Organizing for High Performance*. Mohrman is a senior research scientist at the Center for Effective Organizations in the Graduate School of Business at USC. PETER J. ROBERTSON is an associate professor in the School of Public Administration (USC).
309

Index